REVISING THE REVOLUTION

REVISING THE REVOLUTION

THE UNMAKING OF RUSSIA'S OFFICIAL
HISTORY OF 1917

―∞―

LARRY E. HOLMES

INDIANA UNIVERSITY PRESS

This book is a publication of

Indiana University Press
Office of Scholarly Publishing
Herman B Wells Library 350
1320 East 10th Street
Bloomington, Indiana 47405 USA

iupress.org

© 2021 by Larry E. Holmes

All rights reserved
No part of this book may be reproduced or utilized in any form or by any means, electronic or mechanical, including photocopying and recording, or by any information storage and retrieval system, without permission in writing from the publisher. The paper used in this publication meets the minimum requirements of the American National Standard for Information Sciences—Permanence of Paper for Printed Library Materials, ANSI Z39.48-1992.

Manufactured in the United States of America
First printing 2021

Library of Congress Cataloging-in-Publication Data

Names: Holmes, Larry E. (Larry Eugene), 1942- author.
Title: Revising the revolution : the unmaking of Russia's official history of 1917 / Larry E. Holmes.
Description: Bloomington : Indiana University Press, 2021. | Includes bibliographical references and index.
Identifiers: LCCN 2020039203 (print) | LCCN 2020039204 (ebook) | ISBN 9780253054784 (hardback) | ISBN 9780253054791 (paperback) | ISBN 9780253054807 (ebook)
Subjects: LCSH: Istpart, Otdel TS.K.R.K.P.(b.) po izucheniiu istorii Oktiabr'skoĭ revoliutsii i R.K.P.(b.)—History. | Istpart, Otdel TSK VKP(b) po izucheniiu istorii Oktiabr'skoĭ revoliutsii i VKP(b)—History. | Soviet Union—History—Revolution, 1917-1921—Historiography. | Soviet Union—Politics and government—1917-1936—Historiography.
Classification: LCC DK265.A553 H65 2021 (print) | LCC DK265.A553 (ebook) | DDC 947.084/1072—dc23
LC record available at https://lccn.loc.gov/2020039203
LC ebook record available at https://lccn.loc.gov/2020039204

For Esther Kay and Lois

CONTENTS

Preface ix

Acknowledgments xi

Note on Transliteration xiii

Abbreviations xv

Timeline xvii

Introduction 1
1. Istpart's Origins and Mission 14
2. At the Periphery 36
3. Multiple Scripts for 1905 and 1917 51
4. Viatka's 1917 Revolution in the Past and the Present 66
5. Fractured Finances 89
6. Moscow's Embrace of the Political 104
7. The Passing of Istpart and Professional Civility 130
8. Methodology Ex Cathedra: Stalin Speaks and Istpart's Legacy 141
9. Their Fate 157

    Conclusion 171

   Glossary of Prominent Individuals 177

   Selected Bibliography 179

   Index 185

PREFACE

Fifty years ago, I completed a dissertation on Soviet scholarship on the Russian Revolution of 1917. It had much to say about the work during the 1920s of the Commission for the Collection, Study, and Publication of Materials on the October Revolution and History of the Communist Party (*Istpart*, in abbreviated Russian). After a few articles published on the subject, I moved on to other topics. In so doing, I joined my colleagues in turning away from intellectual and political history, of which my interest in Istpart was a part, to what might broadly be defined as social history. My departure from Istpart also accompanied the profession's relative loss of interest in the 1920s for a greater concern for the late tsarist period, on the one hand, and full-fledged Stalinism in the 1930s, on the other.

But what goes around comes around. My interest in regional history has brought me back to Istpart. For the past two decades, I have focused on Russia's Viatka region (after 1934, Kirov), located about 500 miles northeast of Moscow. A number of publications have resulted, all of which have examined the relationship between the center (Moscow) and the periphery (Viatka/Kirov). The abundance of material in Kirov's two main archives and the warmth and expertise of its archivists have made it all possible.

As it turned out, one of those archives contained an entire collection, 298 folders to be exact, on Viatka's Istpart branch. Curiosity prompted me to look at some of the items, then professional concerns drove me on to read more. I wanted to know the extent to which Viatka's Istpart participated in the quarrelsome struggle by the party's historians to meet the simultaneous demands of scholarship and partisan politics. And I wanted to know of Viatka's involvement in a corresponding contentious discussion of the history of 1917. In the course of these multiple disputes, I asked whether Viatka sought to accommodate demands from the center or resist them. More prosaically, had Viatka acted in accordance with the resources at hand and its own understanding of the region's past?

In Kirov's archive, I found more than I had initially bargained for. What I discovered required a subsequent reexamination of items first read decades before. And it compelled an appraisal of materials on Istpart in Moscow's former Central Party Archive, a collection (and an archive) inaccessible to almost all researchers when I began work on Istpart fifty years ago.

It has been, first in the past and now in the present, a fascinating journey.

ACKNOWLEDGMENTS

I am indebted to the librarians at Kirov's Herzen State Public Library for their untiring assistance. Research for this book could not have been completed without the help of Deborah Cobb and the staff of the interlibrary loan department at the University of South Alabama's library. Archivists at the Russian State Archive of Social and Political History and the State Archive of the Social and Political History of the Kirov Region repeatedly shared their time and expertise: Galina Gorskaia, Elena Chudinovskikh, Vladimir Zharavin, Galina Nagornichnykh, Liubov' Poptsova, Pavel Chemodanov, Natal'ia Rozhkova, and Mikhail Strakhov. Special thanks to Ekaterina Nalesnikova and Liubov' Ryzhakova at Kirov's Regional Museum of Local History for locating rare photographs.

My research has been supported by the University of South Alabama; the University of Illinois Russia, East European, and Eurasian Summer Research Laboratory; and the Kennan Institute.

Aaron Retish, Ben Eklof, and Tat'iana Saburova read earlier versions of several chapters and made excellent recommendations for their improvement. I am immensely appreciative of the insightful suggestions made by two anonymous readers. Keith Holmes enhanced the quality of many illustrations. I am most grateful to Jennika Baines at Indiana University Press for her patience and encouragement.

Marsha Hobbs has stood by me during my prolonged absences while working on this book.

All errors of fact and judgment are, of course, exclusively mine.

Larry E. Holmes
Professor Emeritus of History
University of South Alabama

NOTE ON TRANSLITERATION

I use the Library of Congress transliteration system with several exceptions. Surnames that end in "skii" such as Pokrovskii or Trotskii have been changed to "sky," thus Pokrovsky or Trotsky. The last name of Lenin's wife is rendered as Krupskaya; the poet as Mayakovsky; the party official as Zinoviev. I have also chosen to drop the soft sign at the end of Russian cities, presenting them as Kazan, Perm, Iaroslavl, and Stavropol. In the reference notes, I use the following abbreviations when citing Russian archival material: f. for collection (*fond*), op. for inventory (*opis'*), d. for file or folder (*delo*), l. (*list*) for page and ll. (*listy*) for pages, and ob. (*oborot*) for reverse side of a page. The initial letter of all words in the full name of a political party is always capitalized with the exception of Bolshevik party and Menshevik party.

ABBREVIATIONS

BI	*Biulleten' Istparta*
Comintern	Communist International
GAKO	Gosudarstvennyi arkhiv Kirovskoi oblasti (State Archive of the Kirov Region)
GASPI KO	Gosudarstvennyi arkhiv sotsial'no-politicheskoi istorii Kirovskoi oblasti (State Archive of the Social and Political History of the Kirov Region)
Gosizdat	State Publishing House
IM	*Istorik-Marksist*
Istpart	Commission for the Collection, Study, and Publication of Materials on the October Revolution and History of the Communist Party
Komsomol	Young Communist League
MOPR	International Organization for Aid to Revolutionary Fighters
Orgburo	Central Committee's Organization Bureau
Politburo	Central Committee's Political Bureau
PR	*Proletarskaia revoliutsiia*
RGASPI	Rossiskii gosudarstvennyi arkhiv sotsial'no-politicheskoi istorii (Russian State Archive of Social and Political History)
Zhenotdel	Central Committee's Women's Department

TIMELINE

January–December, 1905, Russian Revolution of 1905

February–March, 1917, February Revolution, overthrow of tsarist autocracy

May 1917, creation of a Bolshevik organization in the city of Viatka

October 25, 1917, Bolshevik revolution in Petrograd

Early November 1917, Bolsheviks take control of Moscow

December 1917, Bolsheviks gain tenuous control over the city of Viatka

Spring 1919, Bolsheviks gain control over the Viatka region

September 1920, creation of Istpart (Commission for the Collection, Study, and Publication of Materials on the October Revolution and the History of the Communist Party)

September 1920, Pokrovsky resigns as Istpart's head, replaced by Ol'minsky

March 1921, rebellion at the Kronstadt naval base

September 1921, creation of Viatka's Istpart

October 1921, appearance of the first issue of Istpart's journal *Proletarskaia revoliutsiia*

December 1921, Istpart placed under the jurisdiction of the party's Central Committee

March 1923, creation of the Lenin Institute

April 22–24, 1923, Second Istpart Conference

March 1924, publication of V. I. Nevsky's *Essays on the History of the Russian Communist Party*

May 26–27, 1924, Third Istpart Conference

October 1924, publication of L. D. Trotsky's *Lessons of October*

1925, Istpart's historians and administrators attack Trotsky's *Lessons of October*

March 16, 1925, Istpart issues secret memorandum condemning its locals for political deviation

May 14, 1925, Istpart's instructions on celebrating the 1905 revolution

June 1925, formation of the Society of Marxist Historians

Late 1925, Viatka's Istpart publishes *The Year 1905 in the Viatka Region*

1927, publication of important books on 1917 by S. M. Dubrovsky, E. M. Iaroslavsky, A. M. Pankratova, A. V. Shestakov, A. G. Shliapnikov, and Viatka's Istpart

January 4–8, 1927, Fourth Istpart Conference

January 27 and March 2, 1927, Viatka Istpart's head, Novoselov, informs Viatka's historians of major cutbacks in publications for the tenth anniversary of the October revolution

May 1927, Novoselov sends letter to Istpart critical of Kuchkin and Kapustin

May 1927, Kuchkin responds to Novoselov's criticism with an article in *Proletarskaia revoliutsiia*

May 24, 1927, meeting of Istpart's auxiliaries, Groups of Assistance, criticism of the value of memoirs

June 1927, Viatka Istpart's collegium supports Novoselov in the conflict with Kuchkin

August 1927, publication of Viatka Istpart's *October and the Civil War in the Viatka Province*

October 30, 1927, opening of Viatka's Museum of the Revolution

May 1928, merger of Istpart with the Lenin Institute

May 1928, Istpart's Groups of Assistance disbanded

October 1928, *Proletarskaia revoliutsiia* publishes Novoselov's criticism of Kuchkin

Late 1928, *Proletarskaia revoliutsiia* publishes Kuchkin's riposte to Novoselov's article

December 28, 1928, to January 4, 1929, First Conference of Marxist Historians

1929, publication of the fourth volume of the *History of the Communist Party*, edited by Iaroslavsky

June 1929, Viatka's Istpart ceases to exist

February 9–13, 1930, Conference of Teachers of Leninism, Party History, and the History of the Comintern

September 8, 1931, Tarle's written plea for help sent to Pokrovsky

October 1931, *Proletarskaia revoliutsiia* prints Stalin's letter condemning the journal

November 12, 1931, V. I. Picheta's written plea for help sent to Pokrovsky

October 1931 to early 1932, Iaroslavsky's multiple responses to Stalin's criticism of his work

January 20, 1932, Stalin summons Iaroslavsky to his office

September–October 1938, publication of *History of the Communist Party: The Short Course*

REVISING THE REVOLUTION

Introduction

THE DEAN OF SOVIET PARTY historians, Mikhail Nikolaevich Pokrovsky, proudly declared that "history is the most political of all existing sciences."[1] In so doing, he spoke for his own and following generations of party historians. Today's historians in the Russian Federation and elsewhere would agree, at least to some extent, with Pokrovsky's assessment of their craft. They readily acknowledge that contemporary politics influence their work. Yet the degree to which these scholars, including those in the former Soviet Union, have written a history for the political present has varied considerably. Such diversity was notably evident during the 1920s, when historians who belonged to the Communist Party wrote about the most delicate of political subjects, the 1917 revolution in Russia and the Bolshevik party's rise to power in October of that year.

The Great October Socialist Revolution ended neither in Russia nor in the year 1917. For decades thereafter, it shaped events in Russia and beyond with an intensity dependent on a continuing construction and reconstruction of its memory. One hundred years later, following a lively discussion in *Revolutionary Russia*'s special issue marking the revolution's centennial, the journal's editors concluded that in the "muddle" of interpretations, "most scholars and pundits agreed that the Russian Revolution and the Soviet system that it bore, for better or for worse, had a lasting impact on global politics in the twentieth century."[2]

Much earlier, in 1920, and already certain of the revolution's future importance, Russia's Council of Peoples Commissars formed a Commission for the Collection, Study, and Publication of Materials on the October Revolution and History of the Communist Party (*Istpart*). Soon after, regional party committees formed Istpart locals. Although Istpart in Moscow and in the Viatka province ceased to exist by 1929, its work continued to be at issue and of immediate relevance to a discussion of historical methodology and of the 1917 revolution until 1931.

THE CENTER AND THE PERIPHERY

This book focuses on the contested discussion in the capital, Moscow, and in a province, Viatka, over the standards of historical scholarship and the interpretation of the 1917 revolution. It joins existing literature on the broader topic of the relationship between the center and periphery. That body of work has emphasized, over and again, the distinctive nature of the provinces and their importance to an understanding of the nation as a whole.[3] In her study of nineteenth-century Nizhnii Novgorod, Catherine Evtuhov found that the area's citizens, not just its nobility, felt strong attachment to their province's life and culture. They created, as she puts it, the "provincial idea" and "a local historical narrative."[4] Other historians have stressed that regional networks of friendship and kinship set practical limits on the power first of St. Petersburg in the late tsarist period and then of Moscow in the first decades of Soviet power.[5] Local officials often pursued their own agenda, not necessarily out of defiance but rather because of the incompetence of the center's own administration; because of ignorance from below of what the capitals wanted; or because of inappropriate, even impossible, demands from above.[6] Most recently, Oleg Khlevniuk underscored the importance during World War II of a sanctioned and spontaneous decentralization of power that was necessary for the production and distribution of goods critical to the nation's survival.[7]

For the past twenty years, I have studied the relationship between Moscow and the province of Viatka (Kirov after 1934). My examination of educational administration has found that during the 1930s, teachers, school directors, inspectors, and local officials in Kirov turned to theatrical displays of their own presumed authority in order to defend their interests in a party-state that otherwise rendered them powerless.[8] A history of one institution in particular, Kirov's Pedagogical Institute from 1941 to 1952, uncovered a tangled web of alliances in which state and party organs exercised power independently of their purported place in a monolithic structure of authority arranged vertically from the top (Moscow) to the bottom (Kirov).[9] My more recent assessment of Soviet wartime evacuation revealed that Kirov's citizens and institutions soon resented the hardships that the central government and evacuation required of them. While not directly challenging the soviet system, they vigorously advanced their own private interests and, in the case of officials, the welfare of the institutions and the region that they represented.[10]

This book finds a similarly tense and complex relationship between the center—in this case, Istpart in Moscow—and its local in Viatka. As we will see over and again, Istpart's personnel in Moscow and Viatka sharply disagreed over how best to write a historically factual yet politically useful history of 1917. Viatka had, in Evtuhov's words, its own "local historical narrative" to tell.

THEMES AND THESES

Istpart's historians in Moscow and Viatka initially believed that they could abide by the traditional canons of scholarship and simultaneously provide a history that was of political service to their party. During the 1920s, this faith in a symbiosis of scholarship and politics began to erode, slowly at first, then rapidly. In Moscow, Istpart soon demanded a master narrative of 1917 that legitimized the party's power, past and present, whatever the facts of the matter. They also altered their understanding (or misunderstanding) of 1917 in order to empower Iosif Stalin in the venomous intraparty struggle of the mid- and late 1920s. But at the center and in Istpart's regional branches, not all historians embraced this politicized agenda. Some did not fully grasp what they were supposed to do. Others knowingly chose to write history as they thought best. Viatka's history of 1917 deviated so sharply from Moscow's emerging master narrative that its Istpart could not easily rearrange the region's past to suit the center's demands.

In their discussions of 1917, historians in Moscow and Viatka understandably disagreed over the selection and use of source material. In the discourse that followed, however, they often acted as combatants freely resorting to pedantic criticism and personal insults. As the decade of the 1920s drew to a close, self-promotion and party politics ignited ever uglier quarrels among them. Their exchanges lacked the civility essential to a lasting respect for scholarship.

Consequently, well in advance of Stalin's 1931 letter to the journal *Proletarskaia revoliutsiia* (a subject of discussion in this book's penultimate chapter), Istpart and its historians portrayed the party's past to fit the politics of its present. Some did this enthusiastically, others reluctantly, but their efforts contributed to a notion of revolution that legitimized the formation of an authoritarian regime at home and abroad with little or no respect for scholarship. In the Soviet Union's specific case, this effort would justify the physical elimination by execution of Istpart's own historians.

Let me hasten to say that this book is not a comprehensive history of Istpart, whether in Moscow or Viatka. It bears mention that Istpart collected tens of thousands of documents and prompted countless individuals to record their reminiscences on the Russian revolutionary movement and the party's past.[11]

No historian of those subjects can manage without use of that material. That part of Istpart's legacy, however, is not part of this book. Other historians, as we will see, have covered it especially well.

Moreover, this work is not an attempt at a history of the 1917 Russian revolution. It examines the literary output on 1917 that Istpart sponsored and encouraged, but only in order to analyze major changes in the way the party's historians approached and interpreted events. In particular, this work focuses on description of the Bolshevik party's activity, real and alleged, in 1917. Although some of that corpus has lasting value, most remains too tendentious for contemporary use in compiling a history of 1917.

In the chapters that follow, I focus on Istpart's founding belief in a compatibility of scholarly principles and political utility. I examine articles and monographs on the 1917 period that flowed from that initial faith. I then analyze the erosion of that conviction and the intense pressure to produce an egregiously politicized narrative. In so doing, this book calls attention to the conflict between Moscow and Viatka over historical methodology and an appropriate rendering of the past.

JUDGING ISTPART

Historians in the former Soviet Union and the current Russian Federation have largely limited their discussion of Istpart to its origins, its collection and preservation of archival documents and memoirs, and its inadequate financial and human resources. That effort, including more than a dozen dissertations and multiple articles on Istpart's locals, says little about the dispute at Istpart over its dual mission of scholarship and political service or its presentation of 1917 (or any other topic). Nor does that body of literature take up the frequently strained relationship between that agency's national office and its regional branches.[12]

In his *Telling October*, Frederick C. Corney discussed exceedingly well the portrayal of 1917 in public celebrations, newspaper articles, cinema, pamphlets, and books designed for a wide audience in the Soviet Union during the 1920s.[13] In doing so, the author presented considerable information on Istpart. It was not his intention, however, to discuss that agency's scholarly mission, the breadth of its scholarship on 1917, and the relationship between its center and local affiliates. By contrast, biographers of Istpart's key personnel have spoken at length about the contradictions in Istpart's initial objectives and how they jostled and competed within the life and work of a single individual. In the best work on Pokrovsky to date, *The Soviet Scholar-Bureaucrat*, George Enteen found a volatile mix of personal, ideological, political, and professional factors that shaped Pokrovsky's career and the first years of Soviet historical scholarship.[14] Pokrovsky's interpretations of the past and his guiding principles as head of several Soviet teaching and research institutions were, to use Enteen's recurring words, ambiguous, vacillating, unstable, and always changing. In the late 1920s, Pokrovsky increasingly equated scholarship with political militancy. He did so in large part, Enteen has argued, for venal personal reasons. In an increasingly envenomed political climate, Pokrovsky hoped to maintain his own prestige and administrative authority.

Aleksei Litvin reached similar conclusions about the historian Sergei Andreevich Piontkovsky, a member of Istpart's collegium in 1921 and an author of multiple articles and monographs on the party's history and 1917.[15] Litvin found that his subject at first combined academic professionalism and political conformism. In a "duality of conduct," Piontkovsky struggled to retain scholarly standards even while succumbing to political pressure to discard them. Although sympathetic to his subject, in the end, Litvin judged Piontkovsky and the first generation of party historians harshly. Even at their best in the 1920s, they were on the ideological offensive, displaying little tolerance for competing points of view. In this way, they contributed to the formation of an inhumane regime that eventually claimed them, Piontkovsky included, as its victims.

Enteen, Litvin, and authors of other monographs on Soviet historical scholarship and Istpart (to be discussed) are keenly aware that their work joins the scholarly corpus on the transition from the relative freedom of the first decade of Soviet power to the early Stalinist period that followed. Some of their colleagues have insisted that Stalin's policies and personality, rather than anything inherent in a "comparatively pluralistic and liberal order" of the 1920s, led to the latter's demise.[16] Other scholars have found not a rupture but a surprising degree of continuity between the 1920s and 1930s.[17] Still others have emphasized that throughout its early years in power, the party aggressively sought a monopoly over most aspects of Soviet life. That effort culminated in the radical social, cultural, economic, and political policies that came with Stalin's so-called Great Break.[18]

Whatever the merits of any insistence on the 1920s as an era of relative tolerance, it inevitably, in the view of some of its adherents, had to end.[19] That has largely been the view of scholars working on the Soviet Union's initial cohort of historians. The very nature of the Bolshevik regime and its ideology, they have argued, demanded a thoroughgoing politicization of writing about the past. Robert Byrnes found that young radicals in the Soviet historical profession, goaded on by political leaders, destroyed any possibility of lasting cooperation and compromise between Marxist and non-Marxist historians.[20] The "largely spontaneous activity of militants," John Barber concluded, wished to impose the militants' interpretations on their colleagues. When some historians resisted, Stalin intervened with his aforementioned letter to *Proletarskaia revoliutsiia*. The Soviet leader wanted to eradicate, as Barber put it, the "disorder and disagreement among intellectuals out of place in a society increasingly characterized by discipline and unanimity."[21]

Scholars who have acknowledged Istpart's early attempts to pursue scholarly and political goals simultaneously have emphasized the poisonous effect of Bolshevik ideology and politics that brought that effort to an end. In their view, the notion of combining scholarship and partisanship was fatally flawed. Istpart's historians sought the impossible, William Burgess has argued, "undone in time by the dilemma in its original mandate."[22] In a work on Istpart's branches in the northern Caucasus, Vasilina Sergeevna Klopikhina likewise has insisted that Istpart's hope for a reasonably objective reading of sources inevitably succumbed to the agency's political mission. It gradually and inexorably became "an ideological institute of state power."[23]

In a monograph on the Institute of Marx and Engels, an organization much like Istpart, Vladimir Gavrilovich Mosolov suggested that politics predictably undermined an initial scholarly agenda. The institute's director until 1931, David Borisovich Riazanov, insisted that it focus not on the incantation of fixed dogma but rather on analysis of the evolution of the thinking of Marx and Engels. To that end, Riazanov employed nonparty specialists and encouraged a free exchange of ideas. The effort, "beautiful and utopian," Mosolov observed, was doomed from the start. Politics inevitably consumed scholarship even before Riazanov's removal as director in 1931 (and later arrest and execution). "The fate of Riazanov and of his Institute," Mosolov concluded, "could only be such as it was."[24]

As will become clear, this book emphasizes the deep faith of Istpart's original cohort of historians in Moscow and Viatka in the possibility to produce works (and museums) worthy of scholarship and politics. It stresses that they were able to succeed momentarily and shares their excitement in so doing. But any such effort to wed scholarship and partisanship, as sincere and committed as it was at the outset, could not likely endure. The Bolshevik party never recognized the intrinsic worth of historical scholarship. Members of the party's ruling faction, at the top of the hierarchy, and many historians below, including the new cohort in the profession as well as some of Istpart's old guard, increasingly ignored traditional standards of research to advance their own personal and political agendas. They did so when rewriting a history of the 1917 period. An emerging national narrative terminated stubborn efforts in Viatka and elsewhere to present a region's own distinctive past. As noted previously, Istpart's original dual mission ended even before Istpart's own demise as an organization. Any respect for a plurality of approaches and conclusions evaporated well before Stalin's Great Break, when the party's historians imposed an orthodoxy on their own ranks (and on their nonparty colleagues).

ARCHIVAL SOURCES

Moscow's Russian State Archive of Social and Political History contains two collections of particular importance to Istpart's story. The first is a body of material produced by Istpart's central office from 1921 to 1928. It holds the records from sessions of the agency's administrative organs and their directives and instructional letters to Istpart's regional branches. Considerable correspondence, including exchanges with the local in Viatka, may also be found there.

The second is the collection for *Proletarskaia revoliutsiia*, a journal founded by Istpart in 1921. It contains extensive correspondence of the editorial board and staff with Istpart's central office and with regional branches. Unpublished manuscripts submitted to the editorial board, including items from Viatka, and the evaluations that followed are also there.

That same archive holds the unpublished commentary by key figures in Istpart's history. Especially prominent among them are the collections for individuals of great importance in the chapters that follow: Ol'minsky, Iaroslavsky, and Pokrovsky.

In the city of Kirov, the State Archive of the Social and Political History of the Kirov Region possesses a large collection exclusively on the activity of the region's Istpart. It contains records from sessions of that agency's governing bodies, its periodic reports, and its circulars and instructional letters. Of particular importance is the correspondence with Istpart's central office in Moscow and with regional party and soviet organizations.

Kirov's archive also possesses materials of the Viatka regional party committee, the body with jurisdiction over the region's Istpart. That depository contains as well records of the agency Truzhenik, responsible for the printing and marketing of Viatka Istpart's publications. That job was fraught with considerable difficulty, as we will see, for both the publisher and Istpart.

STRUCTURE

Chapter 1 evaluates Istpart's efforts to integrate scholarly and partisan pursuits into a single agenda. It also examines the immediate threats posed to that mission by Marxist-Leninist ideology, the heavily politicized discussion of Leon Trotsky's rendition of 1917 in his "Lessons of October" (1924), the personal animosity among Istpart's leaders, and the shortage of human and material resources in Moscow and the provinces. The second chapter focuses on the center's refusal to acknowledge the impoverishment of its locals and a bombardment of them with demands to produce something of value that downplayed regional peculiarities.

As Istpart's historians began to write about the past, they encountered the dilemma of presenting a scholarly but partisan result. Chapter 3 analyzes their work on the 1905 revolution and, of greater importance to this book, on the 1917 period. Viatka's historians produced an admittedly pedestrian volume on 1905 in the region but one that knowingly departed from the center's official template. Their defiant example was duplicated there and elsewhere in the USSR in work on the 1917 revolution. Despite the center's emerging wish for a grand narrative, the result (discussed in detail in chap. 3) provided a remarkably heterogeneous mix of accounts that acknowledged the importance of spontaneity, the Bolshevik party's weakness, and the distinctive nature of events in many of Russia's regions.

The fourth chapter focuses intently on Viatka's efforts to celebrate in print the tenth anniversary of the 1917 revolution. Its plans ran afoul of Moscow's intentions when the local Istpart branch acknowledged the modest achievements, at best, of the Bolshevik party in the region. A spiteful conflict erupted between Istpart's leadership in Viatka and two of the area's own revolutionaries from the past, now ensconced in Moscow, about the appropriate way to remember that past. Even as the head of Viatka's Istpart advanced a reasonably objective account of 1917 in his region, he repeatedly issued shrill declarations of his agency's devotion to a politicized presentation of history. The contradictions in Istpart's dual mission were never more apparent.

"Fractured Finances," the fifth chapter, discusses the party's efforts to slash expenses across the board in the mid-1920s. Viatka's regional party committee closed down the publisher that had previously printed at a considerable loss Istpart's work. And just as Istpart's historians at the center and in the provinces adopted ambitious programs to celebrate the 1917 revolution, their party ruthlessly imposed on them the unforgiving law of supply and demand. The Central

Committee pointed out that Istpart's publications on 1905 (including those in Viatka) remained unsold and rotting in warehouses. It instructed the agency not to repeat the fiasco and proceeded to emasculate publication plans to mark the tenth anniversary of 1917. Viatka's historians, among others, strenuously objected, but they had little choice but to severely abbreviate their work or, in some cases, abandon it altogether.

The sixth chapter analyzes the proceedings of the Fourth Istpart Conference (January 1927). Major addresses by Istpart's leaders and comments by delegates revealed extensive erosion of the agency's earlier faith in a symbiosis of scholarly and political criteria. Istpart now demanded a grand narrative for 1917 in which historians and museums followed a real and imagined succession of events in Petrograd, whatever the facts of the matter elsewhere. Istpart required its historians to embellish the activity of the Bolsheviks and their party, to avoid almost all memoirs as unacceptably subjective sources, and to cite documents of Bolshevik provenance almost exclusively. Nevertheless, as chapter 6 demonstrates, this scheme of research and the story it was meant to produce remained elusive in essays, monographs, memoirs, and collections of documents published by Istpart's locals. Viatka's major publication on 1917 promoted the region's own version, not in keeping with the new orthodoxy. Its local Museum of the Revolution did much the same.

The seventh chapter discusses Istpart's absorption in 1928 by its highly politicized rival, the Lenin Institute. Istpart's demise signified the mortality of scholarly standards and, more broadly, of professional civility. As never before, the party's historians denounced each other and their previously respected nonparty colleagues on a whole range of topics. Warfare on the historical front led to the arrest and imprisonment of many so-called bourgeois historians.

"Methodology Ex Cathedra," the eighth chapter, analyzes the impact of Stalin's letter in fall 1931 to *Proletarskaia revoliutsiia*. His commentary launched a campaign to condemn elements of Istpart's earlier views on 1917 that had reappeared in 1929 in the fourth volume of a party history edited by Emel'ian Mikhailovich Iaroslavsky, an Old Bolshevik and prominent party functionary. Chapter 8 examines Iaroslavsky's always agonizing, sometimes dissimulating, sometimes confessional response.

Iaroslavsky survived. Many other individuals of importance in Istpart's story did not. The final chapter discusses the fate, often tragic, of the agency's leaders and its prominent historians. In so doing, it documents the political absurdity that overtook the head of Viatka's Istpart, Novoselov, after he departed the city in late 1927.

NOTES

1. M. N. Pokrovsky, "Institut istorii i zadachi istorikov-marksistov," *Istorik-Marksist* (hereafter *IM*), no. 14 (1929), 11. Pokrovsky addressed the Society of Marxist Historians, November 18, 1929. Pokrovsky went on to say, "History is the politics of the past without which it is impossible to understand the politics of the present."

2. Aaron B. Retish and Matthew Rendle, "From Lenin's Overcoat? The Global Impact of the Russian Revolution," *Revolutionary Russia* 31, no. 2 (2018): 146. See also the special issue "The Russian Revolution Centennial: New Themes, Scripts and Narratives," *Russian History* 45, no. 2–3 (2018). *Jacobin* published a series of articles on 1917 that can be accessed at https://www.jacobinmag.com/2017/11/the-russian-revolution-at-100. For an earlier work with an especially useful discussion of the revolution's immediate impact on Europe and the Third World, see Paul Dukes, *October and the World: Perspectives on the Russian Revolution* (New York: St. Martin's Press, 1979), 103–168. For a review of the international celebration of the 1917 revolution in print and in other formats, see articles by Vladimir Buldakov, Ol'ga Bol'shakova, and Yingman Li in *Rossiiskaia istoriia*, no. 6 (November–December 2018).

3. For a review of this literature, see Larry E. Holmes, *Grand Theater: Regional Governance in Stalin's Russia, 1931–1941* (Lanham, MD: Lexington Books, 2009), 8–11, and *Stalin's World War II Evacuations: Triumph and Troubles in Kirov* (Lawrence: University Press of Kansas, 2017), 1–3.

4. Catherine Evtuhov, *Portrait of a Russian Province: Economy, Society, and Civilization in Nineteenth-Century Nizhnii Novgorod* (Pittsburgh, PA: University of Pittsburgh Press, 2011), 249.

5. For example, see the work of Tracy McDonald, *Face to the Village: The Riazan Countryside under Soviet Rule, 1921–1930* (Toronto: University of Toronto Press, 2011); J. Arch Getty, *Origins of the Great Purges: The Soviet Communist Party Reconsidered, 1933–1938* (New York: Cambridge University Press, 1985); Yoram Gorlizki, "Scandal in Riazan: Networks of Trust and the Social Dynamics of Deception," *Kritika* 14, no. 2 (Spring 2013): 243–278. A publication on the terror demonstrated its divergent application from region to region as officials used the terror to address local issues and settle personal scores: *Stalinizm v sovetskoi provintsii: 1937–1938 gg. Massovaia operatsiia na osnove prikaza No. 00447* (Moscow: ROSSPEN, 2009).

6. For the early Stalinist period, see esp. Youngok Kang-Bohr, *Stalinismus im der ländlichen Provinz: Das Gebiet Voronež, 1934–1941* (Essen: Klartext Verlag, 2006).

7. Oleg Khlevniuk, "Decentralizing Dictatorship: Soviet Local Governance during World War II," *Russian Review* 77, no. 3 (July 2018): 470–484;

O. V. Khlevniuk, "Sovetskie narkomaty i detsentralizatsiia upravleniia ekonomikoi v gody Velikoi Otechestvennoi voiny," *Rossiiskaia istoriia*, no. 4 (July–August 2018), 58–72; Oleg V. Khlevniuk, "'Tolkachi', Parallel'nye stimuly v stalinskoi ekonomicheskoi sisteme 1930-e–1950-e gody," *Cahiers du Monde Russe* 59, no. 2–3 (2018): 233–254; Oleg V. Khlevniuk, "Administrativnye praktiki v sovetskom tylu: Mezhdu tsentralizatsiei i avtonomiei," in *Sovetskii tyl, 1941–1945:Povsednevnaia zhizn' v gody voiny* (Moscow: ROSSPEN, 2019), 257–276.

8. Holmes, *Grand Theater*.

9. Larry E. Holmes, *War, Evacuation, and the Exercise of Power: Kirov's Pedagogical Institute, 1941–1952* (Lanham, MD: Lexington Books, 2012).

10. Holmes, *Stalin's World War II Evacuations*.

11. For a list of original sources published by Istpart, see G. D. Alekseeva, "Istpart: Osnovnye napravleniia i etapy deiatel'nosti," *Voprosy istorii*, no. 9 (1982), 24.

12. Dissertations on Istpart's locals underscore their obeisance to the center. See dissertations by Ol'ga Iur'evna Shamaeva on the Moscow regional Istpart, "Sozdanie i deiatel'nost' Moskovskogo Istparta (1921–1934 gg.)" (diss., Moscow State University, Moscow, 1984); by Marina Iur'evna Dashinimaeva on the Baikal region's Istpart, "Istoriia sozdaniia i deiatel'nosti Istpartov na territorii Baikal'skogo regiona: 1921–1939 gg." (diss., Institute for Mongol, Buddhist, and Tibetan Studies, Ulan-Ude, 2009); by Elena Anatol'evna Kalinkina on Istpart in the southern Urals region, "Komissii po istorii Oktiabr'skoi revoliutsii i kommunisticheskoi partii na Iuzhnom Urale v 1920–1939 gg." (diss., Cheliabinsk State Pedagogical University, Cheliabinsk, 2009); and by Ekaterina Aleksandrovna Selunskaia on the Tver region's Istpart, "Deiatel'nost' Tverskogo gubernskogo istparta v 1922–1929 gg." (diss., St. Petersburg State University for Culture and the Arts, St. Petersburg, 2010). A welcome exception is the fine dissertation by Vasilina Sergeevna Klopikhina, "Deiatel'nost' istpartov na Severnom Kavkaze (1920–1939 gody)" (diss., Stavropol State University, Stavropol, 2011). In a most informative work, M. V. Zelenov has argued that Istpart, among other party organs, rarely transcended efforts to control and censor information about the past (and present) and to restrict access to archival documents: M. V. Zelenov, *Apparat TsK RKP(b)-VKP(b), tsenzura i istoricheskaia nauka v 1920-e gody* (Nizhnii Novgorod: Volgo-Viatskaia akademiia gosudarstvennoi sluzhby, 2000), 182–238. On Istpart's main functions and for a review of some of the literature on 1917 (but chiefly not by Istpart), see James D. White, "Early Soviet Historical Interpretations of the Russian Revolution 1918–24," *Soviet Studies* 37, no. 3 (July 1985): 330–352.

13. Frederick C. Corney, *Telling October: Memory and the Making of the Bolshevik Revolution* (Ithaca, NY: Cornell University Press, 2004). See, in particular, 97–174 to include a discussion of Eisenstein's film *October*.

See also Corney's introduction to a collection of documents originating with the dispute among party leaders in the mid-1920s over the meaning of the 1917 revolution: Frederick C. Corney, "Anatomy of a Polemic," in *Trotsky's Challenge: The "Literary Discussion" of 1924 and the Fight for the Bolshevik Revolution*, trans. Frederick C. Corney (Boston: Brill, 2016).

14. George M. Enteen, *The Soviet Scholar-Bureaucrat; M. N. Pokrovskii and the Society of Marxist Historians* (University Park: Pennsylvania State University Press, 1978).

15. Aleksei Litvin, *Bez prava na mysl': Istoriki v epokhu Bol'shego Terrora. Ocherki sudeb* (Kazan: Tatarskoe knizhnoe izdatel'stvo, 1994) and Litvin's lengthy introduction to Piontkovsky's diary, *Dnevnik istorika S. A. Piontkovskogo (1927–1934)* (Kazan: Kazanskii gosudarstvennyi universitet, 2009), 3–63. For Litvin's views on Soviet and Russian historical scholarship generally, see Alter L. Litvin, *Writing History in Twentieth Century Russia: A View from Within*, ed. and trans. John L. H. Keep (New York: Palgrave, 2011).

16. Stephen F. Cohen, *Bukharin and the Bolshevik Revolution: A Political Biography, 1888–1938* (New York: Alfred A. Knopf, 1973), 273. On promising efforts toward leniency and noncustodial sentences in the 1920s, see Peter H. Solomon Jr., "Soviet Penal Policy, 1917–1934: A Reinterpretation," *Slavic Review* 39, no. 2 (June 1980): 195–217. On workers' assertions of collective power abruptly ended by Stalin's policies, see Kevin Murphy, *Revolution and Counterrevolution: Class Struggle in a Moscow Metal Factory* (NY: Berghahn Books, 2005).

17. See, e.g., the work on Soviet conservationists by Douglas Weiner, *Models of Nature: Ecology, Conservation, and Cultural Revolution in Soviet Russia* (Bloomington: Indiana University Press, 1988) and by Johanna Conterio on environmental activists of a different type, physicians and medical officials, in "Curative Nature of Medical Foundations of Soviet Nature Protection, 1917–1941," *Slavic Review* 78, no. 1 (Spring 2019): 23–49. In a striking twist of emphasis on continuity, Frances Lee Bernstein has argued that during the 1920s sexual enlighteners, doctors and authors of advice literature, paved the way for the state's repressive measures of the 1930s. They did so by privileging the collective over the individual and by calling for sexual restraint for the good of the health of the nation; Bernstein, *The Dictatorship of Sex: Lifestyle Advice for the Soviet Masses* (DeKalb: Northern Illinois University Press, 2007). Andy Willimott has recently argued that urban communes and communards of the 1920s represented a belief in revolutionary dreams as well as in the importance of the oncoming interventionist socialist state; Willimott, *Living the Revolution: Urban Communes and Soviet Socialism, 1917–1932* (New York: Oxford University Press, 2017).

18. Robert Maguire, *Red Virgin Soil: Soviet Literature in the 1920s* (Ithaca, NY: Cornell University Press, 1989); Michael S. Gorham, *Speaking in Soviet Tongues:*

Language, Culture, and the Politics of Voice in Revolutionary Russia (DeKalb: Northern Illinois University Press, 2003).

19. See, e.g., the work by Richard Stites, *Revolutionary Dreams: Utopian Vision and Experimental Life in the Russian Revolution* (New York: Oxford University Press, 1989). Stalin's most recent biographer, Stephen Kotkin, has argued that any real alternative to Stalin's policies "had to trump his power." In that unlikely event, there would inevitably follow "a willing abandonment or unwilling unhinging of the Bolshevik regime": Kotkin, *Stalin: Paradoxes of Power, 1978–1928* (New York: Penguin Press, 2014), 731–732.

20. Robert F. Byrnes, "Creating the Soviet Historical Profession, 1917–1934," *Slavic Review* 50, no. 2 (Summer 1991): 297–308.

21. John Barber, *Soviet Historians in Crisis, 1928–1932* (New York: Holmes & Meier, 1981), quotes on 11, 126. Konstantin Shteppa, in his *Russian Historians and the Soviet State* (New Brunswick, NJ: Rutgers University Press, 1962), referred to the 1920s as a period of equilibrium that was too unstable to endure (47).

22. William Francis Burgess, "The Istpart Commission: The Historical Department of the Russian Communist Party Central Committee, 1920–1928" (PhD diss., Yale University, 1981), 178. For a similar argument, see the article on Istpart's Smolensk branch: Michael C. Hickey, "Paper, Memory and a Good Story: How Smolensk Got Its 'October'," *Revolutionary Russia* 13, no. 2 (December 2000): 1–19. In an article that Burgess co-authored with me, we took a somewhat more optimistic view of Istpart's embrace of the scholarly canon: Larry E. Holmes and William Burgess, "Scholarly Voice or Political Echo? Soviet Party Historians in the 1920s", *Russian History* 9, pts. 2–3 (1982): 378–398.

23. Klopikhina, "Deiatel'nost' istpartov," 234.

24. V. G. Mosolov, *IMEL—Tsitadel' partiinoi ortodoksii. Iz istorii Instituta Marksizma-Leninizma pri TsK KPSS, 1921–1955* (Moscow: Novyi khronograf, 2010), 37, 581. Michael David-Fox has made a similar argument in his examination of the party's institutions of higher learning in the 1920s. Sverdlov Communist University, the Institute of Red Professors, and the Communist Academy regarded themselves as a "full-fledged revolutionary alternative to all 'bourgeois' science and education." David-Fox, *Revolution of the Mind: Higher Learning among the Bolsheviks, 1918–1929* (Ithaca, NY: Cornell University Press, 1997), 227.

ONE

Istpart's Origins and Mission

FROM THE OUTSET, ISTPART SOUGHT to serve the twin gods of scholarship and politics. Ideological, personal, and financial threats immediately challenged Istpart's self-professed calling.

CREATION

In summer 1920, Vladimir Lenin wanted an official history of the 1917 revolution and the infant Soviet Republic. That August, he invited the party's historian, Mikhail Nikolaevich Pokrovsky, to undertake the project. In the meantime, an impatient Lenin endorsed the creation of a commission at the State Publishing House (*Gosizdat*) to study the party's past. Lenin placed it under the direction of Mikhail Stepanovich Ol'minsky, Old Bolshevik and journalist. Ol'minsky wanted an agency that would produce work with a popular appeal and encourage the publication of memoirs. Pokrovsky returned at the end of August with a proposal for an organization that would promote original scholarship. Lenin informed a surprised Pokrovsky of Ol'minsky's commission and insisted on its cooptation of Pokrovsky's project. Pokrovsky objected. A scholarly history of the October Revolution required specialists—and not just those from the Bolshevik party—who were able to work with a variety of documents. Conversely, Pokrovsky argued, surveys of the party's history would rely primarily on memoirs of party comrades because of the relative absence of documentation, which was either never kept or destroyed during the party's largely underground existence before 1917.[1]

Lenin got his way, although he agreed on the need for "historians-specialists," as Pokrovsky put it. In late September 1920, the Soviet Republic's Council of

Peoples Commissars created Istpart with Pokrovsky as its head. The council placed the new agency under the Commissariat of Enlightenment (*Narkompros*). A little more than a year later, in December 1921, Istpart was removed from Narkompros and put under the jurisdiction of the Central Committee's secretariat.[2]

Pokrovsky had wanted research and the publication of original work as Istpart's chief mission. A majority of the agency's original nine-person collegium, much like Ol'minsky, insisted instead on the preparation of material suitable for party propagandists and on the compilation of memoirs. Within days of the organization's official opening, Pokrovsky resigned because, he said disingenuously, of his burdensome duties as deputy head of the Commissariat of Enlightenment. On September 29, 1920, Istpart's collegium approved Ol'minsky as the new director. Nevertheless, Pokrovsky's designs remained an important part of Istpart's agenda, and he continued as a key and outspoken figure there.

DUAL MISSION

Istpart's charge was unforgivingly political from the outset. Lenin had wanted a useful history. When the Central Committee took control of Istpart in 1921, it hoped for a history to parry multiple challenges at the time to the legitimacy of the party's rule. They came from sailors in rebellion at the Kronstadt Naval Base and from the Bolshevik party's own cadre, among them adherents of the Workers Opposition and Democratic Centralists, who were disappointed with Lenin's harsh policies toward labor unions and with his New Economic Policy. Rebellious sailors and Bolshevik dissidents all believed, albeit for somewhat different reasons, that the Bolshevik government had betrayed the principles of Marxism and of the October Revolution itself. But regardless of the politics associated with Istpart's founding, no one at the time, including Ol'minsky, intended that it generate little else than crude political diatribe. The Central Committee had another apparatus for that purpose, its Department for Agitation and Propaganda (*Agitprop*). In 1922, the Istpart's monthly journal, *Proletarskaia revoliutsiia*, announced the commission's intent to publish not only memoirs but also well-researched articles and monographs. Those publications "must have the characteristics neither of an apologia (especially of an institution) nor of agitational literature." Their content "must be researched and expressed dispassionately." Confident of the rightness of their ideology and their politics, Istpart's personnel believed that such works of scholarship would necessarily provide "a strictly Marxist evaluation."[3]

Figure 1.1. M. N. Pokrovsky, 1925. Courtesy of the Russian State Documentary Film and Photo Archive.

Such hopes for a synthesis of politics and scholarship derived from the careers to date of Istpart's leaders. Pokrovsky possessed impressive professional and political credentials. He had studied under the highly respected historian Vasilii Osipovich Kliuchevsky at Moscow University. He had been the main contributor to a valuable work, *History of Russia since Ancient Times* and author of *Outlines on the History of Russian Culture*.[4] In 1917, Pokrovsky served as chair of the Moscow Soviet. The following year, he joined a commission that drafted the first constitution for the Russian Republic and, as mentioned previously, served as a deputy commissar of Narkompros.

Pokrovsky enthusiastically embraced Istpart's dual mission of scholarship and partisanship. He spoke disparagingly of dilettantes and pamphleteers who paraded about as historians but who neither loved the facts nor respected the principle of documentation.[5] Historical talent, a difficult gift to master, was the first prerequisite for writing history, Pokrovsky insisted in 1926.[6] Those who would throw away the work of the nineteenth-century Russian historian Sergei Mikhailovich Solov'ev and of Kliuchevsky "on the ground that they are not Marxists," he warned that same year, "would prove themselves to be an extraordinary fool."[7]

Another Bolshevik historian, Sergei Andreevich Piontkovsky—one of Istpart's nine original members and an instructor at Sverdlov Communist University—shared Pokrovsky's faith in the compatibility of political and scholarly agendas. In 1922, he praised the journals *Krasnaia letopis'*, *Byloe*, *Golos minuvshego*, and *Dela i dni* (the last three nonparty periodicals) for their publication of reminiscences and documents that represented various points of view.[8] In 1923, in a review of memoirs on 1917 written by non-Bolsheviks, Piontkovsky acknowledged their subjectivity but valued them as a "rich storehouse of testimony and of facts on the history of our present revolution."[9] In 1926, Piontkovsky still believed, or wanted to believe, that the publication and use of a whole range of party and nonparty documents would necessarily portray the Bolshevik party as a progressive force in history. He complained that the Central Archival Administration selected and published documents for political and not scholarly purposes. "Partisanship (*partizanshchina*) and haphazardness (*sluchainost'*)," he declared, "must be eliminated in the publication of materials and in the study of the October Revolution."[10]

MISSION THREATENED

In the early and mid-1920s, Istpart's plan for a mutually supportive arrangement between Bolshevik politics and the traditional canons of scholarship endured multiple challenges. The party's ideology, the publication of Trotsky's version of the events of 1917 in "Lessons of October," conflict among strong-willed leaders at Istpart, and inadequate human and material resources made it difficult, but not yet impossible, for the commission to fulfill its mission.

MARXISM-LENINISM

The very fundamentals of Marxism-Leninism threatened any attempt to balance an objective view of the world, past or present, with Bolshevik politics. In promoting their goal of changing society, Karl Marx and Friedrich Engels took a sharply utilitarian and partisan view of all intellectual endeavor. "For the practical materialist, i.e. the communist," they insisted, "it is a question of revolutionizing the existing world, of practically attacking and changing existing things.... Philosophers have only interpreted the world differently, the point is to change it."[11] Lenin expressed the same sentiments but more forcefully. He demanded that everything become a hammer for the revolutionary transformation of Russian society. Nothing could or should be nonpartisan. And yet in the face of these ideological precepts, as menacing as they might be, Istpart could pursue its initial mission as long as its historians managed to retain the belief that scholarship and political service reinforced each other.

LESSONS OF OCTOBER

After Lenin's death, disputes among his successors turned the story of 1917 into a political battleground. On the occasion in 1924 of the seventh anniversary of the Bolshevik Revolution, Gosizdat printed the third volume of Trotsky's collected works. Entitled *1917*, it covered the months from February to October of that year. Just before its submission for printing, Trotsky hastily wrote a preface, "Lessons of October."[12] He finished it in mid-September. The following month, the publisher released five thousand copies of the volume, with thirty-five thousand more soon to follow.

Trotsky's rambling and egregiously self-serving preface created an immediate sensation. There he presented the party's history in 1917 as an ongoing internal conflict between those militants, himself included, who had demanded that Bolsheviks take power and dissidents—the "right wing" of the party, most notably Lev Kamenev and Grigorii Zinoviev—who opposed any such revolt and a Bolshevik dictatorship to follow. In October, the Petrograd Soviet, not coincidentally led by Trotsky, supported the Petrograd garrison's defiance of any order for its dispatch to the front. At that moment, Trotsky argued, a victorious insurrection in the capital had been three-quarters, even nine-tenths, achieved, even if Lenin was not fully aware of it. The seizure of power on Lenin's orders on October 24 and 25 was, therefore, little more than an anticlimax to events of the preceding days. In the unkindest cut of all, Trotsky made no mention of Stalin at any point in 1917.[13]

On the volume's publication, a so-called literary discussion followed.[14] That November, Kamenev and Stalin denounced Trotsky's essay at a variety of party venues. They did so again at a plenary session of the party's Central Committee in January 1925.[15] A virtual "who's who" of the party, including Zinoviev, Kamenev, Nikolai Bukharin, Aleksei Rykov, Viacheslav Molotov, Nadezhda Krupskaya (Lenin's wife), and Andrei Andreev, wrote scathing pieces that appeared over and over again in 1925 in such volumes as *For Leninism, Against Trotskyism*, and, most notably, *For Leninism: A Collection of Articles*, the latter a 488-page tome printed in a huge press run of seventy-five thousand copies.[16]

They turned Trotsky's argument back on him. The party's entire history had indeed been one of struggle with external and internal enemies, Trotsky most prominently among them, before, during, and after 1917. Critics condemned "Lessons of October" as an attack on the party's leadership in 1917 and again in 1924.

In his contribution in *For Leninism*, Kamenev made it clear that the issue was not primarily a "historical" dispute but a political one: "I do not intend to analyze in detail Trotsky's article. I want only to deal with the social and political meaning of com. Trotsky's effort."[17] "Trotsky," Kamenev hastened to say, "is not an historian; neither are we."[18] Despite this self-proclaimed distance of the discussion from history as a scholarly discipline, the dispute with Trotsky could not but drag Istpart and some of its historians into the fray.

Several years earlier in 1921, when examining the secret police archives, Istpart's researchers found a letter by Trotsky written in early 1913 and sent to Nikolai Semenovich Chkheidze, the head of the Menshevik group in the Fourth Duma. In it, Trotsky reiterated his earlier public attacks on Lenin. But in this private correspondence, Trotsky used uncommonly harsh language. He characterized Lenin as a "professional exploiter of all that is backward in the Russian labor movement." Trotsky added that "the entire edifice of Leninism at the present time is built on lies and falsification and contains the poisonous seeds of its own destruction."[19]

On the letter's discovery, Ol'minsky, then Istpart's head, wrote to Trotsky suggesting its publication. Trotsky opposed its release because, he said, it would dredge up old differences and lead to unnecessary polemical exchanges in the present.[20] Ol'minsky agreed. But now, years later, in the context of the intraparty debates of 1924 and 1925, Ol'minsky and the party's leadership welcomed a polemical exchange with Trotsky. On December 9 and 10, 1924, *Pravda* and *Izvestiia* published not the letter to Chkheidze but Trotsky's letter, embarrassing enough to the author, that he had sent to Ol'minsky.[21] The following year in the introduction of yet another book of essays attacking Trotsky, *Lenin on Trotsky and Trotskyism*, Ol'minsky adopted a more aggressive approach. There he highlighted Trotsky's history of opposition to Lenin and to the party's leadership before 1917. This volume reprinted Trotsky's letter to Chkheidze. Ol'minsky insisted that Trotsky's letters "show through and through a rather obvious contempt for the party."[22]

Ol'minsky technically spoke for himself and not for Istpart. Despite his critical contribution to it, *Lenin on Trotsky and Trotskyism* did not carry Istpart's imprimatur. Yet as an agency of the party's Central Committee, Istpart had no choice but to get involved. It launched its own diatribe against Trotsky in the initial issue in 1925 of *Proletarskaia revoliutsiia*. There, Semen Ivanovich Kanatchikov, Istpart's head since January 1925, repeated the now-official narrative that the party's history had been a struggle with deviants for the purity of revolutionary theory. Trotsky's "Lessons of October" was only the latest "attack on the theoretical foundations of Leninism."[23] Piontkovsky followed with an article, "Mistakes in Trotsky's 'Lessons of October.'"[24] The author began ably enough with cautionary remarks about the reliability and appropriate use of documents. But Piontkovsky then turned fiercely polemical, picking and choosing facts and quotations at will to highlight and embellish the differences between Trotsky and the party's leadership in 1917. He knew better, as we will see later, but at this moment Piontkovsky forswore Trotsky's contention that *Pravda* in March 1917 (then under the leadership of Kamenev, Zinoviev, and Stalin) expressed support for the Provisional Government on the condition that it pursue social and economic reform. Moreover, Piontkovsky knowingly distorted the facts when denying Trotsky any significant role in the October revolt.

However, Piontkovsky and Istpart's leaders, Ol'minsky and Kanatchikov, directed their ire at Trotsky the politician. Istpart's dual mission to serve both scholarship and politics remained in place, if not fully intact.

CLASH OF PERSONALITIES

There were other threats to Istpart's complex agenda. Personal conflicts and spite challenged the agency's initial spirit of intellectual inquiry. Ol'minsky in particular was prone to turn professional disagreements into nasty personal affairs. When evaluating the work of others, he repeatedly displayed what his biographers have called the "exacting, demanding, and severe" features of his personality and a "caustic satirical style."[25] In almost twenty book reviews that appeared in the first three issues of Istpart's *Proletarskaia revoliutsiia* in 1921 and 1922, Ol'minsky demonstrably focused on relatively minor errors of fact and presentation. He seemed almost to prefer memoirs published abroad by former White officers and officials to those of his own comrades. Whatever their purpose, he said, the authors of the former displayed the foolishness and despair of the White cause for all to see. Poor health would soon make Ol'minsky even more abrupt and less tolerant. In summer 1922, he suffered a stroke that deprived him of speech and the use of his right arm and leg. Ol'minsky went abroad for several months of treatment but remained in poor health when he returned to Istpart in autumn 1923.

In the meantime, a bitter, largely personal conflict erupted between Ol'minsky, stationed in Moscow, and his Istpart colleague Vladimir Ivanovich Nevsky, entrenched in Petrograd. The strife between the two both exacerbated and expressed the historical antagonism between the two capitals. An Old Bolshevik, Nevsky had served as an editor of *Pravda* in 1912 and 1913 and in 1913 became a candidate member of the Bolshevik party's Central Committee. One of Istpart's original members, Nevsky worked primarily in its Petrograd branch in the early 1920s. While there, he and Ol'minsky clashed over Istpart's structure and purpose. Ol'minsky believed, and not without justification, that Nevsky's Petrograd branch pursued its own agenda and wished to rival if not dominate the center in Moscow.

Nevsky opened a new Istpart journal, *Krasnaia letopis'*, that challenged Moscow's *Proletarskaia revoliutsiia*. At Nevsky's urging, the new journal published researched articles and documents in proud contrast (it was implicitly understood) to the printing of memoirs in the capital's journal.[26] *Krasnaia letopis*'s second issue, published in 1922, made a particularly conspicuous display of its mission to use archival material. There Nevsky's article, "Strikes in January 1905 in Moscow," relied extensively on police records.[27] That same issue reinforced the point with a reprint of the tsarist police's sketch of Lenin's life to 1900, albeit a bland and unrevealing item.[28] Then to make the journal's assumed greater worth all the more obvious, it printed a review of *Proletarskaia revoliutsiia*'s initial issue that, although largely complimentary, nevertheless hoped that in the future Moscow would print fewer memoirs, freeing up space for analytical pieces based on archival research.[29]

To make matters worse, *Krasnaia letopis*'s fourth issue that year featured Nevsky's lengthy review of the latest five volumes of *Proletarskaia revoliutsiia*.[30] Nevsky did not oppose the publication of memoirs but found that many of them, especially those in *Proletarskaia revoliutsiia*, had at best a "fragmentary character." The journal should therefore enlist researchers to study the broad sweep of the revolutionary past and write articles that integrated revelations in memoirs with knowledge gained from documents. Nevsky ended his review on a caustic note. If *Proletarskaia revoliutsiia* was for only "agitational" purposes, then his criticism was inappropriate. "But as far as we know, Istpart's task is to place a study of the party's history on a scholarly basis, and thus we are right."[31]

Ol'minsky did not like what he heard and read from Petrograd. He insisted that available documents, especially those from the tsarist secret police files, underestimated his party's activity and influence, which, before 1917, had existed mostly underground and largely beyond (he thought) the police's reach. Rather, he and his journal preferred a publication of memoirs by Bolsheviks that emphasized (and embellished) the party's past importance.[32]

It did not help matters when, in early 1923, Nevsky published an article in none other than *Proletarskaia revoliutsiia* in which he dismissed a majority of memoirs published by Istpart's regional branches. The authors of these items,

Nevsky insisted, obsessed over insignificant, petty details and repeated what was already well known.[33] At the same time, Nevsky ostentatiously made his point by picking a particularly egregious example of a memoir that all of his party colleagues would find atrocious. He reviewed the second issue of the émigré journal, *Russkaia letopis'*, published in 1922 in Paris. It was full of "trash and historical evil." Memoirs from monarchists might occasionally be useful, Nevsky admitted, but in this case, he felt compelled to warn potential readers of the volume's "stench of the breath of the Black Hundreds," a notorious antisemitic group. Nevsky contemptuously declared that it portrayed the tsar as a democrat and a patriot, the tsarina as an ideal woman, and Rasputin as a sincere seeker after God.[34]

Professional and personal conflict between Ol'minsky and Nevsky overwhelmed Istpart's Second Conference held in Moscow, April 22–24, 1923, attended by Istpart's leaders and twenty-seven representatives of the agency's locals. Recovering from his illness, Ol'minsky could manage only occasional and brief appearances. It fell to Nevsky to deliver the major report, "On Our Immediate Tasks." Although Nevsky's commentary was not directed explicitly at Ol'minsky, delegates understood all too well, as did Ol'minsky, just whom Nevsky, now the aggressor, had in mind.

Adopting what surely struck many in his audience as an imperious and condescending tone, Nevsky repeatedly emphasized Istpart's scholarly mission. It should focus neither on the preparation of exhibits nor on the publication of memoirs. Rather, it should print documents followed by articles and monographs based on their use. To do so, Istpart needed to rely heavily, if not almost exclusively, on experienced and skilled archivists, including those "from the bourgeois world," and on highly trained historians conversant in many foreign languages. If Istpart settled for anything less, Nevsky warned, it would become little more than a propaganda arm, a subdepartment of the Central Committee's Agitprop.[35] Nevsky put it in a way that would surely insult many of his colleagues. "Our work is serious," he declared, "and it requires highly skilled personnel. But not all of our comrades are able to promote historical work. They lack the acumen, the training, and the necessary knowledge."[36]

As Nevsky no doubt expected, harsh criticism followed. Panteleiman Nikolaevich Lepeshinsky, former schoolteacher and official at Narkompros and at Istpart since 1921, led the way. "Nevsky scares us," he declared, with all of his demands. Lepeshinsky spoke for many when he announced that Nevsky had implicitly targeted Ol'minsky, who was not conversant in foreign languages. Nevsky's ambitions for Istpart, Lepeshinsky continued, might be appropriate well into the future, perhaps in one hundred years.[37] In one of his rare appearances, Ol'minsky curtly remarked that he did not share Nevsky's opinion.[38] Delegates agreed. They repeatedly declared that Istpart at the center and in the provinces lacked the human and material resources to do little more than collect and preserve a few documents and publish, when possible, memoirs. Anna Il'inichna Elizarova, Lenin's sister and official at Istpart since 1921, insisted that although Istpart in Moscow desperately needed all the help it could get, Nevsky had "one leg in Petrograd" and in his *Krasnaia letopis'*. Istpart lacked the means to support a relatively lavish operation in Petrograd and to print a second journal, in addition to *Proletarskaia revoliutsiia*.[39] In response to the criticism, Nevsky held firm. In so doing, he fell victim to his own fanciful ambitions for Istpart. If it did its job at producing genuine historical scholarship, he observed, the government would find the resources to support the agency in Moscow, Petrograd, and the provinces. In the meantime, Istpart should adopt a grand plan of scholarly endeavor obligatory for all its branches.[40]

Nevsky's stubbornness as well as Istpart's initial intent to promote research won the day, at least rhetorically. Lepeshinsky agreed that the agency should continue to support Nevsky's *Krasnaia letopis'*.[41] Elizarova conceded that *Proletarskaia revoliutsiia* should publish researched articles.[42] Nevsky helped his own cause as the conference drew to a close by initiating a successful motion honoring Ol'minsky as Istpart's "founder and soul."[43] The conference's final resolutions stressed the importance of a publication of documents, researched articles, monographs, and memoirs. They also acknowledged the need for well-trained archival specialists (albeit without repeating Nevsky's embrace of such people drawn from "the bourgeois world"). Delegates agreed that the pursuit of Istpart's mission required a compulsory plan of work for the agency at the center and in the provinces. It thereby might eliminate all too prevalent "impulsiveness, fecklessness, and self-indulgence" that admittedly existed throughout its apparatus.[44] The details remained to be determined for any such plan and the extent to which it could be enforced on Istpart's branches.

Nevsky had little time to enjoy his victory. Shortly after the conference's closing, the Petrograd party organization diminished the scale of Istpart's work there and largely limited *Krasnaia letopis'* to the publication of memoirs.[45] Nevsky moved to Moscow to work full time for Istpart's center, as Elizarova had hoped. Yet just when a truce of sorts took hold, the relationship between Ol'minsky and Nevsky took a sudden and nasty turn.

In June 1923, Nevsky completed a lengthy manuscript on the history of the workers revolutionary movement and the Social Democratic Party up to 1898, entitled *Essays on the History of the Russian Communist Party*. In so doing, he relied heavily on archival sources, including records of the tsarist security police, the Okhranka. The Petrograd publisher Priboi submitted galley proofs of the first quarter of the book, well over one hundred pages, to Lepeshinsky. He hastily looked over the material and informed Ol'minsky, who was still recuperating from a stroke, that the work was acceptable. He apparently did not tell Ol'minsky that he, Lepeshinsky, believed the book merited Istpart's imprimatur. In February 1924, Priboi released several advance (*signal'nye*) copies of the book, now more than six hundred pages in length, with Istpart's endorsement on its cover.[46] It contained a preface by Lepeshinsky, "From Istpart." There he called Nevsky's book a "major event," one that eclipsed all earlier work on the subject that had satisfied "neither scholars nor the broader public."[47] In particular, Lepeshinsky praised the author for his knowledge and use of archival materials.

Ol'minsky thought otherwise. As he later put it, "aware of Nevsky's usual sloppiness," he, Ol'minsky, had demanded his own advance copy. Priboi sent him one, which did not include Lepeshinsky's preface but did carry Istpart's imprimatur on its cover. Ol'minsky did not like what he saw. After an admittedly "most cursory examination," Ol'minsky demanded the removal of Istpart's endorsement.[48] He would be even more upset when soon thereafter he saw Lepeshinsky's encomium.

Priboi released the book in March 1924 in a press run of twenty thousand copies.[49] It did not feature Istpart's approval on the cover, but it mentioned Istpart's sponsorship on its title page and retained Lepeshinsky's preface, which Ol'minsky would now read for the first time as an "unpleasant surprise," as he recalled it.[50] Ol'minsky responded with an ill-tempered review in *Proletarskaia revoliutsiia*'s May issue. Even for Ol'minsky, he was unusually insulting while sharing with his readers almost nothing about the volume's content and major theses. He began with biting sarcasm. "We won't make excessively severe demands on the author, we won't search for a profoundly new analysis. So what if the presentation is trite." On four occasions for relatively minor errors, Ol'minsky condemned the book and its author for "sloppiness," in one instance for "'learned' sloppiness." "The 'historian' Nevsky," Ol'minsky almost audibly growled, had written fiction.[51]

Ol'minsky then turned on his deputy, Lepeshinsky. How could he "write a testimonial for Nevsky's book?" Ol'minsky answered his own question with the assertion that Lepeshinsky "had not looked at the volume that he promoted."[52] As if to deny Lepeshinsky's credibility, Ol'minsky pointed out that before Lepeshinsky's arrest in 1898, an event mentioned by Nevsky, he had not been a Social Democrat but rather a Populist.[53] Then turning his sights on

Figure 1.2. M. S. Ol'minsky, 1928. Courtesy of the Russian State Documentary Film and Photo Archive.

Nevsky, Ol'minsky condescendingly remarked that he had not mentioned all of the work's defects. "I only wanted to show," he finished, "why after a cursory acquaintance with Nevsky's book on the eve of its publication, I, as Istpart's head, rushed to remove Istpart's imprimatur from it."[54]

Ol'minsky had more to say about Nevsky elsewhere in that same issue of *Proletarskaia revoliutsiia*. Together with Maksimilian Aleksandrovich Savel'ev—journalist, a member of Istpart's collegium since 1921, and now the agency's deputy head—Ol'minsky wrote an insulting item, "From Istpart." In it, the authors insisted that despite Lepeshinsky's introduction, Istpart did not endorse Nevsky's book. "In view of any possible misunderstanding, Istpart asks that the book not be considered as its publication. Istpart assumes no responsibility for its content."⁵⁵ Ol'minsky and Savel'ev then asked a number of newspapers to print Istpart's disapproval.

Criticism of Nevsky's work broadened to include a denunciation of his sources. In the volume in question, Nevsky had dispassionately discussed at length the relative value of major prerevolutionary studies by such "bourgeois" historians as Kliuchevsky. He also remarked favorably on the reliability of police records.⁵⁶ Led by Ol'minsky, the ensuing attack on Nevsky almost completely dismissed the worth of prerevolutionary gendarme archival material. Critics joined Ol'minsky in declaring that such items underestimated the power of the revolutionary movement and the significance of the Bolshevik party. On September 6, 1924, at a meeting of Istpart's staff, Ol'minsky and his coworkers egregiously distorted the issue (and Nevsky's work) with criticism of unnamed colleagues for an alleged deviation (*na uklon*) toward a "history of the police." They declared that Istpart should "compile a history of revolution and not of the police."⁵⁷ Later that month, Savel'ev sent Istpart's "Letter No. 1" to all locals. At the center and in the provinces, it declared, work on party history had "displayed a deviation toward the use of documents of the Okhranka, police, etc. without sufficient verification. A history of the police but not of the revolution emerges." The letter also objected to uncritical use of documents from so-called counterrevolutionary sources.⁵⁸

Not everyone welcomed the denunciation of police records. That November, Pokrovsky urged caution. Such sources needed to be used, he said, albeit with great care. He insisted that memoirs were also valuable. They were, he said, "interwoven with 'poetry and truth.'"⁵⁹ But later that year, undeterred, an incautious Ol'minsky once again turned on Nevsky. In a note in *Proletarskaia revoliutsiia* about his own (Ol'minsky's) mistakes in a review of a book of no significance to his conflict with Nevsky, Ol'minsky gratuitously insisted that "Nevsky knows neither how to use archival nor published material."⁶⁰ He successfully asked the party's Central Committee to remove Nevsky from Istpart and blocked the publication of a collection of essays edited by him, "The Proletarian Revolution on the Don (the Year 1905 in Rostov-on-Don)."⁶¹

Ol'minsky's behavior did not bode well for the viability of Istpart's dual mission. A modest embrace of the canons of scholarship required tolerance of different approaches and points of view. However, in the midst of this threat, Nevsky remained in reasonably good standing. He became director of Moscow's Lenin State Library. Moreover, he mollified his detractors with the publication in 1924 of two short and tendentious works, one a history of the party from 1917 to 1924 and the other a biography of Lenin, the latter in a press run of fifty thousand copies.⁶² Meanwhile, Nevsky's serious work remained at the forefront, officially acceptable despite its condemnation by Ol'minsky. In 1925, Priboi published a second edition of *Essays on the History of the Russian Communist Party* in a generous press run of twenty thousand copies, despite Ol'minsky's request of Lazar Kaganovich, member of the party's Central Committee, to prevent its appearance. This volume did not, however, contain Lepeshinsky's introduction. In its preface, Nevsky commented wryly that the first edition had provoked considerable "favorable and not-so-favorable" criticism.[63]

COMING UP SHORT

Another challenge threatened Istpart's mission and the existence of the agency itself: Istpart needed considerable financial support to achieve its ambitious program.

With its formation, Istpart was confined to single room at the Main Archival Administration, an agency at the time (like Istpart) under the jurisdiction of Narkompros. Not all of Istpart's forty administrators, researchers, and service personnel worked there at one time, but those who did found themselves in cramped quarters and beset by tobacco smoke, human traffic coming and going, and idle talk all around. They also found it difficult to get their full rations.[64] Elizarova later recalled that Ol'minsky, ever the tough taskmaster, thought well of these Spartan conditions. They would, he believed, put off any careerists who might otherwise seek work there.[65]

Elizarova would have been appalled if she had fully known of Ol'minsky's enthusiastic embrace of adversity. In January 1921, Ol'minsky sent a memorandum to the Presidium of the All-Russian Central Executive Committee in which he alleged that Istpart's employees received more than their fair share of rations. They were double- even triple-dipping, as it were, by acquiring food from Narkompros's cafeteria, from the House of Soviets (where some of them lived), and from the Kremlin. Such conduct, he insisted, had taken on "almost a mass character." Some people even managed to get additional food from a municipal cafeteria. Ol'minsky asked rhetorically if the practice should continue and received, as he expected, a curt reply to end it.[66]

Istpart continued to work in cramped quarters and with few resources to write and publish. Elizarova complained that while under Narkompros's jurisdiction, Istpart "led a recluse's life at the tail of the archive."[67] At the beginning of 1921, notwithstanding his fondness for Spartan conditions, Ol'minsky feared that his Istpart might wither and disappear. Soviet and party organs burdened his personnel with so many other jobs that they had little or no time for Istpart's work.[68] His agency could not publish on time (or sometimes at all) what it did complete. The previous December, it had prepared a collection of items on the October Revolution and submitted it to Gosizdat. The publisher sent it to Rostov-on-Don for printing, and then, Ol'minsky was not sure, perhaps to Dagestan or to an area along the Caspian Sea. When Istpart inquired about the manuscript, Gosizdat could not locate it. "They searched for it for half a year," Ol'minsky sarcastically put it, "and neither from Indochina nor from the Sandwich islands came news about the manuscript's location."[69] On another occasion, in March 1921, Istpart sent the first issue of its journal *Proletarskaia revoliutsiia* to the same publisher. Shortages of materials there and Istpart's relative insignificance meant that the journal was published only in October.[70] Ol'minsky later recalled, "They say that it is impossible to deal with Gosizdat without bribes."[71]

In late 1921, Ol'minsky complained that the state spent 500 million rubles just to put on a ballet. In contrast, Istpart received fifty-two million rubles for the entire year for its central office and regional branches. The state, he continued, had opened three hundred studios for instruction in song and dance and provided the necessary number of apartments for their personnel. Istpart remained confined to its single room, and its research associates, communists all, Ol'minsky sardonically pointed out, "wander about to find a place to spend the night as in the good old days of underground work."[72]

To give Istpart some visibility and funding, Elizarova launched a campaign, initially over the objections of Ol'minsky and Lenin, to place the agency under the Central Committee's jurisdiction. As mentioned previously, she succeeded. On October 31, 1921, Istpart's collegium called for the transfer in order to convert Istpart into a "strike force of an enterprise."[73] On December 2, 1921, the Central Committee declared Istpart a department (*otdel*) of the committee's secretariat. Istpart received a "special room" that was more spacious than its previous abode, albeit still small, in Elizarova's opinion.[74]

Istpart's new home at the Central Committee helped improve its relationship with Gosizdat. *Proletarskaia revoliutsiia*'s first issue in 1922 appeared on time in a huge press run of twenty thousand copies. Nevertheless, delays in printing continued, perhaps the inevitable consequence of shortages at Gosizdat of personnel and materials.[75] Istpart itself continued to suffer from inadequate human and material resources. Its new room was hardly adequate for its needs. Spare accommodations no doubt helped account for Ol'minsky's discovery, though perhaps embellished, of exceedingly poor work discipline. People came late and left early. While on the job, they "babbled on with each other and with visitors."[76]

In late 1921, the Central Committee budgeted for a professional staff of sixty at Istpart. The following April, its Organization Bureau (*Orgburo*) ordered a drastic reduction in the personnel of all departments under the jurisdiction of the Central Committee. The number of positions at Istpart was almost halved to thirty-five.[77] That number would suffice, Istpart's leadership reported in early 1923, if the people remaining were healthy; however, many suffered from a variety of illnesses and took multiple days of sick leave.[78] Of the thirty-five employees left, only sixteen associates worked, when able, on the agency's primary task: the collection, classification, and analysis of documents and memoirs. According to Istpart's report in April 1924, many associates were poorly qualified.[79] That year, Ol'minsky lamented that the Central Committee only tolerated his agency.[80] By the summer of 1924, no one from the committee had visited Istpart's headquarters or even commissioned a report from it.[81] That November, the head of Istpart's archive complained of broken glass in eight of its room's windows and a need for several heating stoves.[82]

For Istpart, poor conditions and inadequate resources seemed even more intolerable with the creation of a rival for funding as well as for dominion over the party's history. In March 1923, Moscow's party committee created the Lenin Institute; in September, the institute came under the jurisdiction of the Central Committee. The new institute, housed in its own building, received a huge quantity of books, documents, and memorabilia on Lenin and party history. After Lenin's death, in January 1924, it inherited his heart and brain. At the Thirteenth Party Congress in May 1924, its head since its origin, Kamenev, announced that the institute would become a "hotbed of Leninism" rather than, in an implicit jab at Istpart, "some kind of isolated academic organ." The congress instructed all individuals and organizations, Istpart included, to transfer materials relevant to Lenin's life to the institute.[83]

Eminently well-funded, the Lenin Institute stood in striking contrast to Istpart. Years later, Elizarova bitterly recalled that unlike Istpart with its single room, its adversary enjoyed "a richly appointed residence." When before Lenin's death she went there for the first time, she asked its staff sarcastically, "Well, it will be interesting. When Il'ich recovers and can visit you and us, where will he feel more at home, in your palace or in our democratic surroundings?" She thought it would have been better to give Istpart responsibility and the funds for the study of her brother's life.[84] She was not alone. At the Third Istpart Conference in May 1924, several delegates blamed the Lenin Institute for consuming at Istpart's expense the Central Committee's funds and attention. Ol'minsky put it bluntly, "We have an extremely powerful competitor in the Lenin Institute. For it, you might say, there is the whole state budget. For Istpart, there are cuts and more cuts." Ol'minsky mused that perhaps the Lenin Institute should take the lead or, as he probably preferred, that Istpart should control the institute.[85] Ol'minsky's colleagues suggested the latter option. The study of Lenin's past and the collection and publication of his writings and speeches were, after all, an integral part of party history for which Istpart was responsible.[86] Nevertheless, Istpart lost out. Between 1923 and 1928, it transferred to the Lenin Institute more than twenty-five thousand documents.[87] As discussed later, the institute took over Istpart in 1928.

Before then, Istpart achieved a great deal, including worthwhile examinations of the 1917 period. Some scholarship came from its regional branches, even as they experienced difficulties (discussed in the next chapter) that exceeded those at the center.

NOTES

1. M. N. Pokrovsky, "O vozniknovenii Istparta," *Proletarskaia revoliutsiia* (hereafter *PR*), no. 7–8 (102–103) (July–August 1930), 138–139. Pokrovsky's comments are also in the Russian State Archive of Social and Political History (hereafter RGASPI), f. 70, op. 3, d. 886, l. 1a.

2. Istpart announced its transfer to the jurisdiction of the Central Committee, effective December 1, 1921, in "Vsem oblastkomam i gubkomam R.K.P.," *PR*, no. 5 (1922), 322. Locals were required to have one of member of the regional party committee as a member of their collegium.

3. "Temy dlia pereraboty po istorii Oktiabr'skoi revoliutsii," *PR*, no. 5 (1922), 323.

4. *Russkaia istoriia s drevneishikh vremen* (Moscow: Mir, 1913); M. N. Pokrovsky, *Ocherk istorii russkoi kul'tury* (Moscow: Mir, 1915).

5. M. Pokrovsky, "N. N. Avdeev, kak istorik," *PR*, no. 5 (52) (May 1926), 217–221. Pokrovsky believed that such attributes were consistent with a historian's reliance on the Marxist method. Speaking of his subject, N. N. Avdeev, Pokrovsky concluded that "the historian in N. N. not at all killed the politician" (221).

6. M. Pokrovsky, "Burzhuaznaia kontseptsiia proletarskoi revoliutsii," in *Istoricheskaia nauka i bor'ba klassov*, vol. 2 (Moscow-Leningrad: Gosudarstvennoe sotsial'no-ekonomicheskoe izdatel'stvo, 1933), 111. It was Pokrovsky's speech delivered at the Society of Marxist Historians, November 5, 1926.

7. M. Pokrovsky, "Novaia kniga po noveishei istorii," in *Istoricheskaia nauka i bor'ba klassov*, 2:216–217. Pokrovsky's article first appeared in *Bol'shevik*, no. 12 (June 30, 1926).

8. See S. Piontkovsky, "Iz istoricheskikh zhurnalov," *Pechat' i revoliutsiia*, no. 2 (5) (April–June 1922), 163–180.

9. S. Piontkovsky, "Obzor literatury po istorii proletarskoi revoliutsii v Rossii," *Pechat' i revoliutsiia*, no. 2 (February–March 1923), 110. Piontkovsky

reviewed the published memoirs of M. Rodzianko, A. Denikin, A. Lukomsky, A. Kerensky, S. Mstislavsky, and Sukhanov.

10. S. Piontkovsky, "K voprosu ob izuchenii materialov po istorii Oktiabr'skoi revoliutsii," *PR*, no. 2 (49) (February 1926), 241.

11. Karl Marx and Friedrich Engels, *The German Ideology*, ed. R. Pascal (New York: International Publishers, 1947), 34, 199.

12. "Ot avtora. Uroki Oktiabria (vmesto vvedeniia)," in L. Trotsky, *Sochineniia* (Moscow: Gosudarstvennoe izdatel'stvo, 1927), vol. 3, 1917, pt. 1, *Ot fevralia do Oktiabria*, IX-LXXVII. An English-language version of "Lessons of October" is in *The Essential Trotsky* (New York: Unwin Books, 1963), 115–177, and in Frederick C. Corney, trans., ed., *Trotsky's Challenge: The "Literary Discussion" of 1924 and the Fight for the Bolshevik Revolution* (Boston: Brill, 2016), 86–138.

13. See references to the party's "right wing" and its "right-wing elements" in Trotsky, *Sochineniia*, vol. 3, XXXI, XXXII, XXXV, XXXVII, XLI. On the insurrection as three-fourths or nine-tenths complete, see XLIX, L.

14. See Corney's discussion of the response in his "Introduction: Anatomy of a Polemic," in *Trotsky's Challenge*, 5–9, 17–41. For a translation of many of these responses, 139–688.

15. *Kommunisticheskaia partiia Sovetskogo Soiuza v rezoliutsiiakh i resheniiakh s"ezdov, konferentsii i plenumov TsK*. Vol. 3, 1922–1925, 9th ed. (Moscow: Izdatel'stvo politicheskoi literatury, 1984), 326.

16. *Za Leninizm, protiv Trotskizma (po povodu "Urokov Oktiabria", tov. Trotskogo)* (Moscow: Molodaia gvardiia, 1925); *Za Leninizm: Sbornik statei* (Moscow-Leningrad: Gosudarstvennoe izdatel'stvo, 1925).

17. L. B. Kamenev, "Partiia i trotskizm," in *Za Leninizm: Sbornik statei* (Moscow-Leningrad: Gosudarstvennoe izdatel'stvo, 1925), 27–28.

18. L. B. Kamenev, "Byl li Lenin deistvitel'no vozhdem proletariata i revoliutsii," in *Za Leninizm: Sbornik statei*, 208.

19. In *Lenin o Trotskom i trotskizme* (Moscow-Leningrad: Gosudarstvennoe izdatel'stvo, 1925), 171–172.

20. Trotsky's letter to Ol'minsky is in *Lenin o Trotskom i trotskizme*, 3–4.

21. *Pravda*, December 9, 1924, 2; *Izvestiia*, December 10, 1924, 4.

22. *Lenin o Trotskom i trotskizme*, 5; Trotsky's letter to Chkheidze is on 171–173.

23. S. Kanatchikov, "V bor'be za partiiu," *PR*, no. 1 (36) (1925), 13.

24. S. Piontkovsky, "Oshibki v 'Urokakh Oktiabria' t. Trotskogo," *PR*, no. 1 (36) (January 1925), 220–231.

25. O. Lezhava and N. Nelidov, *M. S. Ol'minskii: Zhizn' i deiatel'nost'*, 2nd ed. (Moscow: Izdatel'stvo politicheskoi literatury, 1973), 216; B. P. Verevkin, *Mikhail Stepanovich Ol'minskii* (Moscow: Izdatel'stvo, "Mysl'," 1972), 45. Lezhava and Nelidov discuss in detail Ol'minsky's meticulous and often combative style of leadership at Istpart. Verevkin observed that "O'lminsky demanded from every

author exactitude in the use of words, painstaking work on each sentence and on each word." Verevkin, *Mikhail Stepanovich Ol'minskii*, 75.

26. See the statements of purpose for *Krasnaia letopis'* in its initial issue in 1922: *Krasnaia letopis'*, no. 1 (1922), 5–7, 339. Nevsky was surely the author of these items.

27. V. Nevsky, "Ianvarskie zabastovki 1905 g. v Moskve," *Krasnaia letopis'*, no. 2–3 (1922), 7–26.

28. "Spravka departamenta politsii o V. I. Lenine," *Krasnaia letopis'*, no. 2–3 (1922), 306–308.

29. *Krasnaia letopis'*, no. 2–3 (1923), 425.

30. V. Nevsky's review in *Krsnaia letopis'*, no. 4 (1922), 397–402.

31. *Krasnaia letopis'*, no. 2–3 (1922), 400, 401.

32. See Ol'minsky's draft of an article, hand-dated August 1923, in which he questioned archival sources as a reliable source on the Bolshevik party's underground years: RGASPI, f. 70, op. 4, d. 310, l. 14. On the differences between Ol'minsky and Nevsky over historical sources, see M. V. Zelenov, "Kontseptsiia, rozhdennaia v bor'be (Istoriko-partiinoe tvorchestvo V. I. Nevskogo)," *Voprosy istorii KPSS*, no. 8 (August 1991), 124–125, and chap. 3, "Nevskii's Riposte from Petrograd," in William Francis Burgess, "The Istpart Commission: The Historical Department of the Russian Communist Party Central Committee, 1920–1928" (PhD dissertation, Yale University, 1981), 71–95. On the strained personal and professional relations between Ol'minsky and Nevsky, see an entire folder in RGASPI, f. 70, op. 4, d. 310. The clash between Ol'minsky and Nevsky over the relative worth of archival documents and memoirs was recalled years later in 1985 in notes submitted by Ol'minsky's colleagues on the occasion of the ninety-fifth anniversary of his birth. See especially the comments by Khabas in RGASPI, f. 91, op. 1, d. 305, ll. 2–3.

33. V. Nevsky, "Obzor nashei istpartovskoi provintsial'noi literatury," *PR*, no. 4 (16) (1923), 288.

34. *PR*, no. 10 (22) (1923), 261.

35. See Nevsky's report in *Biulleten' Istparta* (hereafter cited as *BI*), no. 2 (1923), 17–20, and additional remarks on 23, 31, 40.

36. *BI*, no. 2 (1923), 18.

37. *BI*, no. 2 (1923), 20.

38. *BI*, no. 2 (1923), 24.

39. *BI*, no. 2 (1923), 33.

40. *BI*, no. 2 (1923), 23, 34, 40.

41. *BI*, no. 2 (1923), 35.

42. *BI*, no. 2 (1923), 32. Elizarova repeated the point later in the year, on October 19, 1923, at a meeting of Istpart's staff: RGASPI, f. 70, op 1. d. 26, l. 1.

43. *BI*, no. 2 (1923), 39.

44. *BI*, no. 2 (1923), 42–43.

45. Nevsky was editor of *Krasnaia letopis*'s ninth issue in 1923 but not its tenth, the first issue that appeared in 1924 after Lenin's death.

46. For these developments, see Nevsky's foreword in V. Nevsky, *Ocherki po istorii Rossiiskoi kommunisticheskoi partii*, vol. 1 (Petrograd: Priboi, 1923), V, and Ol'minsky's "Ot Istparta," *PR*, no. 5 (28) (May 1924), 254.

47. "Ot Istparta" in Nevsky, *Ocherki*, III.

48. As Ol'minsky later recalled it in Ol'minsky, "Ot Istparta," 254.

49. Nevsky's book bears a publication date of 1923, but it appeared only in 1924. In its foreword, Nevsky noted the delay but provided no explanation. Shortages of funding and material at publication houses frequently held up publication of items, including, as we will see below, the initial issue of *Proletarskaia revoliutsiia*.

50. Ol'minsky, "Ot Istparta," 254.

51. Ol'minsky's review of V. Nevsky, *Ocherki po istorii R.K.P*, pt. 1 (Petrograd: Priboi, 1923), is in *PR*, no. 5 (28) (May 1924), 222, 223, 225. An earlier version of Ol'minsky's review is in RGASPI, f. 70, op. 4, d. 314, ll. 41–47.

52. Ol'minsky's review of V. Nevsky, 222.

53. Ol'minsky's review of V. Nevsky, 223. Friendly relations between Ol'minsky and Lepeshinsky were soon restored.

54. Ol'minsky's review of V. Nevsky, 227. Later that year, Ol'minsky's colleague at Istpart, Nikolai Nikolaevich Baturin, reviewed Nevsky's book. In a display of pettiness, Baturin questioned Nevsky's Marxism. In doing so, he demonstrated that medieval scholasticism was alive and well in the infant Soviet state. See N. Baturin, "Po povodu knigi tov. V. I. Nevskogo," *PR*, no. 8–9 (31–32) (August-September 1924), 149–163.

55. Ol'minsky, "Ot Istparta," 254.

56. Nevsky, *Ocherki*, 521–530.

57. RGASPI, f. 70, op. 1, d. 26, l. 9 ob. It also complained of a deviation toward a history of the White Guards.

58. RGASPI, f. 70, op. 1, d. 187, l. 1. Also in *PR*, no. 10 (33) (October 1924), 281.

59. M. Pokrovsky, "Dvadtsatiletie nashei pervoi proletarskoi revoliutsii," *PR*, no. 11 (34) (November 1924), 8–9, quote on 9.

60. M. Ol'minsky, "Moi oshibki," *PR*, no. 12 (35) (December 1924), 335.

61. Zelenov, "Kontseptsiia," 125.

62. V. Nevsky, *Sem' let pobed i porazhenii* (Leningrad: Priboi, 1924); V. I. Nevsky, *Vladimir Il'ich Lenin (Ul'ianov)* (Moscow-Leningrad: Gosudarstvennoe izdatel'stvo, 1924). In 1926, Nevsky published another brief and pedestrian work: V. I. Nevsky, *Istoriia RKP(b). Kratkii ocherk* (Leningrad: Priboi, 1926), in a press run of over twenty-five thousand copies.

63. Nevsky, *Ocherki*, 9. He also took note of some of the substantive criticism of his book—that he should have focused on the history of the Bolshevik party

and not on the Social Democratic Party or on Populism. Nevsky countered that the party had arisen out of the left wing of the Russian Social Democratic Party and that that party, in turn, had a historical relationship with Populism. Nevsky, *Ocherki*, 11.

64. On the room and rations, see A. Elizarova, "Retrospektivnyi vzgliad na istpart i na zhurnal 'Proletarskaia revoliutsiia'," *PR*, no. 5 (100) (May 1930), 156–157. For the staff as of February 1921, see RGASPI, f. 70, op. 1, d. 20, l. 4. The Main Archival Administration remained under the jurisdiction of Narkompros until 1922 when it was transferred to the All-Russian Central Executive Committee.

65. Elizarova, "Retrospektivnyi vzgliad," 158.

66. See Ol'minsky's memorandum and the response from the presidium's business office in the left-hand margin in RGASPI, f. 91, op. 1, d. 236, l. 2. Ol'minsky also reported that the Kremlin sent over rations that exceeded the number of administrators that worked at Istpart. He had ordered the "extra" rations sent to colleagues at the Main Archival Administration.

67. Elizaveta Drabkina, *A. I. Ul'ianova-Elizarova*, 2nd ed. (Moscow: Izdatel'stvo politicheskoi literatury, 1979), 126. Elizarova, "Retrospektivnyi vzgliad," 157. Elizarova noted that Narkompros had so little influence that Istpart could not convince institutions, especially those outside Moscow, to preserve valuable documents.

68. N. M. Mikhailova, "M. S. Ol'minskii—organizator i rukovoditel' Istparta," *Istoriia i istoriki: Istoriograficheskii ezhegodnik, 1981* (Moscow: "Nauka," 1985), 155. At this point, the Central Committee's Orgburo coopted a number of people, Elizarova included, into Istpart's leadership.

69. This information in Ol'minsky's review of a book in *PR*, no. 3 (1922), 303–304 and M. Ol'minsky, "Vozniknovenie Istparta i zhurnala 'Proletarskoi revoliutsii'," *PR*, no. 5 (100) (May 1930), 155.

70. See Ol'minsky's recollection in RGASPI, f. 91, op. 1, d. 177, l. 18.

71. RGASPI, f. 91, op. 1, d. 177, l. 18.

72. These comments in Ol'minsky's review of a book of memoirs, *PR*, no. 3 (1922), 303.

73. RGASPI, f. 70, op. 1, d. 20, l. 32.

74. Elizarova, "Retrospektivnyi vzgliad," 159.

75. See a report at the Twelfth Party Congress, April 1923, in *Dvenadtsatyi s"ezd RKP(b). 17-25 aprelia 1923 goda. Stenograficheskii otchet* (Moscow: Izdatel'stvo politicheskoi literatury, 1968), 80 and Istpart's report on its activity in early 1925 in *PR*, no. 6 (41) (June 1925), 261.

76. Ol'minsky's comments at a meeting of Istpart's research associates, September 6, 1924, in RGASPI, f. 70, op. 4, d. 340, l. 332 and RGASPI, f. 70, op. 1, d. 26, l. 9. The meeting resolved to limit conversations to matters "only about work" and to require from researchers weekly reports.

77. See Istpart's report for the period of its work from March 1922 to March 1923 in RGASPI, f. 70, op. 1, d. 46, l. 155. More reductions occurred in late 1925: see the report on Istpart for the party's Central Revision Commission, November 26, 1927, in RGASPI, f. 70, op. 1, d. 38, l. 3.

78. See comments at Istpart's Second Conference, April 23, in *BI*, no. 2 (1923), 5.

79. RGASPI KO, f. 70, op. 1, d. 46, l. 163.

80. Corney, *Telling October*, 130.

81. RGASPI, f. 70, op. 4, d. 310, l. 19.

82. RGASPI, f. 70, op. 4, d. 340, l. 154. The archive's head, Riabinsky, wrote to the chief of the Kremlin's Buildings Department.

83. *Kommunisticheskaia partiia Sovetskogo Soiuza v rezoliutsiiakh i resheniiakh s"ezdov, konferentsii i plenumov TsK*, 8th ed., 9 vols. (Moscow: Izdatel'stvo politicheskoi literatury, 1970), 4:121–22 and also, for the broader context, 38–44, 52, 57, 94, 114. On the Lenin Institute's creation, *Pravda*, April 1, 1923, 3; on its transfer to the jurisdiction of the Central Committee, *Pravda*, October 27, 1923, 5.

84. Elizarova, "Retrospektivnyi vzgliad," 161–162, quote on 161. Until the creation of the Lenin Institute, Elizarova had been responsible at Istpart for the collection and publication of material on and by Lenin.

85. "Protokol 3-go soveshchaniia Istpartotdelov S.S.S.R.," *PR*, no. 8–9 (31–32) (August-September 1924), 410–412, Ol'minsky's comment on 429. It did not help matters that Ol'minsky and Kamenev had been openly hostile at least since 1917. In March of that year, Ol'minsky, temporarily transferred from Moscow to Petrograd, served on the editorial board of *Pravda*. There he opposed Kamenev's inclusion on the board. See E. N. Burdzhalov, "Eshche o taktike Bol'shevikov v marte-aprele 1917 goda," *Voprosy istorii*, no. 8 (April 1956), 111.

86. See such a suggestion in summer 1924 in RGASPI, f. 70, op. 4, d. 310, l. 19.

87. Iu. N. Amiantov, N. V. Nelidov, and K. A. Ostroukhova, "U istokov sovetskoi istoriko-partiinoi nauki," *Voprosy istorii KPSS*, no. 9 (1970), 116.

TWO

At the Periphery

MOSCOW HARBORED PLANS FOR THE creation of Istpart branches throughout the infant Soviet state. Its ambitions stood in stark contrast to what occurred.

ISTPART'S LOCALS

Shortly after its foundation, Istpart took institutional form well beyond Moscow. By the end of 1921, Istpart claimed twenty-one regional bureaus, each under the jurisdiction of a regional party committee; by mid-1922, there were seventy-two. Thereafter, the number of locals fluctuated depending on the willingness of the party's Central Committee and regional party committees to fund them. It also depended on the readiness of the regional committees to count a branch that did not exist or the readiness of other agencies, often a regional agitprop, to administer and fund the Istpart local. Officially, the number of branches fell to thirty-nine in 1923, then rebounded to fifty-six in May 1924, seventy-two in 1925, and eighty-six in early 1927. Whatever the total, most were poorly staffed. In February 1921, Moscow had stipulated that locals should employ four people.[1] Most of the units at any particular time, however, relied on no more than one person. Many existed only on paper.[2]

Istpart's main office struggled over the extent to which it should and, as a practical matter, could dominate its locals. At the Second Istpart Conference in April 1923, Nevsky had insisted that Istparts everywhere take up serious research according to a plan devised by the national office. Despite objections from those assembled, Nevsky got his way.[3] At the same time, the agency adopted a statute requiring its branches to report monthly to their respective regional party committees and once a year to Istpart in Moscow.[4] That December, the center's new Office for Regional Branches, led by E. E. Shteinman, announced plans to assign locals tasks in accordance with an overall plan of work.[5]

Moscow's inability if not unwillingness to finance Istpart's locals undermined its quest to control them. At Istpart's Third Conference in 1924, delegates addressed the relationship between Moscow and the periphery more realistically than at the preceding assembly. To be sure, some attendees yearned for centralized control. Perhaps they hoped that more authority exercised from above would mean more support for the locals below. But now Istpart's leaders, Savel'ev in particular, resisted such appeals. He rejected what he called "an extreme" (*krainost'*) in proposals for Moscow's domination of the regions. "I would like," he declared, "to warn against absolutely unnecessary centralization." Rather than a single detailed plan for all the branches, he wanted what he called a "localization (*raionirovanie*) of Istpart's work."[6] Branches themselves could best decide what topics to pursue. Savel'ev hastened to add one caveat. The center must navigate upcoming work for the twentieth anniversary of the 1905 revolution. The conference accordingly provided guidelines for publications on the topic—one of many instructions, as we will see, for celebrating the great event.

What the center wanted and what it got were two different things. At Istpart's Second Conference, representatives from locals spoke repeatedly of a lack of human and material resources to do much of anything. Neither the party's Central Committee nor its regional committees supported the agency's branches. The delegate from the Urals Istpart, Ivanov, put it bluntly: "The Urals bureau exists only on paper. We have no money, no staff."[7] At the concurrent Twelfth Party Congress, April 17–25, 1923, a report from the party's Revision Commission noted that Istpart's central office had little or no contact with the Central Committee. Moreover, that office and its branches worked largely in isolation from each other. The agency had no inspectors (*instruktory*) of its own to send into the field to monitor the work of its locals.[8] The congress hoped to resolve the problem by fiat. Its resolutions called on the Central Committee and regional party committees to assign qualified cadres "exclusively for Istpart work."[9] Little improvement followed.

Even the collection of documents, let alone steps for their classification and preservation, exceeded the capability of most locals. Archival records became scrap paper for various household needs, wrapping or bandaging for hospitals, or raw material for recycling.[10] In 1923, Tambov's Istpart managed to purchase (from an unnamed individual) records of the tsarist police that had earlier been stolen from the archive of the Stavropol regional party committee. Their acquisition earned not praise but a reproach from Istpart's central office. The transaction encouraged "systematic theft" of such material for the purpose of resale.[11] Early the following year, documents in the city of Nizhnii Novgorod remained scattered hither and yon, with the exception of those that had been burned.[12]

Responding to the absence of financial and human resources, delegates at the Third Istpart Conference recommended a drastic reduction in the number of locals.[13] The representative from Saratov, Gustav Petrovich Saar, took the sentiment further. "The time has come," he declared, "to liquidate provincial Istparts." He thought agitprop could step into the breach by taking over the task of collecting and preserving documents.[14] If, as one conferee noted, Saar's proposal had "all the characteristics of panic," it nevertheless epitomized the desperate circumstances of the agency's branches.[15] Many had, in fact, already closed. Those remaining received little or no funding from their regional party committee and unsuccessfully begged the center's Istpart and the Central Committee for help.[16]

As noted previously, most branches that existed had only one staff member. However, that person performed few, if any, tasks for Istpart. They had other responsibilities, usually assigned by the regional party committee's agitprop. A report in 1922 noted that Istpart branches "serve local departments of agitation and propaganda." Istpart's people often acted as lecturers at regional soviet party schools that had been created for the training of propagandists.[17] At its second conference in 1923, a delegate from Istpart's Vitebsk branch reported that he had little or no time for the agency's work because he lectured in five different locations and had just been appointed deputy head of the local agitprop.[18] The representative from Kostroma reported that his local, starved for resources, had become a subdepartment of agitprop.[19]

A year later at Istpart's Third Conference, the delegate from Iaroslavl noted that his branch had one worker who was in the employ (*na uchete*) of agitprop. The delegate from none other than the Moscow region's Istpart told the conference that he had been compelled to inform the regional party committee that Istpart's assignment was not to serve agitprop departments but to produce work of scholarly value.[20] Hoping to give Istpart some autonomy from its rival, Central Committee secretary Andrei Andreev and Istpart's head, Kanatchikov, issued a special letter to all party committees and Istparts on February 7, 1925. It called for an end to the "abnormal situation" in which party organs converted Istpart's locals into a "subdepartment of agitprop, often thereby completely liquidating Istpart work."[21]

Little had changed when Istpart delivered its report to the Central Committee on the agency's activity from May 1924 to October 1925. It complained that local party organizations viewed their Istparts as "unnecessary appendages and Istpart's work as deadeningly boring."[22] The center still lacked its own inspectors to visit and instruct its branches. To save the costs of travel, the second and third Istpart conferences were held in conjunction with the twelfth and thirteenth party congresses and consisted largely of delegates sent to the congresses from the provinces. Many locals, therefore, had no voice there. Istpart's central office, still short of its own funds to send its inspectors into the field, did the next best thing by hosting thirty-nine representatives from its regional affiliates in 1924 and 1925.[23]

Istpart's branches had reason for still other grievances. Although there was little physical contact between the center and locals, the latter nevertheless felt overwhelmed by the flood of Moscow's instructions, circulars, and directives. On April 22, 1925, Viatka's Istpart objected. Its head, Aleksandr Abramovich Novoselov, reported that the Central Committee's Istpart had issued "letters and circulars one after the other," but his agency could do little in response. It suffered from a shortage of personnel and resources and from "an indifference of the party's masses."[24] Three weeks later, on May 14, Istpart's head, Kanatchikov, issued an abrupt response. He admitted that the center "sends out one task after another" but then told Viatka to stop complaining and to do as it was told.[25]

Throughout the decade, shortages of financial and human resources continued to plague Istpart's locals. Some of them desperately tried to stay alive by begging agitprops for their takeover. At Istpart's Fourth Conference, January 1927, one delegate asked Istpart's head at the time, Sergei Ivanovich Gusev, if a corresponding trend to convert locals into subdepartments of agitprop would end. Gusev craftily dodged the issue by saying that in only two regions had a branch merged with agitprop. Elsewhere, he said disingenuously, Istparts existed independently. Whatever their relationship with agitprops, most locals soon ceased to exist. In April 1927, the Central Committee ordered the reduction of the number of regional units from eighty-six to fifty-nine.[26] Additional retrenchment followed. By October 1928, only thirty-eight locals remained, twenty-five of which, including Viatka's, had a single employee.[27]

SMOKE AND MIRRORS IN VIATKA

On September 28, 1921, Viatka's provincial party committee created its own Istpart branch. Unlike its parent in Moscow, Viatka's Istpart had few, if any, scholarly ambitions. Its statute, adopted in early 1923, envisioned the collection of materials for an archive and their periodical display in exhibits at Istpart's office.[28] That office's physical location symbolized its primary political mission. It was housed in the building assigned to the soviet party school.

Viatka's Istpart had few resources to implement even this modest agenda. In 1921, the regional party committee appointed three full and two candidate party members to its newly created Istpart.[29] Each of the appointees had other responsibilities and lacked the time, if not the inclination, to breathe life into the agency. More than a year later, in January 1923, the regional party committee created Istpart anew, as it were. It asked Stefan Nikolaevich Poroshin to present a plan within three weeks for Istpart's future work. Two weeks later, on January 24, he presented a statute for the agency, confirmed that day by the committee's secretariat.[30] Yet little changed. Poroshin, the branch's chief, was already overburdened as director of the soviet party school, as a member of the Viatka Pedagogical Institute's Admissions Commission, and as head of the Regional Department of Education.[31] Istpart remained largely a figment of the party's imagination. One year later, Poroshin told the regional party committee's agitprop that Istpart received almost no financial support from Moscow (and, implicitly, little from Viatka).[32]

Finally, in early 1924, Viatka's Istpart showed some life. On February 22, Viatka's regional party committee assigned to it the aforementioned Novoselov for full-time work. Born in 1902, Novoselov had no more than seven years of formal education when he joined the ranks of the party committee in the region's Urzhum district in August 1920. After serving the committee as a clerk, Novoselov became the head of its agitprop in 1921. In that capacity, he diligently submitted reports, some of them marked "secret," to the region's agitprop in Viatka until his transfer to the provincial capital in late 1922 or early 1923.[33]

At Istpart, Novoselov worked almost alone. The agency had a collegium consisting of Novoselov, Poroshin, and Ivan Ipatovich Derishev, the latter the so-called "grandfather" of Viatka's Bolshevik organization, who had joined the party in Viatka in 1903 and remained active there until his arrest in January 1906.[34] It was Novoselov, however, who was solely responsible for the agency's day-to-day operations. On March 21, 1924, Viatka's regional party committee informed the central Istpart that its Istpart had only one employee and asked the central Istpart to finance an additional one. Moscow refused. On at least three other occasions from early 1924 to late 1925, Novoselov repeated that request to fund an additional worker, if only for secretarial duties. The center declined, reporting correctly (as we will see) that it was itself undergoing a sharp reduction in staff.[35]

Figure 2.1. Viatka Province's Congress of Archivists, March 1926. Second row, third from the right A. A. Novoselov, to his right, S. N. Poroshin, to his left, P. G. Falaleev. Third row third from the right, M. K. Liubovikov. Courtesy of Kirov's Regional Museum of Local History.

Novoselov had other duties. By dictate of Istpart's central office, he served as head of the regional archive's special Political Section (*politsektsiia*), as did all heads of Istpart's branches, with control over sensitive party documents.[36] His job became more demanding in 1925 and 1926, when the regional party committee provided Istpart with funds to celebrate the 1905 and then 1917 revolution (as will be discussed). Novoselov was now clearly overwhelmed. On March 4, 1926, he wrote the committee's secretariat, asking for his removal as head of the Political Section. The archive, he said, could appoint its own person to the position.[37] Poroshin no doubt continued to be of little help. Nevertheless, in November 1926, Novoselov took the occasion of Poroshin's transfer by the Central Committee to Samarkand to inform Moscow that he, Novoselov, now had an even greater workload. At the same time, Novoselov complained that the center dismissed the work of its regional Istparts "as unnecessary digging around in the archives."[38]

Viatka's Istpart had only begun "digging around." Its 1923 statute called on party committees in each of the region's rural districts to appoint an Istpart representative to collect materials and arrange exhibits in reading huts and museums. It did not happen. Local party committees lacked the interest, if not the financial and human resources, to support any such initiative. By mid-March 1923, not a single district committee had designated anyone to do Istpart's bidding.[39] Over the next few years, only a few district committees did so,[40] and in those instances, the local committee assigned the representative tasks unrelated to Istpart's mission.[41] A report from Viatka's Istpart in May 1924 complained that, for that very reason, its work "limped along and from time to time even comes to a dead stop."[42]

The party's rank and file likewise cared little about Istpart and refused to support it. As mentioned, in early 1925 Novoselov wrote to his superiors in Moscow to complain of the indifference of the party's members toward Istpart's work. Without anyone representing his agency to provide guidance, individuals, party organs, and state agencies throughout the region discarded their records rather than go to the trouble of selecting the important items and then bundling and preserving them. The problems persisted. In its report for the period from January through November 1927, Viatka's Istpart complained that its cadre in the province was assigned other responsibilities.[43]

Where they did exist, Istpart's rural operatives were untrained and without local encouragement, and they pursued menial and unproductive tasks. Regardless of any good intentions, they earned not Viatka's gratitude but rather abrupt rebuke. In November 1926, Novoselov told Ivan Sergeevich Durkin (his official in the Nolinsk district) that a statistical compilation of party membership for the first quarter of 1920 was a waste of time and paper. "We don't need such figures spread out over a two-meter strip of paper," Novoselov scolded Durkin.[44] In February 1927, Novoselov told Nikolai Nikiforovich Zapol'skikh (Istpart's representative in the Omutninsk district) that the latter's essay on the history of the local party organization was boring (*sukhim*).[45] That same year, Novoselov chastised Zapol'skikh for an attempt to publicly air the agency's troubles in an article submitted to the region's major newspaper, *Viatskaia pravda*. Zapol'skikh had complained that few if any party members, including the party's leaders, showed an interest in Istpart. They refused to help it collect documents and encourage the writing of memoirs. The newspaper sent the item for vetting to Novoselov. He prevented its publication.[46]

A number of documents that Viatka's Istpart managed to collect and classify were, in turn, demanded by the center. Moscow frequently requested materials on the 1905 and 1917 revolutions. It also wanted items on the life in tsarist exile in Viatka of such notable revolutionaries as Feliks Dzerzhinsky, the original head of the Soviet secret police (*Cheka*), and Vatslav Vatslavovich Vorovsky, a

Soviet diplomat assassinated in Switzerland in 1923. It also demanded all previously secret records of the tsarist police. Viatka requested their rapid return, and the center's Istpart duly promised to do so. Moscow eventually sent back most of the items with the apparent exception of the police files.[47]

Under Novoselov's direction, Istpart managed to collect considerable material for its archive. It also erected and maintained monuments and plaques commemorating revolutionary events and heroes. It responded to requests for verification of a person's political credentials so that he or she might receive a pension or a one-time monetary grant. For all that, Istpart remained on the margins when commemorating major anniversaries in the party's history. In 1922 and 1923, not it but the region's agitprop led preparations to celebrate anniversaries of the February and October 1917 revolutions.[48] That would soon change. As we will see in chapters 3 and 4, from 1924 to 1927 Viatka's Istpart played a major role in the observance of the twentieth anniversary of the 1905 revolution and the tenth anniversary of the 1917 revolution.

NEW DIRECTIONS IN 1925

In autumn 1923, Ol'minsky had recovered sufficiently from his stroke to return to Istpart. He remained in poor health and late the following year wrote Molotov at the Central Committee requesting his release as Istpart's director.[49] Reluctant to let Ol'minsky go, by mid-November the committee had altered Istpart's structure in such a way as to keep Ol'minsky on the job if not as the agency's head. It abolished Istpart's collegium and in its stead created a council (*soviet*) responsible for implementation of Istpart's projects. It appointed Ol'minsky as its chair. The director would fulfill chiefly administrative tasks.[50] It remained to be seen whether such a duumvirate could function smoothly.

In January 1925, the party's Central Committee appointed Semen Ivanovich Kanatchikov, previously the chief of the committee's Press Bureau, as Istpart's new director.[51] Like no leader before him, Kanatchikov insisted on the center's dominance over the periphery. At the Press Bureau, Kanatchikov had waged war on Trotsky and oppositionists of every stamp. He was determined to enlist his new agency from top to bottom in an assault on them and on any and all manifestations of political heresy. On March 16, Kanatchikov and Feodosiia Il'inichna Drabkina, the latter as head of Istpart's secretariat, issued a memorandum marked secret to all Istpart locals. It condemned them wholesale for political deviation.[52] Their interest in the broad revolutionary movement and in the activity of other "socialist" parties had allegedly come at the expense of a proper respect for the Bolshevik party. The numerical weakness and relative insignificance of Bolsheviks in a given area was no excuse for, as Kanatchikov and Drabkina put it, the "study of regional peculiarities" that avoided focusing on and, implicitly, exaggerating the party's activity.⁵³

Istpart's two leaders proceeded to tell their locals how best to present a history of the "party of *Bolsheviks*" (emphasis in the original) rather than a history of "Mensheviks, SRs [Socialist Revolutionaries], and others." "Our party is a militant party," they declared. "It finds itself now and will long find itself in hostile surroundings. Thus Istpart cannot be an academic institution engaged in scholarly research." Kanatchikov and Drabkina told their locals to demonstrate, whatever the reality of a region's past, that Mensheviks and SRs "were in essence always counterrevolutionaries, despite their arch-revolutionary outward appearance." Local Istparts should publish far fewer articles and memoirs written by SRs and Mensheviks of which a majority "are subjective and provide an incorrect historical analysis."⁵⁴

Later that year, Istpart drove the same point home once again. It wanted regional history to give way to the center's grand narrative, a tale that left comparatively little room for a leading role of any but the Bolshevik party. In their "passion for regional studies," Istpart's branches had devoted far too much attention to the Populist movement and jubilees of only local or regional importance such as those commemorating Taras Shevchenko, the nineteenth-century Ukrainian poet; or the Decembrists, early nineteenth-century revolutionaries; or Emel'ian Pugachev, the eighteenth-century peasant rebel.⁵⁵ Of greater harm, locals had focused on a history of Mensheviks and SRs "to the detriment of the history of Bolsheviks."⁵⁶

As expected, most Istpart branches responded, if only in a pro forma way, that they would conform to the latest set of demands.⁵⁷ But not everyone did so. In early 1925, Ukraine's Istpart objected to the center's requirements for an almost exclusive interest in the history of Bolsheviks and their party; it wanted to honor Shevchenko. An unsympathetic center summoned the branch's head to Moscow. After "a prolonged conversation with him," he fell into line.⁵⁸ Kanatchikov and Drabkina continued to instruct their locals on how best to proceed. On May 14, 1925, they issued a directive demanding that locals celebrate the 1905 revolution by concentrating on the armed struggle of the Bolshevik party from 1905 to 1907.⁵⁹

Meanwhile, in Moscow, Kanatchikov found himself accused of deviation from the official line of *smychka*—the purportedly unbreakable alliance between the proletariat and the peasantry. In an article published in *Proletarskaia revoliutsiia* in late 1925, he had demonstrably pointed to Lenin's acknowledgement of the instability of any such alliance with a predominantly petty-bourgeois peasantry.[60] In August 1926, the Central Committee removed Kanatchikov from Istpart and appointed in his stead Sergei Ivanovich Gusev, previously secretary of the Central Control Commission and head of the Central Committee's Press Bureau. Savel'ev remained at Istpart as Gusev's deputy and editor of *Proletarskaia revoliutsiia*.[61]

Conflict with Ol'minsky also contributed to Kanatchikov's demise. As noted previously, after his removal as Istpart's head, Ol'minsky remained at the agency as the chair of its soviet. His aggressive and cantankerous personality, so evident in his earlier disagreements with Nevsky, made friction with Kanatchikov unavoidable. On October 15, 1925, Ol'minsky wrote the Central Committee to complain that Kanatchikov refused to cooperate with him and the soviet. According to Ol'minsky, at a meeting of Istpart's staff, Kanatchikov denounced "dual power" (*dvoevlastie*) at Istpart, criticism, as Ol'minsky understood it, of him and of his soviet. Ol'minsky insisted that Kanatchikov could not cope with his duties and that Istpart's work had deteriorated under his tenure.[62] On the same day, Ol'minsky wrote Stalin, making the conflict with Kanatchikov deeply personal. Kanatchikov had neglected his duties at Istpart and left them entirely to Drabkina. Ol'minsky told Stalin that he could work with neither of them.[63] At the same time, Ol'minsky's colleagues wrote the Central Committee to complain of Kanatchikov's imperious style. Istpart was not, they said, like other departments of the Central Committee. It had a research and literary function in which a "mechanical transference of administrative methods from other departments" hindered work.[64]

Istpart's new leadership promptly retreated for the moment from Kanatchikov's narrowly partisan instructions recently issued to locals for a writing of the past. Guidelines released in 1926 for work on the 1917 revolution demanded, as before, a focus on the Bolshevik party. But they also called for an acknowledgment of the activity of other parties and of the possibility that in the provinces, "the October revolution resulted from a spontaneous movement." At Viatka's Istpart, someone, probably Novoselov, drew in pencil a vertical line in the left-hand margin at the mention of spontaneity.[65] The pencil's stroke signified, as we will see, the potential for a conflict about how best to remember 1917. There had already been disagreements about a presentation of the 1905 revolution.

NOTES

1. See provisions adopted by Istpart, February 16, 1921, in RGASPI, f. 70, op. 1, d. 20, l. 4 ob. The four were the local's head, a secretary, a typist, and an assistant for special assignments.

2. On the nonexistence of many of these locals, see Corney, *Telling October*, 126–131. Even the Istpart for the Moscow region, impressive on paper with a staff of five individuals and a network of its own branches throughout the region, amounted to no more than the activity of the head of the main bureau; Corney, *Telling October*, 129. Meetings of the center's Istpart board were poorly attended. On the number of Istpart branches, see *PR*, no. 8 (1922), 231; RGASPI, f. 70, op. 1, d. 46, l. 161 (March 1923); *PR*, no. 8 (20) (1923), 275; *PR*, no. 11 (34) (November 1924), 260; *PR*, no. 12 (47) (December 1925), 266; and RGASPI, f. 70, op. 1, d. 42, l. 47 (1927). At the Fourth Istpart Conference, January 1927, a report indicated the existence of eighty-three locals, sixty-one of which were supported by the Central Committee's budget. Those sixty-one had a staff of 126 people (ninety-one of whom held administrative or research posts); RGASPI, f. 70, op. 1, d. 33, l. 28.

3. Holmes and Burgess, "Scholarly Voice," 384.

4. RGASPI, f. 70, op. 1, d. 3, l. 9 ob. Klopikhina, "Deiatel'nost' istpartov," 45. In mid-1927, Istpart demanded regular reports from its locals at least every three months: State Archive of the Social and Political History of the Kirov Region (hereafter GASPI KO), f. P-45, op. 1, d. 240, l. 54.

5. *PR*, no. 1 (24) (1924), 281.

6. *PR*, no. 8–9 (31–32) (August–September 1924), 436, 443.

7. *BI*, no. 2 (1923), 15. See a summation of the problems experienced by locals in Isidor Vladimirovich Volkovicher's report on the subject at the conference in *BI*, no. 2 (1923), 24–27.

8. See the report by Viktor Pavlovich Nogin in *Dvenadtsatyi s"ezd RKP(b). 17–25 aprelia 1923 goda. Stenograficheskii otchet* (Moscow: Izdatel'stvo politicheskoi literatury, 1968), 80.

9. *Dvenadtsatyi s"ezd RKP(b)*, 706.

10. See reports at the Second Istpart Conference, April 1923, in *PR*, no. 4 (16) (1923), 349, 351.

11. See Ol'minsky's circular to all Istparts in 1923 in *PR*, no. 10 (22) (1923), 267. Ol'minsky reminded his branches that they should compel the surrender of such documents.

12. See a report at Istpart's Third Conference, May 1924, *PR*, no. 8–9 (31–32) (August–September 1924), 419.

13. *BI*, No. 2, 24; "Protokol 3-go soveshchaniia Istpartotdelov S.S.S.R.," *PR*, no. 8–9 (31–32) (August–September 1924), 410, 416–17, 429–35. This desperate situation matched that of the affiliates of the Central Committee's Women's Department (*Zhenotdel*) during the early 1920s, as described in Barbara Evans Clements, *Bolshevik Feminist: The Life of Aleksanda Kollontai* (Bloomington: Indiana University Press, 1979), 170–171, 210–214.

14. *PR*, no. 8–9 (31–32) (August–September 1924), 429–430.

15. *PR*, no. 8–9 (31–32) (August–September 1924), 434.

16. Local Istparts were left to their own financial devices. The center's budget in 1927 projected an allocation of only forty-five thousand rubles to regional branches from its entire budget of 265,000 rubles; see Savel'ev's report at Istpart's Fourth Conference, January 1927, in GASPI KO, f. P-45, op. 1, d. 236, ll. 11–12.

17. *PR*, no. 8 (1922), 234.

18. See comments by Shul'man in *BI*, no. 2 (1923), 16.

19. *PR*, no. 4 (16) (1923), 348. The delegate was Rostopchina.

20. *PR*, no. 8–9 (31–32) (August-September 1924), 416, 420. The delegate was Chernomordik.

21. *PR*, no. 3 (38) (March 1925), 266. Also in RGASPI, f. 70, op. 1, d. 187, l. 6.

22. *PR*, no. 12 (47) (December 1925), 267. It noted that of the seventy-two locals, forty-nine of them had a staff of a single person.

23. *PR*, no. 12 (47) (December 1925), 267.

24. See Novoselov's "Informational Letter No. 1" in RGASPI, f. 70, op. 2, d. 99, l. 11.

25. RGASPI, f. 70, op. 2, d. 100, l. 12.

26. RGASPI, f. 70, op. 1, d. 42, ll. 47, 57; M. V. Zelenov, *Apparat TsK RKP(b)-VKP(b), tsenzura i istoricheskaia nauka v 1920-e gody* (Nizhnii Novgorod: Volgo-Viatskaia akademiia gosudarstvennoi sluzhby, 2000), 211–212, 216.

27. See the numbers in *PR*, no. 11–12 (82–83) (November–December 1928), 362–363.

28. For the resolution creating Viatka's Istpart: GASPI KO, f. P-1, op. 2, d. 17, l. 106. See the statute among materials from the session of the regional party committee's secretariat, January 24, 1923, in GASPI KO, f. 1, op. 2, d. 42, l. 56. The bureau of Viatka's regional party committee confirmed the statute on November 23, 1923: *O sud'bakh i mgnoven'iakh proletevshikh … Ocherki istorii Gosudarstvennoi arkhivnoi sluzhby Kirovskoi oblasti* (Kirov: "O-Kratkoe," 2008), 137.

29. GASPI KO, f. P-1, op. 2, d. 17, l. 106.

30. GASPI KO, f. P-1, op. 2, d. 415, ll. 3, 13.

31. Until his departure from Viatka in 1926, Poroshin was occasionally referred to as the head (*zaveduiushchii*) of Istpart. However, in 1924 and thereafter Novoselov carried out most of Istpart's responsibilities.

32. GASPI KO, f. P-1, op. 2, d. 630, l. 87.

33. See information on Novoselov's career in Urzhum in GASPI KO, f. P-12, op. 3, d. 59, ll. 10 ob.-11, 14 ob.-15 and his reports to Viatka's agitprop in GASPI KO, f. P-12, op. 3, d. 89, ll. 10–11, 37–39, 43–43 ob.

34. GASPI KO, f. P-45, op. 1, d. 197. l. 14. The request officially came from Viatka's Istpart.

35. See requests in RGASPI, f. 70, op. 2, d. 98, l. 4; f. 70, op. 2, d. 98, l. 35; f. 70, op. 2, d. 99, l. 17. See the responses of April 8, 1924, and December 30, 1924, in RGASPI, f. 70, op. 2, d. 97, ll. 3, 5.

36. On July 8, 1924, Viatka's regional archive bureau created the political section; *O sud'bakh*, 20.

37. GASPI KO, f. P-1, op. 4, d. 40, l. 234.

38. GASPI KO, f. P-45, op. 1, d. 213, l. 337.

39. See information in a circular from Viatka's Istpart to all district party committees, March 19, 1923, in GASPI KO, f. P-45, op. 1, d. 201, l. 10.

40. See information from the secretary of the municipal party committee, Bulatov, and secretary of Viatka's Istpart in GASPI KO, f. P-45, op. 1, d. 201, l. 25. Also from May 1926: GASPI KO, f. P-45, op. 1, d. 213, l. 64.

41. See information on the districts in GASPI KO, f. P-45, op. 1, d. 213, l. 55; f. P-45, op. 8, d. 220, ll. 1–2; f. P-45, op. 1, d. 224, l. 13; and f. P-45, op. 1, d. 212, ll. 60, 87. Even when taking up Istpart's tasks, they did so as unpaid volunteers. They understandably preferred to devote their time and energy to other duties in keeping with their salaried position. See Viatka Istpart's report of May 1924 in RGASPI, f. 70, op. 2, d. 98, l. 21 and resolutions adopted by Istpart's representatives in the Viatka region, September 1924, in RGASPI, f. 70, op. 2, d. 98, l. 11.

42. RGASPI, f. 70, op. 2, d. 98, l. 21.

43. See the report in *PR*, no. 2 (72) (January 1928), 202.

44. GASPI KO, f. P-45, op. 1, d. 213, l. 352.

45. GASPI KO, f. P-45, op. 1, d. 233, l. 30. Novoselov frequently chastised Zapol'skikh for other errors: see GASPI KO, f. P-45, op. 1, d. 224, l. 125; d. 213, l. 285; d. 233, l. 12.

46. GASPI KO, f. P-45, op. 1, d. 233, ll. 17, 19–20. Novoselov criticized Zapol'skikh for signing the article with a pseudonym. But Novoselov's real objection was that a subordinate had registered a complaint publicly before vetting it with the regional Istpart office. See also problems in 1925 with the Iaransk district's Istpart in GASPI KO, f. P-45, op. 1, d. 212, ll. 7–8.

47. See *PR*, no. 11 (34) (November 1924), 266; RGASPI, f. 70, op. 2, d. 100, ll. 2, 3, 10 and d. 99, l. 4; *PR*, no. 2 (37) (February 1925), 239. Roles were reversed when in mid-1927 the center's Istpart reminded its branch in Viatka that the latter had not yet returned to the Central Archive materials on Pugachev: GASPI KO, f. P-45, op. 1, d. 242, l. 118. At the Third Istpart Conference, May 1924, the head of the Archive of the October Revolution who was also an associate of Istpart, Vladimir Vasil'evich Maksakov, insisted on the transfer to Moscow of all archival materials of the gendarme administration and of labor unions. See his comments in *PR*, no. 8–9 (31–32) (August-September 1924), 448.

48. On February, see a session of the regional party committee in GASPI KO, f. P-1, op. 2, d. 367, ll. 76–97; on October, September 22 and October 6, 1922, in

GASPI KO, f. P-1, op. 2, d. 239, ll. 89 ob., 111 ob. Also on October, see a session of the regional party committee's secretariat, October 4, 1923, in GASPI KO, f. P-1, op. 2, d. 418, l. 53 and plans devised by the Commission for Celebrating the October Revolution in GASPI KO, f. P-1, op. 2, d. 148, l. 74a and f. P-1, op. 2, d. 408, l. 107 ob.

49. See this information in Savel'ev's letter to Ol'minsky written no later than early November in RGASPI, f. 91, op. 1, d. 255, ll. 1–2.

50. A number of Ol'minsky's colleagues had written Molotov to encourage the Central Committee to keep Ol'minsky at Istpart. See RGASPI, f. 70, op. 4, d. 314, ll. 5–6.

51. For biographical information on Kanatchikov, see M. Chugunov, "Soldat leninskoi gvardii: Kanatchikov Semen Ivanovich," in *Oni borolis' za vlast' Sovetov* (Novosibirsk: Zapadno-sibirskoe knizhnoe izdatel'stvo, 1970), 86–93; and Reginald E. Zelnik, *The Fate of a Russian Bebel: Semen Ivanovich Kanatchikov, 1905–1940* (Pittsburgh, PA: Center for Russian and East European Studies, University of Pittsburgh, 1995). See also S. Kanatchikov, *A Radical worker in Tsarist Russia: The Autobiography of Semen Ivanovich Kanatchikov*, ed. and trans. Reginald E. Zelnik (Stanford, CA: Stanford University Press, 1986).

52. The memorandum, marked secret, is in GASPI KO, f. P-45, op. 1, d. 210, ll. 3–4.

53. Corney writes that with this memorandum Kanatchikov demanded a "zealous focus on the Bolshevik party as the sole *legitimate* measure of past political activity" and hoped to give the party an "aura of organizational coherence and revolutionary continuity." Corney, *Telling October*, 153.

54. GASPI KO, f. P-45, op. 1, d. 210, ll. 3–4.

55. "Otchet o rabote Istparta TsK(b) za ianvar'-aprel' 1925 goda," *PR*, no. 6 (41) (June 1925), 262–263. The report indicated that Istpart locals had been told of the error of their ways and of Istpart's proper "essence and tasks."

56. *PR*, no. 6 (41) (June 1925), 263.

57. *PR*, no. 6 (41) (June 1925), 263.

58. See the report on Istpart's work from January to April 1925 in *PR*, no. 6 (41), 263.

59. GASPI KO, f. P-45, op. 1, d. 211, l. 38.

60. S. Kanatchikov, "Lenin i revoliutsiia 1905 goda," *PR*, 1925, no. 11 (46), 62–80. See the discussion of this article in Burgess, "Istpart Commission," 167–170. Kanatchikov did manage to stay on at Istpart for a time.

61. Burgess notes that the "circumstances of Kanatchikov's removal are obscure." Burgess, "Istpart Commission," 171. In July 1926, Bukharin denounced Kanatchikov as a member of the opposition. It may not have helped Kanatchikov that in 1926 *Proletarskaia revoliutsiia* began publication of a series of articles on 1917 by Shliapnikov, then considered a member of the opposition. For biographical information on Gusev, see *U istokov partii: Rasskazy o soratnikakh*

Lenina (Moscow: Gosudarstvennoe izdatel'stvo politicheskoi literatury, 1963), 69–82; for information on Savel'ev, see L. V. Akhapkina, "Maksimilian Aleksandrovich Savel'ev," *Voprosy istorii KPSS*, no. 3 (March 1974), 105–108. Gusev's real name was Iakov Davidovich Drabkin. The previously mentioned Fedosiia Drabkina was his spouse. In 1905, he had served first as secretary of the party's Odessa municipal committee and then, later in the year, of the party's Moscow committee. In 1917, he held the same position in the party's Petrograd committee. A Bolshevik since 1905, Savel'ev had served as an editor of several newspapers, including *Pravda* and *Kommunist*, the latter the press organ of the Ukrainian Communist Party. During the 1920s, Savel'ev edited several economic journals. In 1930, he once again edited *Pravda*. From 1930 to 1934, Savel'ev was a candidate member of the party's Central Committee.

62. RGASPI, f. 70, op. 4, d. 310, l. 113. In his letter to Molotov, November 18, 1926, Ol'minsky retrospectively complained that Kanatchikov had not adhered to the requirement that the soviet oversee the implementation of Istpart's work. Under Kanatchikov, "this 'supervision' was in no way apparent." RGASPI, f. 91, op. 1, d. 261, l. 1 ob. (quotation marks in the original)

63. RGASPI, f. 70, op. 4, d. 310, l. 113. This note to Stalin is handwritten.

64. RGASPI, f. 70, op. 4, d. 310, l. 167. Years later, Ol'minsky remained bitter. In 1927, he recalled that under Kanatchikov's tenure, *Proletarskaia revoliutsiia*'s press run fell by half and the quality of its content declined markedly as well: RGASPI, f. 70, op. 4, d. 310, l. 69 and f. 91, op. 1, d. 179, l. 37a. In fact, under Kanatchikov the press run of each issue declined from 8,000 to 4,000. However, as we will see in chapter five, economic factors, not Kanatchikov, played the critical role in this decline. Ol'minsky remained at Istpart as the chair of its soviet, although his poor health limited his activity. On November 18, 1926, he wrote Molotov: "Illness and age are taking their toll." At work, he tired quickly. Ol'minsky continued to suffer from a "blockage of brain vessels," as he put it. After each attack (*pripadok*), "I irrevocably become stupid." If he were to remain in Istpart's soviet, he added, it could not be as its chair. RGASPI, f. 91, op. 1, d. 261, l. 1. In 1927, Ol'minsky remained dissatisfied, as ever, with Istpart and especially with its journal, *Proletarskaia revoliutsiia*. "In general, the journal is a dying collection of random, poorly edited articles written in haste and terribly wordy." RGASPI, f. 70, op. 4, d. 310, l. 72.

65. GASPI KO, f. P-45, op. 1, d. 202, ll. 59–60.

THREE

Multiple Scripts for 1905 and 1917

WHEN ISTPART'S HISTORIANS TOOK UP writing about the past, they abruptly encountered the dilemma inherent in Istpart's mission to present a recognizably scholarly but politically usable result. The difficult task became all too readily apparent when they addressed the history of the 1905 and 1917 revolutions.

FALLOUT OVER 1905

Istpart's central office planned to guide all its branches in their celebration of 1905. In late 1923 and again in early 1924, it devised a template for a presentation of this, the so-called first, Russian revolution. The regional narrative would follow the outline of major events as they had unfolded in St. Petersburg and Moscow. Local exhibits and publications would focus on popular resistance both before and after Bloody Sunday on January 9 in St. Petersburg, events surrounding the strikes in the capital in October, and action taken in response to news of the revolt in December in Moscow. They would also discuss, as extensively as possible, Bolshevik activity throughout the year.[1] Pokrovsky thought the task eminently possible. Writing in *Proletarskaia revoliutsiia*'s November 1924 issue, he told locals that he was certain that in December barricades had been erected well beyond Moscow. "The wave of armed revolt," he confidently wrote, "rolled throughout the country."[2] He and his colleagues were soon to learn otherwise.

With more funds at last provided by Viatka's regional party committee in 1925, its Istpart proceeded to commemorate the 1905 revolution. Istpart's central office asked its Viatka local, as it did other branches, for reports on its corresponding arrangement of exhibits and plans for publications. In particular, Moscow wanted from Viatka, first, a detailed prospectus and then, later, the manuscript of a major book in preparation, *The Year 1905 in the Viatka Region*.[3] The center would then make recommendations for changes and consider a subsidy for the book's publication.[4]

Istpart's national office was not pleased with what it heard from below. Rather than follow Moscow's instructions, Viatka's local collected and displayed materials on multiple political parties and groups from across the political spectrum, including so-called monarchist parties.[5] It also sponsored a number of publications, which acknowledged the limited influence of Social Democrats, whether Mensheviks or Bolsheviks.[6]

Moscow told its local that Viatka's exhibits improperly highlighted the activity of Mensheviks, SRs, and other political groups at the expense of proper glorification of the Bolsheviks. An obstinate Viatka disagreed. On April 11, 1925, when Viatka's local discussed Kanatchikov's memorandum of March 16, it denied any wrongdoing. Poroshin responded that Viatka was guilty of only a few unspecified deviations. Novoselov insisted that his Istpart committed only a minor error when it sponsored a display that included photographs and archival materials from various political parties and groups in 1905.[7]

For many of the same reasons, in early 1925, Istpart found fault with Viatka's prospectus for its major publication on 1905. Moscow demanded less attention to any cooperation of the Bolsheviks with the Mensheviks and more to the presumed militant posture and armed struggle waged by the former in the region from 1905 to 1907.[8] In July, Isidor Vladimirovich Volkovicher, who had recently compiled and edited an Istpart publication on the history of the Bolshevik party, harshly evaluated the draft of Novoselov's contribution to the volume.[9] He wanted the author "to throw out much of what was said about the activity of SRs" and instead focus intently on the armed struggle of the Bolsheviks. For the book, Novoselov might also consider the publication of reminiscences, in their entirety, of those Bolsheviks who wrote specifically about that subject.[10]

Later that year, Viatka's Istpart published *The Year 1905 in the Viatka Region*. The book consisted of 340 pages in a generous press run of five thousand copies.[11] Despite Moscow's instructions, a stubborn Novoselov discussed at length in his three chapters the strength and activity of Mensheviks and SRs while, to be sure, saying much about the Bolsheviks.[12] The volume's introduction, probably also written by Novoselov, noted that Viatka's workers staged protests and strikes, led by the example of their compatriots in St. Petersburg. He underscored, however, that Viatka's proletariat did not seek major political change but rather an eight-hour workday and better wages. He also pointed out that in his region, one without a history of large landed estates and serfdom, the peasantry did not seek land but rather political equality and lower taxes and did so using peaceful means. They did not coordinate any of their activity with workers' protests. [13]

Moscow's Istpart objected. One of its research associates, R. Khabas, reviewed the book in *Proletarskaia revoliutsiia*'s April 1926 issue. Novoselov's contributions in particular failed to highlight the activity and purportedly leading role of Bolsheviks in 1905. Khabas also wanted more said about what he believed to be the peasants' revolutionary movement.[14] For the moment, he appealed in vain and not just about the telling of 1905. Literature on the revolution that occurred in 1917, published in Viatka and elsewhere, provided a heterogeneous mix of accounts.

COMPLEXITIES OF 1917

From its origins, Istpart had issued something of a template for a proper rendition of 1917. Questionnaires sent out by Istpart in 1920 asked respondents to privilege the party's activity "as the unmistakable yardstick of revolutionary commitment and clarity." They also asked recipients to relate local developments to the main story at the center, in Petrograd, and to a lesser degree in Moscow.[15] Nevertheless, the party's historians in Moscow and elsewhere (Viatka included) wrote about 1917 with little regard for such tutelage.

Until 1927, Istpart's leadership still thought it possible to simultaneously satisfy political and scholarly demands. Its thinking corresponded with the politicized but important work by party historians on the 1917 revolution. To be sure, even the best of these historians based their research and subsequent publications on several partisan assumptions. First, they took for granted the existence of distinct classes, regardless of how people at the time identified themselves. The urban population correspondingly consisted of the bourgeoisie, petty bourgeoisie, and proletariat. The rural population included the feudal aristocracy and the rich, middle, poor, and landless peasantry. A distinct political party represented the interests of each class. The Bolshevik party, for example, spoke for the proletariat and poor peasantry. Second, the party's historians embraced the necessity, and thereby the inevitability, of the October Revolution. Russia had reached a turning point in its history. Only the introduction of socialism and the creation of a Bolshevik dictatorship could end Russia's economic dislocation and its participation in the war.[16] Third, these historians projected the Bolshevik revolution as the beginning of a successful assault against a united front of the international bourgeoisie or, as Lenin had put it, a break in the imperialist chain at its weakest link. These three politicized assumptions, however, were far too broad and sweeping to preclude significant work. The party's historians recognized that many people in 1917, even members of the so-called proletariat, did not think of themselves in terms of sharply drawn class lines. These same historians also readily acknowledged the public's concerns about immediate material improvement rather than political revolution. Finally, they recognized, even emphasized, the Bolshevik party's limited popularity and influence. Its program and ideology were, at best, far in advance of popular sentiment and behavior.

In 1923, Istpart sponsored a book by Piontkovsky, *October Revolution in Russia, Its Prerequisites and Progress*, released in a run of seven thousand copies. The author spoke of "waves of the workers movement," "waves of agrarian terror," and, more generally, "processes of spontaneous dissatisfaction."[17] Sergei Mitrofanovich Dubrovsky, one of Pokrovsky's students at the Institute of Red Professors and an instructor in history at the Timiriazev Agricultural Academy, peppered his publications with references to impulsive outbursts of popular anger. In a book published in 1923 and in another released in 1927—the latter a work sponsored by Istpart and the Central Committee's Agitprop that appeared in a handsome print run of twenty-five thousand copies—Dubrovsky spoke in turn of "the agrarian movement, agrarian revolution, spontaneous peasant movement, and spontaneous destruction."[18] The peasant movement, he wrote, exhibited "such a strength of spontaneity, that it would have been madness to try to control it. The peasant masses would have ground into dust anyone who would stand in their way."[19]

Like Dubrovsky and Piontkovsky, Anna Mikhailovna Pankratova and Andrei Vasil'evich Shestakov, both of whom would become prominent Soviet historians, emphasized widespread popular demands for better conditions at home, at work, and at the front rather than for sweeping political change. Factory committees demanded higher wages and better working conditions; soldiers thought mainly of ending the war and improving conditions in their units; and the poor peasantry, subject to "petty bourgeois illusions," desired private ownership of land. Even the landless peasantry sought not political revolution but rather better pay. No political party controlled such manifestations of "spontaneity."[20]

Historians acknowledged that the overthrow of the tsarist government in February caught Bolsheviks off guard. That spring in Petrograd and elsewhere, Bolsheviks and Mensheviks formed united organizations dominated numerically by the latter. Even the Old Bolshevik, Iaroslavsky—a member of the party's Central Control Committee, chair of the League of Godless, and an editor of the Central Committee's *Pravda* and of its journal *Bol'shevik*—underscored the Bolshevik party's weakness in February and March. He did so in an article published in 1927 in *Proletarskaia revoliutsiia* and in a widely distributed booklet, *The Party of Bolsheviks in 1917*, sponsored by Istpart and Agitprop and printed in a huge press run of sixty-five thousand copies.[21] United organizations had appeared everywhere—an indication, in his estimation, that Bolsheviks suffered from "organizational and ideational (*ideinyi*) confusion" (*razbrod*). Some united groups, Iaroslavsky conceded, continued well into the year 1917.[22] At the same time and in *Proletarskaia revoliutsiia*, David Iakovlevich Kin, a young historian and a recent graduate of the Institute of Red Professors, published an article, "The Struggle against the Intoxication of Unification." He emphasized the existence of such groups both at the center and in the provinces throughout much of the year.[23]

Historians freely acknowledged that not just Kamenev but most Bolsheviks in March and early April advocated conditional support of the Provisional Government as long as it pursued socioeconomic and democratic reforms. Many party members supported Russia's war effort until a time in the future when negotiations could bring it to a halt. They adhered to those positions well after Lenin's return to Russia and his denunciation of them in his "April Theses." In his 1927 article on the Bolsheviks in the first few months of 1917, Iaroslavsky quoted at length Stalin's own recognition of the difficulties that Bolsheviks experienced in finding a correct policy toward the Provisional Government and war.[24] He did not mention Stalin's own heresy on the matter. But in his subsequent and widely distributed book (mentioned earlier), he called attention to Stalin's conditional acceptance of the Provisional Government's rule. "Stalin himself," Iaroslavsky confided, "has declared more than once and openly that he then shared this mistaken position with a majority of the party." Understanding the delicate nature of this commentary, Iaroslavsky hastened to add that Stalin supported the April Theses and never repeated his mistake.[25]

Not the Bolshevik party's leadership and numbers but rather spontaneity emerged as the major dynamic of 1917. The revolt, Dubrovsky wrote in 1923, was "a floodgate through which the wave of popular dissatisfaction burst forth."[26] The best that the Bolsheviks could do with the peasant revolution in 1917, he continued, was to adopt an indulgent attitude and join forces with it. Dubrovsky began *The Peasantry in 1917*, published in 1927, with the comment that "one of the particular features of the October revolution as a socialist revolution was its unbreakable and direct bond with a massive peasant revolt." Throughout most of 1917, he continued, the Bolshevik party encouraged the "most 'plebeian' resolution of the agrarian question" from the peasants themselves.[27]

Piontkovsky agreed. In October, under the party's leadership, the "waves of the petty-bourgeois peasant revolution and waves of the proletarian revolution merged." "The combination of spontaneity and Bolshevik organization was," he allowed, "one of the characteristic traits of October. The proletariat and peasants provided spontaneous strength; the party provided organization and leadership."[28]

Party historians were uncomfortable, however, with their characterization of the October Revolution as, implicitly, a "people's revolution," a "quasi-anarchist revolt," or a "popular uprising." As the triumphant event in the party's short and difficult history, it deserved the socialist label. They made it so using several crafty maneuvers. The February revolution, they insisted, inevitably developed into the October revolt. The events of October 24 and 25 in Petrograd thereby completed the first (bourgeois-democratic) revolution that had begun in February. It simultaneously introduced the second (socialist) revolution. In 1923, Dubrovsky had written of a "union" (*soiuz*) in late 1917 of the peasantry and proletariat.[29] Four years later, he phrased it somewhat differently. Now he insisted that in October, "the revolutionary movement of the peasantry merged with the proletarian revolution under the direct leadership of the proletariat and its party."[30] Shestakov spoke of "two lines" (*dve linii*) of revolution in 1917, the proletarian and peasant. In October, they coalesced: "The peasant revolution formed a single current with the revolution of urban workers and soldiers."[31] Pokrovsky described the Bolsheviks' seizure of power in Petrograd as "the last act of the bourgeois revolution and ... the first act of the proletarian revolution."[32] Piontkovsky insisted that October "weaved together two currents," the bourgeois-democratic and socialist, under the hegemony of the proletariat and its party.[33] October thereby had "two faces" or a "double character as it completed the bourgeois-democratic revolution and began the socialist."[34] In *The Party of Bolsheviks in 1917*, Iaroslavsky similarly referred to the "dual character of the October revolt."[35] As we will see, this readily apparent unease with their own work would take a radical turn in the later 1920s.

Some of most interesting work on 1917 came from the pen of a Bolshevik with no historical training, Aleksandr Gavrilovich Shliapnikov. A Bolshevik since 1903, Shliapnikov chaired the Petrograd Union of Metal Workers in 1917 and, from July of that year, the newly organized All-Russian Union of Metal Workers. Following the October Revolution, Lenin appointed him as the first commissar of labor. Shortly thereafter, Shliapnikov became a leader of the "Workers Opposition," a group within the Bolshevik party that advocated labor's control over unions and that disapproved of the New Economic Policy (NEP). He continued to criticize the NEP as an unwarranted concession to capitalism and denounced the party's Central Committee as consisting of bureaucratic careerists dedicated to the creation of a "petty bourgeois order."

Throughout his career, Shliapnikov had kept or copied thousands of documents generated by the party and other organizations. On October 10, 1921, Istpart's collegium proposed to give him the handsome sum of one million rubles for the classification, reproduction, and use of the items.[36] Whether Istpart managed to lavish on Shliapnikov such a huge amount is unknown. It did sponsor a substantial number of his books and articles in the early and mid-1920s, most of them on the 1917 period. They included a two-volume work, *The Eve of 1917*, three volumes of *1917* (*Semnadtsatyi god*), and eight articles in *Proletarskaia revoliutsiia*.[37]

In those works, Shliapnikov relied extensively on a wide range of archival sources, memoirs of others, and his own recollections. Workers and soldiers in 1917 sought not political revolution but rather improved material conditions. In the capital, the Bolshevik party's propaganda failed to resonate with workers interested primarily in better wages and working conditions and not in the party's acquisition of political power. He repeatedly acknowledged deep divisions within the Bolshevik party over how best to deal with the Provisional Government and Russia's involvement in World War I.

Reviewers judged Shliapnikov's work largely by scholarly standards. They appreciated the research behind it, its honest appraisal of popular attitudes, and the recognition of the many difficulties facing the Bolshevik party.[38] Iaroslavsky's aforementioned article in *Proletarskaia revoliutsiia* published in early 1927 used Shliapnikov's *The Eve of 1917* to demonstrate the weakness of the Bolshevik party in 1917. Everywhere, Iaroslavsky correspondingly concluded, Bolsheviks were small in number and in the provinces joined Mensheviks in united organizations that continued to exist well into the year.[39]

Meanwhile in 1927, historians in Moscow and Leningrad published two major books on 1917. In the first, Pankratova returned to her earlier discussion of organized labor but this time with a book on labor unions rather than on factory committees. Her new work, *The Political Struggle in the Russian Labor Movement, 1917–1918*, relied on a wide range of sources, including newspapers, memoirs, and archival records of Leningrad's unions. There she emphasized workers' desires at the center and in the provinces for continued employment (in the face of lockouts and shortages of raw materials), better wages, and improved working conditions. Throughout much of 1917, they believed that their unions as well as the Menshevik party and the Provisional Government would best help them achieve their objectives. Pankratova said relatively little about the activity of the Bolshevik party. Workers and their unions accepted the Bolshevik program for dramatic political change in the country, but they did so at their own pace and in their own way. The proletariat, she wrote, came to such a conclusion through a nebulous process of "political self-determination." Textile workers "spontaneously came over to the side of the Bolsheviks." Woodworkers "proceeded along a path of bolshevization." In the provinces, support for Bolsheviks proceeded even more slowly because of the "amorphous nature of the working masses there and the Bolshevik party's passivity." Even at the center, the politically advanced steelworkers union lacked a permanent Bolshevik faction in its leadership until late 1918.[40] When the Bolsheviks seized power in October, most unions called not for a Bolshevik dictatorship but for a coalition government of all socialist parties and a quick convocation of the Constituent Assembly.[41] Moreover, Pankratova presented Trotsky and Kamenev, both in opposition to Stalin's leadership in 1927 (the year of her book's publication), as champions of the Bolshevik cause.[42]

The second book of note published in 1927, a collection entitled *Essays on the History of the October Revolution*, appeared under the editorial guidance of Pokrovsky and had Istpart's imprimatur. It consisted of lectures recently delivered by Pokrovsky's students, graduates of the Institute of Red Professors. Esfir' Borisovna Genkina wrote about the month of February, Mikhail Simonovich Iugov about March and June, and Otto Avgustovich Lidak about the period from July through August.[43] All of the authors relied on an impressive array of sources, including memoirs and documents from Istpart's archive.

Pokrovsky launched the book in an overtly pugnacious way. "It is not for the historian of the October Revolution," he wrote in the foreword, "to act in the role of a supreme judge to decide who was right or who was not right in their attempts to lead the masses."[44] A proper Marxist analysis of the past, Pokrovsky continued, demonstrated that "history" had already ruled in favor of the Bolsheviks. In the chapters that followed, his students duly avoided any contrary judgment. They largely refrained, however, from the politicized posturing so evident in their mentor's opening remarks.

Genkina, Iugov, and Lidak focused on workers' desire not so much for political change but for an improvement of their wages and working conditions and on the quest of soldiers for peace. In so doing, they relied time and again on the work of Shliapnikov and of the Left Menshevik, Nikolai Nikolaevich Sukhanov (whose work will be discussed in detail later). Workers and soldiers expressed their needs spontaneously. Iugov in particular underscored the absence in early 1917 among the proletariat, soldiers, and political parties of hardened class lines. He found instead "political amorphousness, an amalgamation of class elements, and social formlessness." In the provinces, Iugov continued, many Bolshevik organizations failed to go beyond the limited demands for a democratic republic, an eight-hour day, and confiscation of land.[45] In some areas, soviets led by Mensheviks and SRs, not Bolsheviks, took power well in advance of the October revolt in Petrograd.[46]

Of the three essays, Lidak's was the most tendentious. Along with his colleagues, he emphasized workers' demands for improved living conditions in the midst of an economic crisis in mid-1917. But he also highlighted, with little evidence, a consistent opposition to Lenin's directives throughout the year by Trotsky, Kamenev, and Zinoviev, with the latter two individuals representing a "right deviation" in the party. At the same time, Lidak embellished Stalin's role as Lenin's single best comrade and lieutenant who understood the "dialectic of revolution" and the need for an armed revolt.[47] He thereby advanced a tale remarkably similar to the version of 1917 that would soon become dominant.

MIXED MEMORIES

Scholarly standards had compelled a respect, if grudging, for reminiscences by non-Bolsheviks. As mentioned previously, Ol'minsky thought memoirs by former White officers were valuable because they demonstrated, in his opinion, the hopelessness and despair of forces aligned against the Bolsheviks in 1917 and in the civil war that followed. So did a frequent contributor to *Proletarskaia revoliutsiia*, G. Lelevich (Laborii Gilelevich Kalmanson), who would become a prominent spokesperson for the "On Guardists," a group that agitated for a distinct proletarian literature. Whatever the intent of their authors, Lelevich argued that these reminiscences revealed a fear of revolution by both the bourgeoisie and the nobility, the bankruptcy of all non-Bolshevik parties, the weakness of the Provisional Government, and the broad support for the October Revolution among soldiers.[48] Piontkovsky included excerpts from the memoirs of officials of the Provisional Government and its army in his reader on the history of the October Revolution published in 1924.[49]

In late 1924, *Proletarskaia revoliutsiia* printed a favorable review of the seven-volume memoir on 1917 published in Berlin, *Notes on the Revolution*, written by the left Menshevik, Sukhanov. There Naum Mikhailovich Lentsner, a student at the Institute of Red Professors, wrote that although Sukhanov had opposed the Bolshevik seizure of power in October, his reminiscences were of "undoubted interest." They revealed that Mensheviks and SRs admired, albeit reluctantly, the "steadfastness (*stoikost'*) of the masses" in Petrograd and the "iron cohesiveness of the party of Bolsheviks." Here and elsewhere the timid Sukhanov and like-minded memoirists demonstrated that unlike Bolsheviks they feared power worse than fire.[50] For the same reasons, Piontkovsky included excerpts from Sukhanov's *Notes on the Revolution* (and from Shliapnikov's *1917*) in the appendices of his popular booklet published in 1924 on the February Revolution. In *Proletarskaia revoliutsiia*, a reviewer praised Piontkovsky for doing do.[51]

Istpart itself encouraged the compilation and publication of a heterogeneous mix of first-hand accounts of the past. The Society of Old Bolsheviks, created in 1922 and at first under Istpart's jurisdiction, became a source of interesting, sometimes conflicting reminiscences. Moreover, Istpart sponsored the transcription of memoirs by former revolutionaries regardless of political affiliation and the variety of points of view expressed in them. In 1925, the agency formed auxiliaries (Groups of Assistance) to encourage the telling, by Bolsheviks and non-Bolsheviks alike, of events in 1905 that had occurred outside Russia's capital cities.[52] By 1926, a large number of the groups existed, now focusing their attention on compiling accounts of 1917. Their meetings were often loud and contentious affairs, their storytellers insisting on their own versions of the past and engaging in mutual recriminations. Some attendees spoke of the sordid behavior by Bolsheviks, among others.[53]

These reminiscences, published and otherwise, repeatedly demonstrated the inapplicability of any grand narrative for the history of 1917. Time and again, local memoirists underscored the "absence of a distinct class struggle" in their region and a history "independent of events in the center."[54] In 1924, a review of literature on 1917 published in the provinces, much of it dependent on such recollections, noted a preoccupation with the Bolshevik party's weakness, an emphasis on the protracted dominance of Mensheviks and SRs, and a recognition of the tardiness of the "October" revolution in nonindustrial areas when "October" did finally occur.[55] Memoirs published in *Proletarskaia revoliutsiia* on 1917 in the provinces remarked on the presence, if that, of a weak and poorly financed Bolshevik party whose members cooperated and joined with Mensheviks in a united organization.[56]

In 1926 *Proletarskaia revoliutsiia* published a survey of events following the Bolshevik revolt in Petrograd that reported that in many cities "a coalition of politically formless groups" continued to retain power.[57] In his work on the countryside, Shestakov made it clear that the actions of the peasantry in 1917 varied considerably from place to place, dependent on the economic situation, the degree of power exercised there by the Provisional Government, the strength of the left SRs, and the extent of the "ideational (*ideinoe*) influence" of the Bolsheviks.[58]

So it was in Viatka. As we will see in the next chapter, Viatka's Istpart insisted on its own version of events in the region in 1917.

NOTES

1. See the circular of December 6, 1923, in *PR*, no. 2 (25) (1924), 241.
2. M. Pokrovsky, "Dvadtsatiletie nashei pervoi proletarskoi revoliutsii," *PR*, no. 11 (34) (November 1924), 7.
3. RGASPI, f. 70, op. 2, d. 97, l. 5 and RGASPI, f. 70, op. 2, d. 100, l. 1.
4. RGASPI, f. 70, op. 2, d. 100, l. 1.
5. See a report on Istpart's exhibit in mid-1924 in GASPI KO, f. P-45, op. 1, d. 203, ll. 19- ob.-20 and materials from sessions of the regional party committee's secretariat, February 13 and 23, 1925, in GASPI KO, f. P-45, op. 1, d. 216, l. 8 and GASPI KO, f. P-1, op. 3, d. 32, l. 56. See also agitprop's instructions of November 12, 1925, in GASPI KO, f. P-1, op. 4, d. 281, l. 7, and Novoselov's report to agitprop, November 18–19, 1925, in GASPI KO, f. P-1, op. 4, d. 281, l. 9.
6. See articles by N. K. Solonitsyn in *Viatskaia pravda*, November 17, 19, and 20, 1925, all on page 3; and articles by Solonitsyn and Novoselov in *1905 v Viatskoi gubernii: Sbornik statei, vospominanii i materialov*, a work edited by Poroshin and sponsored by Istpart (Viatka: Truzhenik, 1925). See also, S. Semakov, *Iz revoliutsionnogo proshlogo molodezhi Viatskoi gubernii (1905–1908 g.g.)* (Viatka: Truzhenik, 1926).
7. GASPI KO, f. P-45, op. 1, d. 215, l. 9 ob. See Novoselov's "Informational Letter No. 1" in RGASPI, f. 70, op. 2, d. 99, l. 11.
8. RGASPI, f. 70, op. 2, d. 100, ll. 7, 12.
9. Novoselov had sent it to Moscow on June 16, 1925: RGASPI, f. 70, op. 2, d. 99, l. 14. Volkovicher's work: *25 let R.K.P. (bol'shevikov), 1898–1923: Illiustrirovannyi iubileinyi sbornik* (Moscow: Gosudarstvennoe izdatel'stvo, 1923). Earlier, in April 1923, Volkovicher had delivered a report at Istpart's Second Conference on the state of the agency's locals.
10. RGASPI, f. 70, op. 2, d. 100, l. 14. Volkovicher is identified as a research associate at Istpart's central office.
11. *1905 god v Viatskoi gubernii* (Viatka: Truzhenik, 1925). See many of the contributions for the volume in manuscript and typescript form in GASPI KO, f. P-45, op. 1, d. 33, 1284 ll.
12. *1905 god*, 180–191.
13. *1905 god*, I, III.
14. R. Khabas's review in *PR*, no. 4 (51) (April 1926), 261–263. Khabas did think that overall the book had value. For a similar critical review of a work sponsored by another Istpart local on 1905, see Klopikhina, "Deiatel'nost' istpartov," 156–157.
15. Corney, *Telling October*, 122–124, quote on 124.
16. S. A. Piontkovsky, *Oktiabr'skaia revoliutsiia v Rossii, ee predposylki i khod. Populiarno-istoricheskii ocherk* (Moscow-Petrograd: Gosudarstvennoe

izdatel'stvo 1923), 29, 34; M. N. Pokrovsky, "Prolog Oktiabr'skoi revoliutsii" in *Oktiabr'skaia revoliutsiia: Sbornik statei, 1917–1927* (Moscow: Izdatel'stvo Kommunisticheskoi akademii, 1929), 73–75.

17. Piontkovsky, *Oktiabr'skaia revoliutsiia*, 25, 48.

18. S. M. Dubrovsky, *Krest'ianstvo v 1917 godu* (Moscow-Leningrad: Gosudarstvennoe izdatel'stvo, 1927), 25–31, 65, 106–108, and *Ocherki russkoi revoliutsii*, 2nd ed. (Moscow: Izdatel'stvo Narkomzema "Novaia derevnia," 1923), 182, 185. In 1981, in his examination of Soviet historical literature, E. N. Gorodetsky spoke well of Dubrovsky's publications on the peasantry: Gorodetsky, *Sovetskaia istoriografiia Velikogo Oktiabria* (Moscow: Izdatel'stvo "Nauka," 1981), 173.

19. Dubrovsky, *Ocherki*, 183.

20. Dubrovsky, *Ocherki*, 183; Dubrovsky, *Krest'ianstvo*, 65–66, 93, 114; A. Pankratova, *Fabzavkomy Rossii v bor'be za sotsialisticheskuiu fabriku* (Moscow: Krasnaia nov', 1923), 189–234; P. Lepeshinsky, "Oktiabr' 1917 g.," *PR*, no. 4 (1922), 321; A. V. Shestakov, *Bol'sheviki i krest'ianstvo v revoliutsii 1917 goda* (Moscow-Leningrad: Gosudarstvennoe izdatel'stvo, 1927), 22–24; V. Miliutin, *Agrarnaia politika SSSR* (Moscow-Leningrad: Gosudarstvennoe izdatel'stvo, 1926), 151–158. The peasant movement proceeded "in a typically peasant fashion by uncoordinated and unorganized agrarian disorders": G. Lelevich, "Ob istorii krest'ianskogo dvizheniia v Mogilevskoi gubernii nakanune Oktiabr'skoi revoliutsii," *PR*, no. 11 (1922), 127.

21. Em. Iaroslavsky, "Bol'sheviki v fevral'sko-martovskie dni 1917 g.," *PR*, no. 2–3 (61–62) (February–March 1927), 36–60; E. Iaroslavsky, *Partiia bol'shevikov v 1917 godu* (Moscow-Leningrad: Gosudarstvennoe izdatel'stvo, 1927), 23–35. Corney suggests that Iaroslavsky's book "rendered the party synonymous with the Russian revolutionary movement": Corney, *Telling October*, 198. However, as noted here and below, the book failed to meet official expectations.

22. Iaroslavsky, "Bol'sheviki v fevral'sko-martovskie dni," 40–41.

23. D. Kin, "Bor'ba protiv 'ob"edinitel'nogo ugara' v 1917 godu," *PR*, no. 6 (65) (June 1927), 3–17.

24. Iaroslavsky, "Bol'sheviki v fevral'sko-martovskie dni," 48–49. Iaroslavsky quotes from Stalin's *On the Pathway toward October*, published in 1925.

25. Iaroslavsky, *Partiia bol'shevikov*, 34.

26. Dubrovsky, *Ocherki*, 183.

27. Dubrovsky, *Krest'ianstvo*, 5, 132.

28. Piontkovsky, *Oktiabr'skaia revoliutsiia*, 51, 56.

29. Dubrovsky, *Ocherki*, 197.

30. Dubrovsky, *Krest'ianstvo*, 13–14.

31. Shestakov, *Bol'sheviki i krest'ianstvo*, 8, 17.

32. M. Pokrovsky, "Dva Oktiabria," in *Oktiabr'skaia revoliutsiia: Sbornik statei, 1917–1927* (Moscow: Izdatel'stvo Kommunisticheskoi akademii, 1929), 95–96 (first published in *Sputnik agitatora*, no. 18, 1925).

33. Piontkovsky, *Oktiabr'skaia revoliutsiia*, 117–118.

34. Piontkovsky, *Oktiabr'skaia revoliutsiia*, 114.

35. Iaroslavsky, *Partiia bol'shevikov*, 99. In a recent essay, Richard Sakwa noted that "the October Revolution turned out to be a number of revolutions, all rolled into one." He spoke of a social revolution, democratic revolution, liberal revolution, and a national revolution. See Sakwa, "The Rise of Leninism: The Death of Political Pluralism in the Post-Revolutionary Party," in *Was Revolution Inevitable? Turning Points of the Russian Revolution*, ed. Tony Brenton (New York: Oxford University Press, 2017), 266–267.

36. RGASPI, f. 70, op. 1, d. 20, l. 29.

37. See Shliapnikov's articles in *Proletarskaia revoliutsiia*, no. 10 (1922); no. 1 (13) (1923); and no. 3 (50) (March 1926) through no. 8 (55) (August 1926). A. Shliapnikov, *Kanun semnadtsatogo goda*, vol. 1 (Moscow: Gosudarstvennoe izdatel'stvo, 1920), and vol. 2 (Moscow: Gosudarstvennoe izdatel'stvo, 1922). A Shliapnikov, *Semnadtsatyi god*, vol. 1 (Moscow-Petrograd: Gosudarstvennoe izdatel'stvo, 1923), vol. 2 (Moscow-Leningrad: Gosudarstvennoe izdatel'stvo, 1925), vol. 3 (Moscow-Leningrad: Gosudarstvennoe izdatel'stvo 1927). A fourth volume of the series appeared in 1931 (Moscow-Leningrad: Gosudarstvennoe izdatel'stvo, 1931). I have written elsewhere about Shliapnikov's life and of his work on 1917. See Larry E. Holmes, "Soviet Rewriting of 1917: The Case of A. G. Shliapnikov," *Slavic Review* 38, no. 2 (June 1979): 224–242. See also Larry E. Holmes, "For the Revolution Redeemed: The Workers Opposition in the Bolshevik Party, 1919–1921," *Carl Beck Paper No. 802* (Pittsburgh, PA: University of Pittsburgh Center for Russian and East European Studies, 1990). See the biography of Shliapnikov: Barbara C. Allen, *Alexander Shlyapnikov, 1885–1937: Life of an Old Bolshevik* (Chicago: Haymarket Books, 2016). See also the foreword by A. S. Smol'nikov and A. A. Chernobaev in A. G. Shliapnikov, *Kanun semnadtsatogo goda*, vol. 1 (Moscow: Izdatel'stvo politicheskoi literatury, 1992). Shliapnikov also published: *Po zavodam Frantsii i Germanii* (Leningrad: Priboi, 1926); *Zametki o Frantsii* (Leningrad: Priboi, 1926); *Revoliutsiia 1905 goda* (Moscow-Leningrad: Gosudarstvennoe izdatel'stvo, 1925); and *Fevral'skie dni v Peterburge* (Khar'kov: Proletarii, 1925).

38. See separate reviews by S. Mitskevich, G. Lelevich, and Feliks Kon in *Pechat' i revoliutsiia*, no. 3 (1923), 191–193; no. 2 (1924), 215–217; and no. 5–6 (1925), 414–417. See also V. Petrov's comments in *Krasnaia letopis'*, no. 6(21) (1926), 176–179.

39. Iaroslavsky, "Bol'sheviki v fevral'sko-martovskie dni," 38–41. See also a considerable reliance on Shliapnikov's work in A. Stanchinsky, "Vserossiiskaia aprel'skaia partiinaia konferentsiia 1917 g.," *PR*, no. 4 (63) (April 1927), 11–66.

40. A. M. Pankratova, *Politicheskaia bor'ba v rossiiskom profdvizhenii, 1917–1918 gg.* (Leningrad: Izdatel'stvo Leningradskogo gubprofsoveta, 1927), quotes in succession on 187, 81, 86, 27. On the Bolshevik fraction, 125. The book was published in a press run of three thousand copies.

41. Pankratova, *Politicheskaia bor'ba*, esp. 111–112.
42. Pankratova, *Politicheskaia bor'ba*, 60, 74, 100.
43. *Ocherki po istorii Oktiabr'skoi revoliutsii: Raboty istoricheskogo seminariia Instituta krasnoi professury*, ed. M. N. Pokrovsky, vol. 2 (Moscow-Leningrad: Gosudarstvennoe izdatel'stvo, 1927). See E. B. Genkina, "Fevral'skii perevorot," 3–110; M. Iugov, "Sovety v pervyi period revoliutsii (mart-iiun')," 113–253; and O. Lidak, "Iiul'skie sobytiia 1917 goda," 257–346. This collection also included an article by N. L. Rubinshtein, "Vneshniaia politika Kerenshchiny," 349–452. In his review of historical literature on the occasion of the fiftieth anniversary of the 1917 revolution, James Billington described this work as "still the best attempt to apply Marxist forms of analysis to the events of 1917": Billington, "Six Views of the Russian Revolution," *World Politics* 18, no 3 (April 1966): 462. The first volume contained articles on the period from 1914 to February 1917; M. N. Pokrovsky, ed. *Ocherki po istorii Oktiabr'skoi revoliutsii. Raboty istoricheskogo seminariia Instituta krasnoi professury*, vol. 1 (Moscow-Leningrad: Gosudarstvennoe izdatel'stvo, 1927). Plans for a third volume never materialized.
44. *Ocherki po istorii Oktiabr'skoi revoliutsii*, vol. 2, IV.
45. Iugov, "Sovety v pervyi period," 147, quote on 153. As the Bolsheviks had in 1917, Iugov referred to these three demands as the "three whales," an analogy to a fable in which the earth was supported on the backs of three whales. In his conclusion for the initial volume on the period from 1914 to 1917, Pokrovsky depicted the party in other, more glowing, terms. Despite suppression, it remained strong and became the vanguard of the revolutionary proletariat in Russia and in Europe: Pokrovsky, *Ocherki po istorii Oktiabr'skoi revoliutsii*, vol. 1, 506–508. At the same time in mid-1927, Iugov reviewed a book on factory committees in October 1917, insisting that the book's author exaggerated the role of the committees at the expense of the significance of the Bolshevik party: *PR*, no. 7 (66) (July 1927), 258–264.
46. Iugov referred to the "spontaneous formation of power in the provinces": Iugov, "Sovety v pervyi period," 220.
47. Lidak, "Iiul'skie sobytiia," esp. 341–344.
48. G. Lelevich, "Oktiabr' v belogvardeiskom opisanii," *PR*, no. 9 (21) (1923), 31–38; G. Lelevich, "Fevral' v belogvardeiskom opisanii," *PR*, no. 1 (13) (1923), 187–219. See also Lelevich's praise of Piontkovsky's use of such literature in his review of S. A. Piontkovsky, *Khrestomatiia po istorii Oktiabr'skoi revoliutsii* (Moscow: Krasnaia nov', 1923) in *PR*, no. 8 (20) (1923), 253.
49. S. A. Piontkovsky, *Khrestomatiia po istorii Oktiabr'skoi revoliutsii*, 2nd ed. (Moscow: Krasnaia nov', 1924).
50. N. Lentsner, review of N. Sukhanov, *Zapiski o revoliutsii*, 7 vols. (Berlin: Izdatel'stvo Z. I. Grizhebina, 1922), in *PR*, no. 10 (33) (October 1924), 267–270. Quotes on 269. Lentsner's assessment is reminiscent of Lenin's which the Soviet

leader dictated in January 1923. Sukhanov's memoirs reminded Lenin of the "pedantry of our petty-bourgeois democrats" and how "in all their conduct they reveal themselves to be cowardly reformists." V.I. Lenin, *Polnoe sobranie sochinenii*, 5th ed., vol. 45 (Moscow: Izdatel'stvo politicheskoi literatury, 1970), 378. Later Lentsner wrote articles and several books about international communism and the Communist International (*Comintern*). From 1927, he worked as an official in the Comintern and spent some time in Germany. Back in the USSR, he was arrested and shot in 1936. I am grateful to Mikhail Mikhailovich Panteleev for information on Lentsner's career.

51. N. Avdeev, review of S. Piontkovsky, *Fevral'skaia revoliutsiia* (Leningrad: Priboi, 1924), in *PR*, no. 5 (28) (May 1924), 234.

52. See the report on Istpart's work from January to April 1925 in *PR*, no. 6 (41) (June 1925), 259.

53. On the auxiliaries, see V. Iu. Korovainikov, "Gruppy sodeistviia Istpartu TsK VKP(b)," *Voprosy istorii KPSS*, no. 1 (January 1991), 112–123. See information on the formation of such an auxiliary by Viatka Istpart's collegium on May 12, 1926, in GASPI KO, f. P-45, op. 1, d. 202, l. 58. On the nature of these meetings, see V. S. Klopikhina, "U istokov otechestvennoi ustnoi istorii (opyt raboty Istpartov Severnogo Kavkaza po formirovaniiu korpusa istochnikov lichnogo proiskhozhdeniia)," in *Gumanitarnye i iuridicheskie issledovaniia*, vol. 1 (Stavropol, 2014), 34. For more on such evenings and constructed memory, see Frederick C. Corney, "Rethinking a Great Event: The October Revolution as Memory Project," *Social Science History* 22, no. 4 (Winter 1998): 405–407.

54. See memoirs published in *PR*, no. 10 (33) (October 1924).

55. Review of literature published by Istpart: *PR*, no. 10 (33) (October 1924), 222–233.

56. See, e.g., E. Bosh, "Oblastnoi partiinyi komitet s.-d. (b-kov) Iugo-Zapadnogo kraia (1917 g.)," *PR*, no. 5 (28) (May 1924), 128–149; A. Petrenko, "Fevral'skaia revoliutsiia v Tomske," *PR*, no. 2 (49) (February 1929), 91–101.

57. V. Leikina, "Oktiabr' po Rossii," *PR*, no. 2 (49) (February 1929), 185.

58. A. Shestakov, "Oktiabr' v derevne," *PR*, no. 10 (69) (October 1927), 91–109; Shestakov, *Bol'sheviki i krest'ianstvo*, 13–24, quote on 45.

FOUR

Viatka's 1917 Revolution in the Past and the Present

ISTPART'S BRANCH IN VIATKA PLANNED for an extensive celebration of the tenth anniversary of the 1917 revolution. Its campaign quickly ran afoul of Moscow's ambition for the great event when Viatka insisted on the party's relatively modest achievements in the province in 1917. A nasty personal and professional conflict erupted between Istpart's leadership in Viatka and two of the region's own revolutionaries, now ensconced in Moscow, over how best to remember that past.

MAKING GOOD ON ISTPART'S PROMISE

With the regional party committee's encouragement, Viatka's Istpart adopted grand plans for the tenth jubilee of the October Revolution. On January 14, 1926, the committee reissued instructions to all district party organizations to appoint a special Istpart representative, this time for the purpose of helping celebrate the decennial. It also asked Viatka's Istpart to submit a plan for publications to mark the occasion. For the implementation of this impressive agenda, the committee appointed Novoselov and Poroshin, among others, to a Commission for Celebrating the October Revolution.[1] On March 25, the commission elected Novoselov as its chair.[2]

The commission proposed the publication of thirteen books. That number included several items devoted to the party's activity in Viatka in 1917 and during the civil war and a volume each on the history in Viatka of unions, cooperatives, the Young Communist League, women, education, enlightenment, and the economy.[3] By October 1926, however, only a few of the manuscripts—chiefly, those on 1917—were ready for publication.[4] And most of those (as discussed in the next chapter) were soon reduced in size or abandoned altogether. Nevertheless, Istpart now had, if in abbreviated form, something of importance to say.

The commission's major volume, *October and the Civil War in the Viatka Province* (fig. 4.1), edited by Novoselov, appeared in August 1927 under Istpart's imprimatur in a print run of three thousand copies.[5] Its 188 pages included articles by Novoselov on the history of the Bolshevik party in Viatka and an item, "October in Viatka," by Mikhail Aleksandrovich Favorov, historian and rector of Kirov's Pedagogical Institute.

It was not Novoselov's first venture into writing the history of 1917. On October 23 and 24, 1926, *Viatskaia pravda* printed his two-part article, "October in Viatka." In that article, he denied its very title. There was no "October" in Viatka in 1917. The Bolshevik party neither controlled nor significantly influenced events. SRs and Mensheviks were far more numerous and popular in the region.[6] That December, in an item intended for the *The Great Soviet Encyclopedia*, Novoselov broadened his emphasis on the party's weakness in Viatka to include the entire period from 1905 to 1917.[7] Two months later, he failed to mention the Bolshevik party in an article on events in February 1917 that appeared in Viatka's regional journal, *Sputnik bol'shevika*, a monthly publication of Viatka's regional party committee and something of a practical guide for party members.[8] In March 1927, Novoselov acknowledged in *Viatskaia pravda* that in February and March 1917, Bolsheviks' opposition to the war had run aground on what he called "popular illusions" of a quick military victory.[9]

In his contribution to *October and the Civil War in Viatka Province*, Novoselov again called attention to the Bolsheviks' impotence and Menshevik strength and popularity throughout 1917.[10] Early in the year, Bolsheviks were so few in number in the city of Viatka that they had joined a united organization with Mensheviks. In it, they represented at best an "exceedingly weak tendency."[11] On May 28, for example, a "representative of that Bolshevik tendency," a thirty-year-old land surveyor, Mikhail Mikhailovich Popov, delivered a major speech at a joint session of Mensheviks and Bolsheviks. Popov denounced the war and Russia's participation in it. Mensheviks raised such a ruckus that Popov could not continue. He and a small group of Bolsheviks left the meeting. Only then did they declare an end to organizational cooperation with Mensheviks. On June 4, this handful of Bolsheviks created their own independent unit.[12] To deny any such previous cooperation by Bolsheviks with Mensheviks, Novoselov declared, was an "elementary sin."[13] As we will see, Novoselov's mention of "sin" was highly calculated. He had someone in particular in mind.

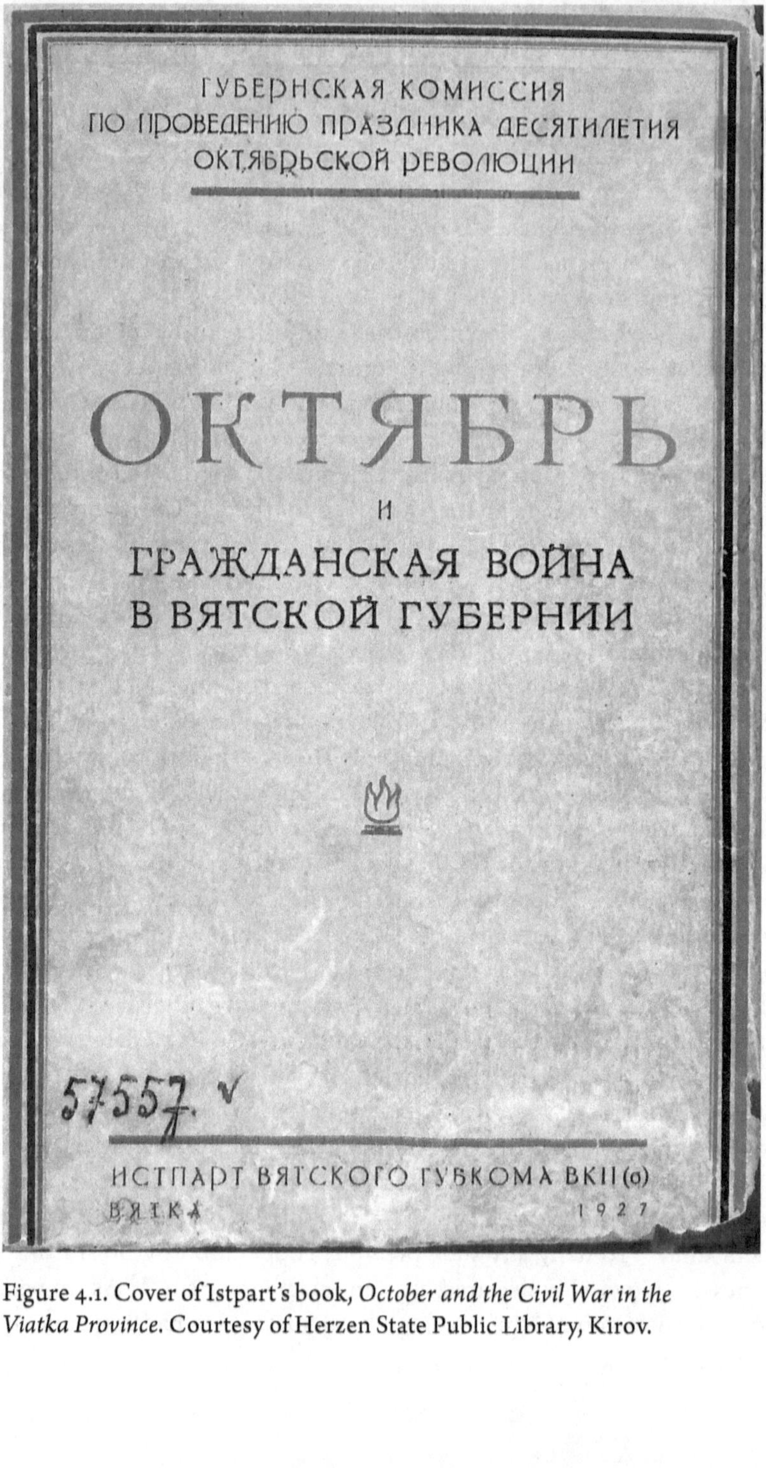

Figure 4.1. Cover of Istpart's book, *October and the Civil War in the Viatka Province*. Courtesy of Herzen State Public Library, Kirov.

Whatever his reasonably accurate interpretation of 1917, Novoselov simultaneously advanced, if somewhat incongruously, Istpart's mission for a heavily politicized rendition of the past. It was too much of a stretch for his imagination to give Bolsheviks a prominent role in events in Viatka in 1917. But Novoselov was a professional propagandist, having served as head of agitprop of the Urzhum district's party committee before his appointment at Istpart. Now as Istpart's head, even as he denied Bolsheviks a major role in Viatka in 1917, he demanded as a matter of principle that his agency manipulate the past to serve the party's present. Something of a double person emerged. As an author on 1917 and then as Istpart's chief, his public stance lurched abruptly in pendulum-like fashion from a subdued description of Bolsheviks in 1917 to intemperate expressions of an agenda for the rewriting of them into the past.

Months before his articles on 1917 in *Viatskaia pravda*, Novoselov published an item of a far different sort in the same venue. He declared that precisely because Istpart was not "some kind of scholarly-historical society," it had an important political role in celebrating the tenth anniversary of the October Revolution.[14] In December 1926, at a conference convened by Viatka's Istpart of authors working on publications to celebrate the decennial, Novoselov lamented that histories written about the region had given the Bolshevik party insufficient attention. Without mention of any particular work, including, of course, his own, he complained that the party had lost pride of place, its role had been obscured or "masked" (*zatushevyvanie*). It had even disappeared completely from view, buried underneath all the verbiage given Mensheviks, SRs, anarchists, and other groups.[15]

And yet in this same presentation, Novoselov felt the pull of his agency's scholarly mission, one largely consistent with his own published work to date. He hoped that Viatka's Istpart might support serious research and produce something other than superficial sketches with only the general reader in mind. "It is not necessary," he declared, "to become overly zealous in the pursuit of popular history."[16]

But months later, Istpart's partisan agenda again dominated Novoselov's thinking. In February 1927, he scolded Istpart's representative from the Malmyzh district, Petrovsky, for a chronology of the period from 1918 to 1922 that contained insufficient information on the Bolshevik party. Every chronology, Novoselov insisted, must be a history of "our party."[17] At the same time (as discussed in chapter 6), Novoselov responded to resolutions of Istpart's Fourth Conference with yet another shrill and politicized declaration of Istpart's mission.

LITTLE HISTORY

In his work on 1917, Novoselov had avoided manipulating Viatka's past in order to condemn contemporary enemies of the party's leadership in Moscow. Perhaps the Kremlin's campaign against Stalin's critics had little resonance for him and others far away in the provinces. To be sure, in 1926, Viatka's regional and municipal party committees duly responded to signals from above with their own sweeping condemnations of Mensheviks, SRs, Kadets (members of the Constitutional Democratic Party), and the opposition within the party itself. They did so, however, largely by rote and without a sustained effort directed against any particular individual or readily identifiable group within the party then present in Viatka.[18] The party there purged some of its members but primarily for drunkenness or a failure to attend meetings.

Nevertheless, it was more likely that actual events in Viatka in 1917 limited Novoselov's room for political maneuver, as he understood it. Viatka had its own distinct history of 1917. It was not alone. Recent scholarship on other regions from Nizhnegorod to Kazan, Odessa, Voronezh, and Saratov, among others, has emphasized the diversity of economic conditions and the multiplicity of arrangements that year among powerful individuals, political parties, and institutions.[19]

And so it was in Viatka. There the Bolshevik party could not reasonably lay claim to a glorious past. In 1917, 96 percent of the province's population lived in rural areas. With only forty-one thousand inhabitants and little industry, the city of Viatka served primarily as an administrative center.[20] The province's city of Izhevsk had a large armaments factory and a number of steel factories, but it was located four hundred kilometers southeast of the capital, Viatka. Moreover, as of 1920, Izhevsk was no longer part of the Viatka province but of the Votsk Autonomous Republic, which from 1922 had its own Istpart branch.

As Viatka's historians have recently documented, the Bolshevik party had "little history" in the region in 1917. Mensheviks and SRs enjoyed far more popularity than Bolsheviks among soldiers stationed in the province and among workers and peasants. The vast majority of the region's population wanted reform, not revolution, and looked to the Provisional Government and the upcoming Constituent Assembly for it.[21] Only in May 1917 did the small number of Bolsheviks in the city of Viatka break away from cooperation with Mensheviks to form their own independent party. When Bolsheviks formed a faction in Viatka's municipal soviet at the end of August, it consisted of a mere ten members. By October, no more than seventy people had joined the city's party unit. Bolsheviks in the province numbered from 1,500 to 2,000, a high percentage of them in Izhevsk.[22] While in August, Bolsheviks gained a majority in elections to the soviet there, they attained dominance in Viatka's municipal soviet only that November. Even then SRs and Mensheviks maintained control over much of the remainder of the province.

When news of the Bolshevik seizure of power in Petrograd reached Viatka, the municipal soviet's executive committee, the municipal duma, and the province's central bureau of trade unions condemned it. The Regional Zemstvo Assembly also opposed it. The assembly called for the creation of a council (*soviet*) to form a new government for an independent Viatka republic until such time when order could be restored throughout the country. Accordingly, on October 27, representatives from the Zemstvo Assembly and the Soviet of Workers and Soldiers Deputies formed a Supreme Soviet (fig. 4.2), one dominated by Mensheviks and SRs, to govern the province. That same day, Viatka's Soviet of Workers and Soldiers Deputies declared the "seizure of power by Bolsheviks tantamount to the beginning of a fratricidal civil war." It demanded all power go to the future Constituent Assembly. Several days later, that soviet's executive committee met in a special session with other organizations in a vote to recognize only the authority of the recently formed Supreme Soviet.[23]

On November 8, Viatka's Bolshevik Petr Pavlovich Kapustin appealed to the party's Central Committee for help because, he said, the party in Viatka was numerically weak and its leaders timid. Petrograd responded by sending several people including Naum Markovich Antselovich and Derishev, the latter born in Viatka province and a Bolshevik propagandist there until his arrest in 1906. As we will see, their arrival became a contentious issue in Istpart's subsequent study of the period. At the same time, a detachment of "revolutionary soldiers" arrived from Kazan to help local Bolsheviks. On November 23, the 106th reserve infantry regiment stationed in Viatka expressed support of the Bolsheviks, but it did so primarily out of a hope that the party, if and when in power, would rapidly demobilize the unit.[24]

On the night of November 25, a newly elected Viatka municipal soviet, now led by Bolsheviks, voted to seize power in the city. In response, at the beginning of December, employees of the telegraph, post office, and other public services went on strike. In the province's elections to the Constituent Assembly at the end of November and beginning of December, Bolsheviks received 22 percent of the votes, and SRs received 57 percent.[25] By year's end, the Bolshevik party could claim tenuous control, at best, over the city of Viatka only and that thanks largely to the arrival of an armed detachment of sailors from the Baltic fleet recently sent from Petrograd.

Figure 4.2. Supreme Soviet of the Viatka Province, November 1917.
Courtesy of the State Archive of the Kirov Region.

At the beginning of January 1918, the first Provincial Congress of Soviets, dominated by Bolsheviks and SRs, declared soviet power in the province. However, the Bolshevik party's authority remained limited and its program unpopular. In what Viatka's historian Iurii Nikolaevich Timkin has called the "amorphous nature of the structure of power," the provincial soviet (with considerable representation of left SRs), the armed detachment of sailors mentioned above, and Viatka's municipal soviet all competed against each other for power.[26] In early 1918, armed groups loyal to the city and regional soviets almost came to blows.[27]

Well into 1918, rebellion by armed detachments, including the very units sent by the Soviet government to requisition grain, peasant resistance to confiscation of that grain, a revolt of Izhevsk's workers against their draft into the Red Army, divisions among Bolsheviks over the Treaty of Brest-Litovsk, and a purge of 25 percent of the party's membership precluded Bolshevik control over the province. In early 1919, the anti-Communist army led by Admiral Aleksandr Kolchak seized eastern portions of the region. His success prompted the January descent on the region by Stalin and Dzerzhinsky and in April by Trotsky to rally Bolshevik forces. "The fate of the world revolution," Trotsky thundered at a gathering of workers, "is being decided right here in the Viatka province."[28] Later that spring, Bolsheviks finally secured power in the region if not worldwide, as Trotsky had hoped.

TROUBLE IN THE VIATKA FAMILY

In his contribution to Istpart's *October and the Civil War in the Viatka Province*, Novoselov made it a point to emphasize that denial of an organization in Viatka that united Bolsheviks and Mensheviks in early 1917 was "an elementary sin."[29] He did not tell his readers—perhaps some of them already knew—that for Novoselov, the issue was a highly personal one.

In late 1926, two of Viatka's young historians, Sergei Vasil'evich Tokarev and Ivan Vasil'evich Tsaregorodtsev, finished a draft of an article, "The Prerequisites of October in the Viatka Province." They hoped to publish it in the major collection of essays (discussed earlier), sponsored by Istpart and Viatka's Commission for Celebrating the October Revolution.[30] Both authors had just graduated from the social sciences department of Viatka's Pedagogical Institute, Tokarev was now an instructor of history there, and Tsaregorodtsev was director of a school in the nearby town of Omutninsk.[31] In more than seventy typescript pages, they discussed socioeconomic conditions, policies of the Provisional Government, the activity of Mensheviks and SRs, and the mood of workers, soldiers, and peasants. However, they had next to nothing to say about the Bolshevik party except to mention its numerical and organizational weakness. The story of the "prerequisites of October," Tokarev and Tsaregorodtsev believed, was one best written with the Bolsheviks largely left out.[32] Novoselov sent the essay to Istpart's central office for vetting. That office sent the item, in turn, to two of Viatka's favorite sons from the year 1917, Andrei Pavlovich Kuchkin (fig. 4.3) and the aforementioned Kapustin (fig. 4.4). They were not kind.[33]

A party member since 1912, Kuchkin had been one of the few Bolsheviks in the city of Viatka in 1917 and was the region's delegate to the First All-Russian Congress of Peasant Deputies that May. He left Viatka in midyear to serve as a party official in the Ufa province and then as a political commissar in the Red Army during the civil war.[34] In 1927, he was studying party history at Moscow's Institute of Red Professors. The other reader, Kapustin, had been a student in 1917 in one of Viatka's schools (*realschule*), whose administration expelled him for political activity. Later that year, he joined the city's Red Guards and became a delegate in Viatka's municipal soviet and a member of its executive

Figure 4.3. Viatka's Municipal Party Committee, June 1917. A. P. Kuchkin, first person seated on the left. Courtesy of Kirov's Regional Museum of Local History.

Figure 4.4. P. P. Kapustin, 1917. Courtesy of Kirov's Regional Museum of Local History.

committee. The following year, he headed the region's Cheka and thereafter held a number of positions in Viatka's regional and municipal governments until his transfer to Rostov-on-Don in 1920.[35] Both Kuchkin and Kapustin opposed the article's publication without substantial revisions to enhance by exaggeration the importance of Viatka's Bolsheviks in 1917.[36]

Kuchkin's negative response should have surprised no one. On multiple occasions, he had already exhibited a capacity for mean-spirited and polemical reviews. In late 1926, *Proletarskaia revoliutsiia* published his commentary on a book, *The Civil War in the Urals, 1917–1919*. That volume's author focused on economic developments with a heavy reliance on statistical information. Kuchkin wanted instead a text that hammered away incessantly on the class struggle and the revolutionary activity of the working class. The book, he concluded, "is unacceptable slander of workers!" Its author was "a Marxist in quotation marks."[37]

In its November 1926 issue, *Proletarskaia revoliutsiia* published another abrupt dismissal by Kuchkin of a book, this one sponsored by Viatka's Istpart, *From the Revolutionary Past of Viatka Province's Youth*. Kuchkin thought it discussed its subject without due praise of the revolutionary movement in the region. He singled out Novoselov for a failure to do so in the volume's preface. Kuchkin ended on a condescending note: "Despite its shortcomings and rather boring and insipid prose, the book is of interest to today's progressive youth."[38]

Novoselov did not respond.[39] He did, however, take issue in May of the following year with the dismissal by Kuchkin and Kapustin of the article by Tokarev and Tsaregorodtsev. In a letter to Moscow's Istpart, he made it clear that he spoke not only for himself but for all those associated with his local and, perhaps, members of the regional party committee. "Viatka's Istpart," Novoselov insisted, "believes that it is necessary to raise the following objections." Both reviews, "in our opinion, are unsatisfactory." Kapustin and Kuchkin had demanded the article's complete makeover to focus almost exclusively on the activity in 1917 of the Bolshevik party. Novoselov thought such criticism misguided. The article, he said, was scheduled to appear in a larger collection that would include a special contribution on Viatka's party organization (one, as it turned out, submitted by Novoselov himself). Neither critic, especially Kuchkin, "had approached their task and the authors in a comradely manner."[40]

Novoselov then proceeded with a lengthy commentary on Kuchkin's review. He was not so much concerned with the author's overall appraisal as he was with an apparently minor point about the critic's own behavior in 1917. Kuchkin had dismissed as a falsehood the article's mention of cooperation between Viatka's Bolsheviks and Mensheviks early that year. Novoselov retorted that documents in Viatka Istpart's archive as well as memoirs "completely refute

Kuchkin's claim." The archive contained proclamations (*vozzvaniia*) issued by Mensheviks, one of which had been signed by none other than the Bolshevik Kuchkin. Kuchkin had rejected the article by Tokarev and Tsaregorodtsev, Novoselov charged, in an effort to conceal such unacceptable activity on his, Kuchkin's, part. In so doing, the critic had inappropriately exploited his connections in Moscow. "Comrade Kuchkin uses his position in order once again to prove that he had no relationship whatsoever with Viatka's Mensheviks." Novoselov added that this very issue had already been a subject of correspondence between Kuchkin and Viatka's Istpart.[41] It would continue to be a sore point between the two.

Novoselov then took up Kapustin's evaluation. He equated the critic's rejection as part of a continuing effort to embellish his, Kapustin's, role in 1917. It was not the first time that Kapustin had done so. Years earlier, in 1919, in an autobiographical sketch for his party cell, he had demonstrated a proclivity for self-promotion. From the middle of July 1917, Kapustin had, as he would have it, "stood at the head" (*stoial vo glave*) of the Bolshevik organization in the city of Viatka as its secretary, agitator, organizer, and propagandist.[42] Now in 1927, he continued his exercise in self-promotion in his comments on the article by Tokarev and Tsaregorodtsev. He demanded that its authors emphasize his, Kapustin's, and Kuchkin's activity in Viatka. Thanks to their efforts, by late 1917 the Bolshevik party in the city and province had purportedly become "a large political force with considerable influence among the masses." If Antselovich had arrived earlier or if he, Kapustin, a nineteen-year-old "leader" (*vozhd'*) of Viatka's party organization had been more experienced, the party could have taken power immediately after the October revolt in Petrograd. The article, Kapustin concluded, would have much greater value if it "gave the work of our party greater place than it does now."[43]

Novoselov found particularly objectionable Kapustin's comments on the allegedly unrealized potential of himself, Kapustin, and Antselovich in October. Novoselov insisted that it was an exaggeration of the role of the individual and thereby a "completely non-Marxist approach to history. Where is the Marxist point of view here?" To drive home the point, Novoselov sarcastically dismissed Kapustin's claim to have been an "actual leader" of the Bolsheviks in October at only nineteen years of age. The boast, Novoselov insisted, was "neither Bolshevist nor Leninist." Not any one person but rather social and economic conditions, the subject matter of the essay by Tokarev and Tsaregorodtsev, were responsible for the delay in taking power. The article by Tokarev and Tsaregorodtsev, Novoselov said, would be "revised and resubmitted for another evaluation."[44]

Kapustin did not respond. Kuchkin, however, answered Novoselov in rapid fashion with an egregiously self-serving article published in the May 1927 issue of *Proletarskaia revoliutsiia*. There he underscored, clearly by exaggeration, his own and the party's importance in Viatka. As Kuchkin would have it, in February 1917 he was the only Bolshevik in the city, a municipality otherwise "clean (*chisto*) of Bolsheviks." Defying the popularity of Mensheviks, SRs, and other groups supportive of the Provisional Government, he had organized and led underground circles of soldiers and factory workers. It was true, Kuchkin admitted, that in April he had signed a proclamation written by Mensheviks that called on all Social Democrats without distinction, Mensheviks and Bolsheviks alike, to attend a meeting to draft a common agenda. But he had done so, he now insisted, as a ploy to attract Bolsheviks unknown to him at the time. Under his direction, they would all walk out to form their own independent organization. According to Kuchkin, five people had subsequently left with him.[45] Then that May, he organized and chaired an independent Bolshevik party committee in Viatka.

On June 6, 1927, the collegium of Viatka's Istpart addressed the dispute between Novoselov and Kuchkin. In addition to Novoselov, who chaired the session, it was attended by Derishev and two local party officials, Mikhail Konstantinovich Liubovikov (fig. 4.5) and Petr Grigor'evich Falaleev. None of them had had any quarrel in 1917 with Kuchkin before his departure from Viatka in midyear. Born in 1902, Novoselov had joined the party only in 1920. Derishev, the "grandfather of Viatka's Bolshevik party," had been in Petrograd almost the entirety of 1917. He arrived in Viatka only late that year. A Bolshevik since 1905 and imprisoned from 1909 to 1915, Liubovikov had been in Irkutsk until he came to Viatka in February 1918. Only Falaleev was in Viatka in 1917, as one of the organizers of the Bolshevik party there, but neither he nor Kuchkin mentioned any contact between them, hostile or otherwise. But now, ten years later, in a deeply personal way, Derishev, Liubovikov, and Falaleev resented Kuchkin's behavior. All three had been born in the province, spent their early careers there, and after 1917 had held multiple party and state posts in its administration. Proud of their native region, they preferred a reasonably accurate portrayal of its recent past.

In mid-1927, dismayed at Kuchkin's recent rewrite of Viatka's history and out of loyalty to Novoselov and the province, the collegium declared its full support for Istpart's head and of his "protest letters to the Central Committee's Istpart." It then commissioned Novoselov to use Istpart's archival materials to submit to *Proletarskaia revoliutsiia* a response to Kuchkin's "incorrect facts and implausible rendition of the history of Viatka's party organization."[46]

Figure 4.5. M. K. Liubovikov, c. 1906. Courtesy of Kirov's Regional Museum of Local History.

By the end of June, Novoselov had done so and sent the result to *Proletarskaia revoliutsiia*. He insisted that Kuchkin had mistakenly depicted himself as the "founder and organizer" of Viatka's party organization. Moreover, Kuchkin had seriously erred when denying any organizational relationship between Mensheviks and Bolsheviks before the end of May. A number of documents and memoirs demonstrated otherwise, including Kuchkin's own signature on the Menshevik appeal for a joint meeting of Mensheviks and Bolsheviks. Kuchkin had distorted the "real history of Viatka's party organization." Then, more charitably but condescendingly, Novoselov allowed that perhaps Kuchkin's "memory had betrayed him."[47]

At the same time, Novoselov took issue with Kuchkin, although without naming him, in the preface to Viatka Istpart's major publication on 1917, the aforementioned *October and the Civil War in the Viatka Province*. Making it clear that he represented not just his own but the Viatka Istpart's opinion, Novoselov emphasized that early in 1917 Bolsheviks in the city of Viatka had committed serious tactical and ideological errors. In particular, they had joined an organization dominated by Mensheviks. With Kuchkin in mind, Novoselov caustically declared, "It is absolutely unwarranted that some comrades try to obscure this fact or for various reasons bypass it in silence. A denial that initially Bolsheviks joined with Mensheviks in a Viatka organization is an elementary sin. It is so because first of all it is against the historical truth."[48]

Meanwhile, on May 30, Kapustin asked Novoselov to help him and others (Antselovich included) to publish their reminiscences about 1917. Novoselov took it as an opportunity to enlist Kapustin, he hoped, in Viatka's campaign against Kuchkin. In a letter sent to Kapustin's home in Moscow in early June, he asked the recipient to help Viatka's Istpart vet memoirs in order to preclude "such incidents as those which occurred with the article by com. Kuchkin," recently published in *Proletarskaia revoliutsiia*. It was a "concoction," Novoselov added, with false information about Viatka's party organization in 1917.[49]

Novoselov had little chance to draft Kapustin into his and Viatka's cause. The latter had promoted both Kuchkin and himself as major actors in 1917. Novoselov made Kapustin's cooperation even less likely when he insisted, for understandable reasons (as discussed in the next chapter), that Viatka's Istpart could not find room for memoirs by Kapustin or anyone else in its volumes scheduled to mark the tenth anniversary of the October Revolution. He offered the possibility of publication in two of Viatka's journals, the previously mentioned *Sputnik bol'shevika* and *Viatsko-Vetluzhskii krai*, the latter a monthly focusing on the region's economy and sponsored by Viatka's regional soviet.[50] Kapustin declined.

Proletarskaia revoliutsiia delayed publication of Novoselov's response to Kuchkin's review for over a year, printing it in the October 1928 issue. In the interim, Kapustin and Kuchkin continued to promote their revolutionary credentials and antagonize further Viatka's Istpart. In July 1927, Kapustin sent *Proletarskaia revoliutsiia* a review of an article submitted by Viatka's Nikolai Karpovich Solonitsyn. The author, a party and state official in the region, had been a member of the local Istpart collegium in 1925 and headed the Statistical Bureau of the regional soviet's executive committee in 1927. He had been a frequent author of articles on the area's economic history published in *Viatsko-Vetluzhskii krai*. In the article now under review, Solonitsyn described extensive peasant resistance to troops sent from Moscow to confiscate grain in Viatka's province in 1918. Kapustin responded that the author had exaggerated the importance of the peasants' opposition by making "outbreaks" (*vspyshki*), as Kapustin preferred to call them, into "revolts" (*vosstaniia*), as Solonitsyn had labeled them.[51] Kapustin had good personal reasons to minimize peasant resistance. In 1918, he had been the official in the province responsible for maintaining order. In May 1918, he headed the newly formed Cheka and in September became the region's military commissar. *Proletarskaia revoliutsiia* asked Aleksandr Grigor'evich Shlikhter, the head of a food detachment sent to Viatka in summer 1918, to evaluate Kapustin's criticism. Shlikhter responded that the author's assessment oversimplified the situation and, in particular, had underestimated the "significance of the atmosphere of peasants' exasperation," as Shlikhter awkwardly put it.[52]

That November, Kapustin reviewed a manuscript for *Proletarskaia revoliutsiia* submitted by Ivan Vasil'evich Popov, who was a Bolshevik in 1917 in Glazov, a city in the Viatka province. Kapustin quarreled with Popov's assertion that the party in the region experienced a "complete collapse" in February. Kapustin disagreed with the characterization because at the time, he said correctly, there had been no Bolshevik organization in the city. But after denying Bolsheviks any substantial presence in February, Kapustin insisted that Popov grossly underestimated the party's numerical strength and influence later in the year. As in his earlier review of the article by Tokarev and Tsaregorodtsev, Kapustin argued that the party enjoyed enough popular support to take power in Viatka in October. It had not done so because it lacked "sufficiently powerful leadership." Kapustin pointed out that one of the leaders—namely, he—was then too young and inexperienced.[53] *Proletarskaia revoliutsiia* published neither Solonitsyn's nor Popov's submissions.

While Kapustin was busy promoting himself at Viatka Istpart's expense, Kuchkin was doing much the same. In July 1927, *Proletarskaia revoliutsiia* published another of his self-serving memoirs, "July Days in Beloretsk." After his departure from Viatka in June 1917, Kuchkin had traveled to his hometown, Beloretsk, a small industrial town in the southern Urals. He remained there until September, when he left for the city of Ufa. The article discussed in detail the heroic behavior of the Bolshevik Pavlych, a play on Kuchkin's patronymic Pavlovich. Tirelessly and bravely, Pavlych denounced the war and the Provisional Government. Confronted time and again by hostile Mensheviks, SRs, and, initially, nonaligned members of the proletariat who at one point beat him, Pavlych prevailed. Through his courageous activity, workers came "to understand the essence of the Bolshevik message. The veil was lifted from the traitorous face of the Mensheviks and SRs."[54]

Proletarskaia revoliutsiia's next issue featured Kuchkin's account of his purportedly glorious service as a delegate from the military garrison of the Viatka and Perm regions to the First All-Russian Congress of Peasant Deputies held in Petrograd in May 1917.[55] SRs dominated the proceedings, but Kuchkin and his fellow Bolsheviks tirelessly addressed soldiers and workers day and night. With this article, however, Kuchkin temporarily met his match for sarcastic commentary. The ever critical Ol'minsky privately dismissed the item as "a decent bauble suitable for the amusement of the journal's readers."[56]

As noted previously, *Proletarskaia revoliutsiia* postponed printing Novoselov's response to Kuchkin's article until its October 1928 issue. Such delays were not uncommon.[57] Yet perhaps Moscow paused on this occasion with the hope that the open hostility between Kuchkin, representing Istpart at the center, and Novoselov, its affiliate in Viatka, might somehow abate in the meantime. It knew well that Novoselov wished to leave Viatka. Since May 1927, he had repeatedly asked Viatka's provincial party committee to release him and his spouse, Matrona Ivanovna Vylegzhanina, an official in the provincial party committee's Women's Department (*Zhenotdel*). Novoselov wanted reassignment to one of the USSR's warmer southern regions because of his tuberculosis.[58] In August, they left for the North Caucasus.[59]

In Novoselov's absence, hostility between Viatka's Istpart and its detractors in Moscow continued unabated. The relationship between the center and its local deteriorated further when, in October 1927, Kuchkin received a copy of Novoselov's response that had been submitted in June to *Proletarskaia revoliutsiia*. Kuchkin countered with his own assessment of Novoselov and events in Viatka in 1917. His bellicosity struck even the journal's staff as extreme. Before its publication in the November 1928 issue, which followed the delayed appearance the month before of Novoselov's article, editors removed or toned down a series of personal attacks on Novoselov.[60] Kuchkin had begun his draft with an angry characterization of Novoselov's letter and a sarcastic comment about its author: "The letter is written in a malevolent tone. It would not hurt the head of a provincial Istpart to be more tactful and proper in his remarks." The editors at *Proletarskaia revoliutsiia* deleted the offending passage. "Yes, com. Novoselov," Kuchkin had written, he, Kuchkin, had helped create a Bolshevik organization in Viatka. The editors removed the caustic reference to Novoselov. Kuchkin asked belligerently how Novoselov would interpret his, Kuchkin's, election as a Bolshevik delegate to the First All-Russian Congress of Peasant Deputies. "As happenstance?" The editors reduced it to a statement that Kuchkin's election was not "happenstance, as com. Novoselov suggests."[61] The editors did retain Kuchkin's false modesty. "I don't want to say," he wrote, "that I am worthy of a special 'rank', but the facts are the facts."[62]

The editors allowed, happily no doubt, something of a mea culpa on Kuchkin's part. He admitted that his signature on a Menshevik proclamation was a mistake. He had acknowledged it as such, he said, in a reference note removed by *Proletarskaia revoliutsiia* when it published his earlier memoir. He insisted that he had always opposed Mensheviks before and during 1917.[63] Few Bolsheviks, he said, cooperated with Mensheviks in 1917. The party organization had not, in any way whatsoever, hatched out of a Menshevik egg. The editors kept Kuchkin's confrontational assertion that Novoselov should have been busy with that very point, that the Bolsheviks had mercilessly fought against the enemy, the Mensheviks, throughout 1917.[64]

By the time *Proletarskaia revoliutsiia* published Novoselov's article followed by Kuchkin's retort, Novoselov had left Viatka. Even if he had stayed, it was unlikely that he could have done much to counter Kuchkin. As he and his colleagues in Viatka's Istpart had already discovered, their nemesis was well entrenched in Moscow, modifications of Kuchkin's draft by *Proletarskaia revoliutsiia* notwithstanding. Moreover, Viatka's Istpart faced two serious threats that limited what it could do in any event. One was political and the other financial.

NOTES

1. GASPI KO, f. P-1, op. 4, d. 34, ll. 9–10, 98. On March 19, 1926, the regional party committee's bureau confirmed the appointments: GASPI KO, f. P-1, op. 4, d. 15, l. 135. At its origin in March, the commission was under the sole jurisdiction of Viatka's regional party committee. In April, it was also made subordinate to the executive committee of the regional soviet. The party committee, however, continued its dominance over the commission. See GASPI KO, f. P-45, op. 1, d. 223, l. 18 and d. 239, ll. 28–29.

2. GASPI KO, f. P-1, op. 4, d. 50, ll. 1–2.

3. See sessions of the Commission for Celebrating the October Revolution in May, June, and July in GASPI KO, f. P-1, op. 4, d. 50, ll. 24, 48, 36 ob., 39, 58.

4. On the state of preparation of twelve of the works, see the commission's session, October 11, 1926, in GASPI KO, f. P-1, op. 4, d. 50, ll. 84–85.

5. *Oktiabr' i Grazhdanskaia voina v Viatskoi gubernii* (Viatka: Istpart, 1927). On the book's publication, see a report in late August in GASPI KO, f. P-1, op. 5, d. 22, l. 190 and a session of the commission in GASPI KO, f. P-1, op. 4, d. 50, l. 170.

6. A. Novoselov, "Oktiabr' v Viatke," *Viatskaia pravda*, October 23, 1926, 2 and October 24, 1926, 2.

7. See the handwritten item in GASPI KO, f. P-45, op. 1, d. 219, ll. 77–87, esp. ll. 80–83. In somewhat revised form, yet still with its acknowledgment of Bolshevik weakness, the piece appeared in 1929 in *Bol'shaia sovetskaia entsiklopediia*, vol. 14 (Moscow: Aktsionernoe obshchestvo "Sovetskaia entsiklopediia," 1929), columns 134–135.

8. See Novoselov's piece in the section, "Iz proshlogo," in *Sputnik bol'shevika*, no. 2 (February 1927), 61–64.

9. A. Novoselov, "Fevral' v Viatke," *Viatskaia pravda*, March 12, 1927, 2.

10. *Oktiabr' i Grazhdanskaia voina v Viatskoi gubernii*, 67–70. In early 1928 in *Proletarskaia revoliutsiia*, N. Nelidov noted without a hint of criticism that Viatka Istpart's major publication, *Oktiabr' i Grazhdanskaia voina*, emphasized the weakness of Bolsheviks in the city and region in 1917 and 1918 and the cooperation between Bolsheviks and Mensheviks in early 1917. See the review by N. Nelidov in *PR*, no. 1 (72) (January 1928), 180–183.

11. A. Novoselov, "Viatskaia organizatsiia VKP (bol'shevikov) v 1917–18 g.g.," in *Oktiabr' i Grazhdanskaia voina*, 67.

12. Novoselov, "Viatskaia organizatsiia," 68. Here Novoselov relied heavily, often almost word for word (and without attribution), on a memoir written by Popov in 1921. Popov's memoir is in GASPI KO, f. P-6807, op. 1, d. 7, esp. ll. 1–2.

13. See Novoselov's introduction to the volume, *Oktiabr' i Grazhdanskaia voina v Viatskoi gubernii*, V.

14. Novoselov did so in an article on the upcoming second conference of the province's archivists: A. Novoselov, "K vtoromu soveshchaniiu rabotnikov Istparta," *Viatskaia pravda*, March 17, 1926, 2.

15. GASPI KO, f. P-1, op. 4, d. 50, ll. 127–128. Novoselov did not speak of 1905 or 1917 in particular. A copy of Novoselov's remarks is also available in GASPI KO, f. P-45, op. 1, d. 106, ll. 17–19, 22.

16. GASPI KO, f. P-1, op. 4, d. 50, l. 132.

17. See Novoselov's communication to Petrovsky in GASPI KO, f. P-45, op. 1, d. 233, l. 28.

18. See, e.g., sessions of the regional party committee's secretariat, April 12, 1926, in GASPI KO, f. P-1, op. 4, d. 34, l. 123; of the regional party committee's bureau, October 4, 1926, in GASPI KO, f. P-1, op. 4, d. 17, l. 159 and of October 10, 1926, in GASPI KO, f. P-1, op. 4, d. 280, ll. 34–34 ob.; and of October 17, 1926, held jointly with the presidium of the municipal party committee, in GASPI KO, f. P-1, op. 4, d. 17, l. 169. For a brief discussion of limited oppositional activity among Viatka's Bolsheviks in the mid-1920s, see *Vo glave mass: Iz istorii Kirovskoi gorodskoi organizatsii KPSS* (Kirov: Volgo-Viatskoe knizhnoe izdatel'stvo, Kirovskoe otdelenie, 1980), 95–96.

19. Sarah Badcock, *Politics and People in Revolutionary Russia: A Provincial History* (New York: Cambridge University Press, 2007); Stefan Karsch, *Die bolschewistische Machtergreifung im Gouvernement Voronež (1917–1919)* (Stuttgart: Franz Steiner Verlag, 2006); Donald J. Raleigh, *Revolution on the Volga:1917 in Saratov* (Ithaca, NY: Cornell University Press, 1986); Tanja Penter, *Odessa 1917: Revolution an der Peripherie* (Cologne: Böhlau Verlag, 2000). See the work on Smolensk that emphasizes a highly fragmented society, the result of multiple public identities and elected local committees that undercut state authority:

Michael C. Hickey, "Discourses of Public Identities and Liberalism in the February Revolution: Smolensk, Spring 1917," *Russian Review* 55, no. 4 (October 1996): 615–637, and "Local Government and State Authority in the Provinces: Smolensk, February–June 1917," *Slavic Review* 55, no. 4 (Winter 1996): 863–881. For a review of recent historical literature that speaks of the "multiplicity of local experiences," see Liudmila Novikova, "The Russian Revolution from a Provincial Perspective," *Kritika* 16, no. 4 (Fall 2015): 769–785, quote on 769. See also the introduction and multiple articles in Aaron Retish, Sarah Badcock, and Liudimila Novikova, eds., *Russia's Home Front in War and Revolution, 1914–1922*, bk. 1, *Russia's Revolution in Regional Perspective* (Bloomington, IN: Slavica Publishers, 2015). The editors speak of "developments in Russia between 1914 and 1922 as a kaleidoscopic process whose dynamic was not solely determined in the capitals" (1). An earlier but still useful work is John Keep, "October in the Provinces," in *Revolutionary Russia*, ed. Richard Pipes (Cambridge, MA: Harvard University Press, 1968), 180–216.

20. *Kirovskaia oblast' k 50-letiiu Oktiabria: Statisticheskii sbornik* (Gor'kii: Izdatel'stvo "Statistika," 1967), 7.

21. See, esp., the work of the Viatka/Kirov historian, Iu. N. Timkin, especially his *Smutnoe vremia na Viatke: Obshchestvenno-politicheskoe razvitie Viatskoi gubernii vesnoi 1917-osen'iu 1918 gg.* (Kirov: Izdatel'stvo VGPU, 1998). Timkin emphasized over and again the Bolshevik party's narrow range of support and its heavy reliance on outside military units to seize and hold power. See also Timkin's "K voprosu ob ustanovlenii sovetskoi vlasti v g. Viatke" and "'Lapinskaia avantiura' v g. Viatke v fevrale-marte 1918 g.," both in *Viatskaia zemlia v proshlom i nastoiashchem. Materialy III nauchnoi konferentsii, posviashchennoi 50-letiiu pobedy Velikoi Otechestvennoi voiny*, vol. 1 (Kirov: Kirovskii gosudarstvennyi pedagogicheskii institut, 1995), 18–21, 121–124. Of considerable interest is V. I. Bakulin, *Drama v dvukh aktakh: Viatskaia guberniia v 1917–1918 gg.* (Kirov: ViatGGU, 2008). Although Bakulin insists on the inevitability of the Bolshevik party's seizure of power, he repeatedly shows the party's weakness in 1917. Bakulin acknowledges that Soviet power was not fully established in the region until well into 1918 and then only in large part thanks to outside armed intervention. Bakulin and Timkin have contributed to a comprehensive study of the region and city of Viatka in 1917 and 1918: V. I. Bakulin, A. S. Makarova, A. S. Pozdniakova, Iu. N. Timkin, M. A. Borchina, *Viatskaia guberniia v 1917–1918 godakh: Revoliutsiia i evoliutsiia regional'noi politiko-upravlencheskoi sistemy* (Kirov: "Raduga-PRESS," 2017). For an earlier, considerably more tendentious account of this period, but one that nevertheless acknowledges the Bolshevik party's weakness, see E. S. Sadyrina, *Oktiabr' v Viatskoi gubernii* (Kirov: Kirovskoe knizhnoe izdatel'stvo, 1957). On Viatka's peasantry in the period of revolution and civil war, see Aaron B. Retish, *Russia's*

Peasants in Revolution and Civil War: Citizenship, Identity, and the Creation of the Soviet State, 1914–1922 (New York: Cambridge University Press, 2008). For continued squabbling and divisions among Bolsheviks in 1918 and 1919, see A. V. Mamaev, "Osobennosti vzaimootnoshenii Viatskogo gorsoveta i gubispolkoma v 1918-nachale 1919 gg.," in *Gorod na Viatke: Istoriia, kul'tura, liudi* (Kirov: Oblastnaia tipografiia, 2014), 67–71.

22. For the city of Viatka, see *Vo glave mass*, 59; for the province, *Kirovskaia oblastnaia organizatsiia KPSS v tsifrakh, 1917–1985* (Kirov: Volgo-Viatskoe knizhnoe izdatel'stvo, Kirovskoe otdelenie, 1986), 18.

23. Tat'iana Saburova and Ben Eklof, *Druzhba, Sem'ia, Revoliutsiia: Nikolai Charushin i pokolenie narodnikov, 1870-kh godov* (Moscow: Novoe literaturnoe obozrenie, 2016), 336.

24. On the regiment, see Timkin, *Smutnoe vremia*, 31–32 and E. A. Sharin, "Rol' 106-go zapasnogo pekhotnogo polka v zhizni Viatskoi gubernii s marta po oktiabr' 1917 g.," in *Voprosy istoricheskoi nauki: Materialy IV Mezhdunarodnoi nauchnoi konferentsii* (Moscow: Buki-Vedi, 2016), 50–53. This source is available at https://moluch.ru/conf/hist/archive/241/11313/ (accessed May 12, 2017).

25. For a detailed discussion of these events in Viatka, see Timkin, *Smutnoe vremia*, 29–39. Mensheviks garnered 1.8% of the votes.

26. Timkin, "Lapinskaia avantiura," 124. The two soviets jostled for control over the detachment, which increasingly acted independently in its requisition and confiscation of property. For a survey of events in Viatka province from 1918 to 1920, see Retish, *Russia's Peasants*, 130–212. Much like Timkin's characterization of power in Viatka, Michael Hickey described it in Smolensk in late 1917 as a "messy sort of power sharing": Hickey, "Paper, Memory and a Good Story," 2.

27. V. I. Bakulin, "Letuchie otriady—'tiazhelaia kavaleriia revoliutsii' v Viatskoi gubernii," *Voenno-istoricheskii zhurnal*, no. 11 (November 2012), 18.

28. GASPI KO, f. P-45, op. 1, d. 186, l. 3. On difficulties in Izhevsk, see Aaron B. Retish, "The Izhevsk Revolt of 1918: The Fateful Clash of Revolutionary Coalitions, Paramilitarism, and Bolshevik Power," in Retish et al., *Russia's Home Front*, 299–322.

29. See Novoselov's introduction to the volume, *Oktiabr' i Grazhdanskaia voina v Viatskoi gubernii*, V.

30. The work had been one of the brochures initially considered by Viatka's Commission for Celebrating the October Revolution. See the commission's session of October 11, 1926, GASPI KO, f. P-1, op. 4, d. 50, l. 84.

31. For biographical information on Tokarev, see I. A. Solov'eva, "Pervyi dekan istoricheskogo fakul'teta Kirovskogo gosudarstvennogo pedagogicheskogo instituta," in *Viatskaia zemlia v proshlom i nastoiashchem: Sbornik materialov*, vol. 1 (Kirov: Izdatel'stvo ViatGGU, 2014), 28–33. On

Tsaregorodtsev, see *Prepodavateli ViatGGU, 1914–2004* (Kirov: Izdatel'stvo ViatGGU, 2004), 184.

32. Various undated typescript copies of Tokarev's and Tsaregorodstev's essay exist. See GASPI KO, f. P-45, op. 1, d. 94, ll. 108–173 and d. 98, ll. 28–297 and d. 88, ll. 1–36. In the latter typescript, the authors referred to a "social revolution" (*sotsial'nyi perevorot*) in the province in 1917 (l. 36). In another draft, someone, presumably one of the authors, self-consciously inserted a brief handwritten note with some generalities about Bolshevik activity in the city of Viatka: GASPI KO, f. P-45, op. 1, d. 94, ll. 133–133 ob.

33. *Proletarskaia revoliutsiia*'s editorial staff also sent a copy of the article by Tokarev and Tsaregorodtsev to Antselovich, now chair of the central committee of the union of workers of agriculture and forestry and a candidate member of the party's Central Committee. Antselovich did not respond until April 1927. He had little to say about the item other than it was not suitable for publication. It was, he said, "hardly of interest to party and non-party readers." RGASPI, f. 72, op. 3, d. 888, l. 1.

34. Kuchkin had been in Viatka since February 1916. On Kuchkin's life, see E. S. Sadyrina, *Andrei Kuchkin, 1888–1973* (Kirov: Volgo-Viatskoe knizhnoe izdatel'stvo, Kirovskoe otdelenie, 1982).

35. For biographical information on Kapustin, see V. I. Bakulin, *Trudnyi perekhod ot voiny k miru: Viatskaia guberniia v 1920–1921 godakh*, bk. 1, *1920 god* (Kirov: ViatGGU, 2009), 85.

36. The response was not published and I did not locate it at RGASPI or at GASPI KO. For its content, I rely on Novoselov's reaction, discussed below. See Novoselov's handwritten response, written on or about May 4, in GASPI KO, f. P-45, op. 1, d. 237, ll. 9–11 and a typed copy in GASPI KO, f. P-45, op. 1, d. 242, ll. 54–56.

37. A. Kuchkin, review of I. Podshivalov, *Grazhdanskaia bor'ba na Urale, 1917–1919 gg.* (Moscow: Gosudarstvennoe voennoe izdatel'stvo, 1925) in *PR*, no. 12 (59) (December 1926), 260–264.

38. A. Kuchkin, review of S. Semakov, *Iz revoliutsionnogo proshlogo molodezhi Viatskoi gubernii (1905–1908 gg.)* (Viatka: Istpart, 1926), in *PR*, no. 11 (58) (November 1926), 266–267, quote on 267.

39. Novoselov might have responded. There is correspondence between Novoselov and Kuchkin that is not available in the archives.

40. GASPI KO, f. P-45, op. 1, d. 242, ll. 54, 56. Novoselov sent it to E. Shteinman, who was head of Istpart's Office for Regional Branches.

41. GASPI KO, f. P-45, op. 1, d. 242, l. 55–56. Regarding the proclamation, l. 57. Novoselov had in mind an appeal for membership published on April 8 in the newspaper *Viatskaia rech'* from the united organization of Mensheviks and Bolsheviks.

42. The sketch, written on March 11, 1919, is in the Research Collection 5432 in Kirov's Regional Museum of Local History.
43. RGASPI, f. 72, op. 3, d. 937, l. 1–2.
44. GASPI KO, f. P-45, op. 1, d. 242, ll. 55–56.
45. A. Kuchkin, "Bol'shevistskaia organizatsiia v Viatke v nachale 1917 g.," *PR*, no. 5 (64) (May 1927), 185.
46. GASPI KO, f. P-45, op. 1, d. 237, l. 3. The collegium also included Poplaukhin, a representative of the Provincial Archive Bureau. The collegium expressed displeasure at the center's demands for delivery of archival materials from Viatka to Moscow without the prior permission of Viatka's Istpart (l. 1).
47. GASPI KO, f. P-45, op. 1, d. 242, quotes in turn on ll. 87, 89, 90, 91. A copy is also in RGASPI, f. 72, d. 134, ll. 1–5. The letter was printed in *PR*, no. 10 (81) (October 1928), 229–231. Novoselov did not say so, but Kuchkin had probably exaggerated his, Kuchkin's, role in the formation of an independent Bolshevik organization in Viatka. His sympathetic biographer, Sadyrina, implies that when the organization was created at the end of May, Kuchkin was probably on the way back from Petrograd where he had represented Viatka at the First All-Russian Congress of Peasant Deputies. See Sadyrina, *Andrei Kuchkin*, 44, 58–59. Kuchkin did become a member of the organization's bureau.
48. "Predislovie," *Oktiabr' i Grazhdanskaia voina v Viatskoi gubernii*, V.
49. GASPI KO, f. P-45, op. 1, d. 245, l. 48.
50. GASPI KO, f. P-45, op. 1, d. 245, l. 48 ob.
51. RGASPI, f. 72, op. 3, d. 938, l. 2. The article also dealt with the rebellion by a Moscow food regiment led by A. A. Stepanov against local Bolshevik forces and its seizure of power in several districts of the Viatka province. For a discussion of the "Stepanovshchina," see Retish, *Russia's Peasants*, 175–179.
52. RGASPI, f. 72, op. 3, d. 938, l. 8 ob. Shlikhter blamed Kapustin, who as head of the region's Cheka, unnecessarily exacerbated tension between local authorities and representatives sent to the region by the center (l. 8). In early 1918, Shlikhter had served as the Russian Republic's commissar of food supply and, later that year, as a special commissar for food supply in Siberia, Perm, Viatka, and other provinces. At the time of his comments about Kapustin's review, he was Ukraine republic's commissar of agriculture. On Shlikhter's activity in Viatka, see Iu. P. Alekseev, "Ekspeditsiia A. G. Shlikhtera i S. P. Sredy za khlebom v 1918 g.," *Istoriia SSSR*, no. 3 (May–June 1966), 135–143.
53. RGASPI, f. 70, op. 3, d. 435, ll. 1–3, quote on l. 3.
54. A. Kuchkin, "Iiul'skie dni 1917 g. v Beloretske," *PR*, no. 7 (66) (July 1927), 162–163.
55. A. Kuchkin, "I Vserossiiskii s"ezd Krestianskikh Deputatov (Vospominaniia delegata)," *PR*, no. 8–9 (67–68) (August–September 1927), 295–308. Here somewhat surprisingly, Kuchkin noted that Trotsky's address to the

delegates was well received: 306. After the congress, "chaos," a word Kuchkin put in quotation marks, gripped the country and led to a takeover of power by the soviets: l. 308. *Proletarskaia revoliutsiia* also published two reviews by Kuchkin of books on developments in the city of Ufa and republic of Bashkiriia in which Kuchkin demanded from their authors far more attention to the activity of the Bolshevik party in 1917 and of the Red Army during the civil war. See Kuchkin's review of *Proidennyi put'* (Ufa: Izdatel'stvo Bashistparta, 1927), *PR*, no. 3 (74) (March 1927), 225–227 and of M. L. Murtazin, *Bashkiriia i bashkirskie voiska v Grazhdanskuiu voinu* (Leningrad: Izdatel'stvo Voennoi tipografii upravleniia delami Narkomvoenmor i RVS SSSR, 1927), in *PR*, no. 7 (66) (July 1927), 266–270.

56. RGASPI, f. 70, op. 4, d. 310, l. 70. Ol'minsky's comment is not dated.

57. A folder of *Proletarskaia revoliutsiia*'s correspondence for the years 1927 to 1930 reveals over and again the journal's slow response to requests from individuals to review their submissions for publication. Many submissions were abruptly rejected as "unnecessary." RGASPI 72, op. 1, d. 16, 149 ll.

58. See Novoselov's requests of May 27, July 16, and August 10, 1927, in GASPI KO, f. P-1, op. 5, d. 31, l. 210; d. 32, l. 136; and d. 22, l. 165.

59. On August 12, 1927, the provincial party committee's bureau assigned them both to the Northern Caucasus regional party committee; GASPI KO, f. P-1, op. 5, d. 14, l. 129.

60. Kuchkin's handwritten response to *Proletarskaia revoliutsiia* is in RGASPI, f. 72, op. 2, d. 134, ll. 10–11 ob. A typed copy is on ll. 12–15. The published version is in the section, "Pis'mo v redaktsiiu," *PR*, no. 11–12 (82–83) (November–December 1928), 364–365. Kuchkin's draft is undated.

61. RGASPI, f. 72, op. 2, d. 13, ll. 12, 13, 14.

62. *PR*, no. 11–12 (82–83) (November–December 1928), 365.

63. *PR*, no. 11–12 (82–83) (November–December 1928), 364–365. For years thereafter, Kuchkin remained sensitive to criticism of his relationship with Mensheviks. I will return to this point in chap. 9.

64. RGASPI f. 72, op. 2, d. 13, l. 15; *PR*, no. 11–12 (82–83) (November–December 1928), 365.

FIVE

Fractured Finances

VIATKA'S ISTPART DEPENDED ON THE regional party committee for financial support. Initially, that organ provided little if any help, dooming the agency to a mere paper existence. In the mid-1920s, when the committee promised ample assistance for a proper celebration of the 1905 and 1917 revolutions, it soon reneged.

FOUND WANTING

In 1926, party and state organs throughout the Viatka region slashed expenses. The regional party committee instructed all party units, including factory cells, to cut staff, roll back salaries of employees who remained, and reduce daily operating expenses.[1] Retrenchment extended to previously untouchable efforts to spread the party's ideological and political message. The soviet party school increased class size, slashed staff and salaries, and canceled repairs to its building.[2] The journal *The Path of Enlightenment* (Put' prosveshcheniia) lost the support of its patron, the provincial soviet's department of education, and ceased publication.[3] The regional party committee reduced funding for the campaign to liquidate illiteracy, despite a personal appeal from Krupskaya not to do so.[4] That December, the committee withdrew its promise of 16,500 rubles for the erection of a monument to Lenin. It decided to honor him in another, unspecified but less expensive way.[5]

Publishers of Istpart's work no longer could be as generous as before. In 1926 and 1927, the regional party committee ordered *Viatskaia pravda* to reduce staff and salaries.[6] It also told the publishing house, Truzhenik, to limit expenses, collect what creditors owed it, and cease publishing items that it could not sell.[7]

In mid-1926, it closed the press down altogether.[8] Viatka's Istpart could get by with a reduced *Viatskaia pravda*. The loss of Truzhenik, however, was another, most serious matter.

Created in 1922, Truzhenik held a monopoly on the printing and sale of items submitted by the region's state and party organs. It was also the only agency empowered in the region to purchase and sell state-sponsored literature printed elsewhere. Truzhenik published a variety of materials: brochures by and about Lenin; manuals on agriculture, chemistry, medicine, and hygiene; and plays designed for village theaters. From 1925, it issued the regional party committee's journal *Biulleten'* and the regional department of education's monthly, *Put' prosveshcheniia*.[9] The committee expected Truzhenik to lose money; however, an overly ambitious publication program and sloppy business practices made its losses exceed all expectations.

At its liquidation in 1926, Truzhenik had not paid bills for literature it had ordered for resale and owed the post office for items it had mailed.[10] Numerous organizations had not reimbursed Truzhenik for the considerable sums due for materials they had received from it. Unfortunately for the publisher, it had lost the paperwork verifying the transactions and amounts owed.[11] A year earlier, Truzhenik had hoped to augment its income by opening a shop selling musical instruments and office supplies. That August, toilets upstairs overran. Their contents penetrated the ceiling and came into the shop below, forcing its closure and expensive repairs.[12]

Truzhenik lost money on the party committee's *Biulleten'*. Few Bolsheviks in the region cared enough about party news and instructions to subscribe. It lost even more on *Put' prosveshcheniia*. The regional department of education had promised an annual subsidy of 3,400 rubles and 1,500 paying subscribers. Instead, the department provided half the amount and far fewer subscribers.[13]

Truzhenik piled up more losses with the publication of items by Viatka's Istpart. In 1925, in celebration of the twentieth anniversary of the 1905 revolution, Truzhenik printed five books (four of them under a hundred pages each) sponsored by Viatka's Istpart and the Commission for Celebrating the 1905 Revolution.[14] The fifth and heretofore mentioned *1905 in the Viatka Province*, a hastily written and uninspiring collection of essays, memoirs, and documents, consisted of 340 pages in a press run of five thousand copies.[15] Sales of all of the volumes lagged badly. By year's end, many of them, including multiple copies of *1905*, remained unsold. Viatka's regional party committee ordered Truzhenik to take measures "for the most rapid sale of literature lying around and going nowhere."[16] It did so in vain. Truzhenik tried to convince the Russian Republic's State Publishing House and the publisher for Moscow's municipal party committee to buy copies of *1905* for resale. Both agencies turned Viatka down because the book, they said, "has only local significance."[17] The situation had not improved in November 1927, when the regional party committee slashed prices of all five items by 50 to 75 percent. The price for *1905* fell from one ruble to thirty kopecks.[18] In the meantime, as was learned at Truzhenik's liquidation, much of Istpart's unsold material had vanished from its warehouse without explanation.[19]

SUPPLY AND DEMAND

The center's Istpart knew all too well the problems of the marketing and sale of printed material. Gosizdat had lost manuscripts sent to it by Istpart and delayed the publication of others, including issues of *Proletarskaia revoliutsiia*. Ol'minsky had entertained the thought that only bribes might induce the publisher to do better. Yet from Gosizdat's point of view, it was compelled to print items that could not be sold. And it, not Istpart, suffered the loss. In late 1923, Istpart returned to Gosizdat as many as five thousand copies of volumes that it, Istpart, had sponsored and purchased from Gosizdat but could not sell. Istpart now wanted a reimbursement of 5,500 rubles. These items included both volumes of Shliapnikov's *The Eve of 1917* and 8 percent of the issues of *Proletarskaia revoliutsiia* published in mid-1923.[20] Elsewhere, other agencies experienced similar problems in moving Istpart's literature. For the remainder of 1923, Istpart and Gosizdat slashed the journal's press run from a high of ten thousand per issue in May to five thousand in November. Thereafter, with only two thousand subscribers, chiefly libraries, Istpart encouraged party members to purchase the journal and, in a burst of optimism, printed from eight to ten thousand issues until late 1925.[21] Nevertheless, sales of the journal lagged even as Istpart still insisted that the monthly and other publications were of value and marketable. It blamed Gosizdat. The publisher allegedly made little or no effort to promote Istpart's items, leaving them unattended in its warehouses, or worse, Ol'minsky charged, preferring to pulp them.[22]

Whatever its problems with Gosizdat, Ol'minsky thought his agency might publish still more, not less. At Istpart's Third Conference, May 1924, he boasted that Istpart had an arrangement with Gosizdat and other unnamed firms for the publication of an unlimited amount of material. He suggested that Istpart's locals, loudly complaining that they lacked resources to print their own work, should send their manuscripts (best if already copyedited) to the central office for publication as brochures or small books. The honorarium, Ol'minsky added, would go to the local. Savel'ev seconded the suggestion.[23]

Istpart proceeded in 1925 with ambitious plans to mark the twentieth anniversary of the 1905 revolution. By autumn, its central office had prepared for publication three major volumes on 1905 and nine smaller items of essays and documents, a total aggregate of 8,800 pages. That figure exceeded the initial publication plan by 85 percent. Istpart planned for still more: a fourth major volume, seven brochures for a mass audience, an index of literature on 1905, and two more volumes of documents and articles.[24] The following year, it launched a more aggressive program for the upcoming celebration of the tenth anniversary of the October revolution. It planned to publish twenty-four thousand pages of monographs, documents, and memoirs.[25] While adhering to its own such fanciful schemes, Istpart's center sanctimoniously cautioned its locals to avoid lengthy and costly works of little public interest. Volumes of collected essays must not, it cautioned, consist of the "dry and somehow improvised material as had occurred in a significant number of collections on 1905."[26]

Plans for these volumes came precisely at a time when the Soviet Union experienced a severe paper shortage. In early 1925, it planned to import for the year more than 127,000 tons at a considerable cost.[27] This planning also occurred when the Soviet publishing industry had a growing backlog of unsold books. In 1925 and 1926, the Central Committee's Press Department imposed limits on the publishing activity of those agencies that had its own press. It also closed a number of journals.[28] Istpart could not long remain an exception. That became apparent at Istpart's Fourth Conference, January 4–8, 1927.

The conference had been a long time in the making. The urge to micromanage remembrance of 1917 and disagreements over the cost and content of publications planned by Istpart and other organizations had forced multiple postponements. In November 1925, the party's Orgburo had created a Commission for Celebrating the October Revolution to set and limit, when necessary, the agenda and expenses for commemorating the upcoming tenth anniversary. It appointed eminent party officials to the commission, including Bukharin as chair, Molotov as his deputy, and Stalin, Rykov, Dzerzhinsky, Mikhail Tomsky, Kamenev, Mikhail Kalinin, Andrei Bubnov, Zinoviev, Pokrovsky, Krupskaya, and Trotsky. Kanatchikov represented Istpart and Gusev the Central Committee's Press Department.[29] In early April 1926, the Orgburo set the conference's opening for May 10 with an agenda to discuss directives issued in the meantime by the commission. It did not happen. The commission was far too large, and its members were too preoccupied with other duties and with quarrels over the politics of the past and present to achieve much of anything. They found neither the time nor the inclination to meet.

On April 26, 1926, Kanatchikov announced the conference's postponement until autumn to give time for the Central Committee's commission to

Figure 5.1. S. I. Gusev, 1922. Courtesy of the Russian State Documentary Film and Photo Archive.

convene.[30] By year's end, it still had not met. On December 1, an immediate convocation of the conference was suggested by Shteinman, Istpart's official in charge of its locals, to the agency's head, Gusev (fig. 5.1), who had replaced Kanatchikov months earlier. The convocation was needed to provide directions to Istpart's impatient branches, which had already launched their own plans for celebrating October.[31] Days later, Istpart issued a circular announcing the conference's opening in Moscow on January 4.[32]

On that day, sixty-four delegates assembled, fifty-one of them male (78 percent of the total). Forty-seven, Novoselov included, headed Istpart's regional locals.[33] They were not pleased with what they heard. The Central Committee's Press Department, which Gusev headed until his appointment to Istpart, had already informed several of the conference's leaders of the full dimensions of the disaster that had overtaken the publication and sale of literature for the 1905 jubilee. At least 250 books had been printed by various organizations, with an average of ninety-six pages and a press run of four to five thousand copies. In total, more than a million volumes had been released at a cost of two hundred thousand rubles. A good half of these items remained unsold and on the shelves, awaiting, as Gusev put it sarcastically, the twenty-fifth or fiftieth anniversary of 1905. Istpart's performance was particularly poor. Mercifully, some of the material it had prepared had not yet been printed. Many volumes that had been published remained unsold.[34] Mariia Moiseevna Essen, head of the Georgian party's agitprop from 1921 to 1925, Istpart member since 1927, and deputy chair of the Russian Republic's State Planning Commission, confided privately that for the 1905 jubilee, "each city, district, and village wrote in bloodstained letters its history of this revolution in thousands of copies. Who will read it and who will buy it? The market is flooded with such literature."[35]

Proposals for celebrating in print the 1917 revolution suggested far worse to come, nothing short of a catastrophe. Essen warned that any repetition of the errors in celebrating 1905 would mean that "the market will be completely saturated and literature for the tenth jubilee will lie like a heavy stone alongside the grave of jubilee literature for 1905."[36] In remarks at the Fourth Conference, Gusev reported that organizations, first among them Istpart, intended to publish a glut of literature on 1917—a total of five hundred volumes, on an average of 160 pages each, eighty thousand pages in all, a "whole library." He had learned of the plan from former associates at Central Committee's Press Department. As Gusev put it, he "decisively protested" against such extravagance. As a result, the number of pages permissible for publication by all agencies combined dropped to 19,200, a reduction by 76 percent. And Gusev hoped that far less, perhaps only half of that allotment, would be printed.[37]

Delegates at the conference fully grasped the reality of such harsh restrictions. Savel'ev made it worse. He informed those assembled of just what the retrenchment meant for the agency's current plans for literature marking the tenth anniversary. At the center and locally, it was permitted to print only 4,640 pages of material.[38]

Delegates objected. Their locals had already commenced to compile books and brochures. The printing of some of them had begun. Among other complainants, the head of Kostroma's Istpart, Ivan Vasil'evich Mishin, spoke on two occasions. His branch had been told that it could not publish items even when it had successfully solicited local resources to finance them. "It's an abnormal situation," Mishin declared, for Moscow to make such decisions.[39] Zakhar Semenovich Petrov from Samara insisted that the State Publishing House, not Istpart, bore responsibility for lagging sales. Gosizdat had not promoted what local Istparts had published. It considered Istpart's work as junk and left it to rot in warehouses.[40] Ida Finkel'shtein, the representative of the Central Asian Istpart in Tashkent, hoped to turn the tables on the center. She wanted to know if Moscow might provide resources to expand rather than abbreviate the program for printing items in the five major languages of her region.[41]

As the conference drew to a close, forty delegates, Viatka's Novoselov among them, signed an appeal to the conference's presidium. They claimed that speakers had not provided an accurate picture of Istpart's work for the tenth anniversary. They implicitly meant, as surely everyone knew, that the center had unjustifiably restricted plans for the celebration of October. The petitioners asked the presidium to invite Pokrovsky, so far absent from the proceedings, to speak at the conference.[42] He had been scheduled to deliver the major opening address. At the last moment, a day before the conference's convocation, it became apparent that illness would prevent him from doing so.[43] Delegates appealed in vain. Pokrovsky remained too ill to come. If he had spoken, he might well have supported the collective dissentient voice from below. As we will see, he believed restrictions on Istpart's publications, at least when they affected his own agenda, had gone too far.

Despite the contrarian murmurs from below, the conference's resolutions mimicked what conferees had been told by their leaders, Gusev and Savel'ev. Locals' efforts to commemorate the 1905 revolution in print had been a disaster. The experience had demonstrated that Istpart's literature had "a limited circle of readers." For the October jubilee, the slogan "Less Quantity, Better Quality" should rule. Yet delegates' protests had been loud and vigorous enough to achieve a compromise of sorts. In sharp contrast to rhetoric in particular from Gusev, the conference called for a rejection of "an extreme and purely mechanical reduction of the publication activity of local Istparts." They asked Istpart's central office to seek permission from the Central Committee for an increase, not a decrease, in the number of pages that locals could print and a subsidy for their publication. And they wanted the center to permit its branches to publish jubilee literature to the greater extent allowed by local resources.[44]

It was a hollow victory. After the conference, Istpart's central office proceeded as if no accommodation had been reached with its protesting branches. On January 29, its collegium discussed an ongoing campaign in the press against what it called the "littering of the market with jubilee literature that was junk." It still had in mind, to be sure, items on 1905 that were unsold and languishing in warehouses.[45] However, it clearly intended its harsh criticism to be a warning not to repeat the calamity when commemorating October. On February 26, Gusev made it all frighteningly public in an article in *Pravda*, "On Jubilee Literature."[46] Istpart's program for publication of materials on the 1905 revolution had produced a disaster. Intent on avoiding its repetition, the Central Committee's Press Department had slashed what Istpart and other organizations could sponsor for the October jubilee, as he had reported at Istpart's Fourth Conference. Further cutbacks were now in order. On July 29, 1927, Istpart duly admonished its locals and instructed them to print no more than a specifically assigned number of pages to be assigned to each.[47]

Voices of dissent continued. With the appearance of Gusev's article in *Pravda*, Pokrovsky protested. In a letter to Gusev, he agreed with efforts to end publication of insignificant and unnecessary "junk." But he could not agree with plans to curtail serious scholarship on the history of 1917.[48] Pokrovsky had in mind volumes of documents and articles being prepared under his general direction. One that subsequently appeared in a generous press run of three thousand copies contained, as previously discussed, important articles by Genkina, Iugov, and Lidak, That same year, Pankratova released her work *The Political Struggle in the Russian Labor Union Movement, 1917–1918*, sponsored by Leningrad's Regional Council of Labor Unions, and published in a press run of three thousand copies. However, other items planned in Moscow and in the provinces, many already written and submitted to a publisher, did not survive or appeared with dramatically diminished content and press runs. *Proletarskaia revoliutsiia* could not avoid downsizing. In 1926 and 1927, its issues appeared in a press run of four thousand, half of what it had been during much of 1925. In each of the last three months of 1927, it fell to 3,500 (while the average number of pages per issue remained about three hundred). The journal still languished on the shelves, unsold. In 1927, Gosizdat told Savel'ev that because of lagging sales, it printed the journal at a major loss.[49]

Three days after the close of the Fourth Istpart Conference, on January 11, 1927, Novoselov departed Moscow for Viatka. He brought an unwelcome message.

A LESSON NOT LEARNED IN VIATKA

Viatka's Commission for Celebrating the October Revolution and Viatka's Istpart had failed to learn from Truzhenik's demise. Even as sales of publications on 1905 lagged, they hoped to print at least twelve volumes to commemorate October's tenth anniversary. On June 8, 1926, Novoselov informed the commission that the total cost for eleven of the books—not including the major and most expensive item, *October and the Civil War in the Viatka Province*—came to 14,800 rubles.[50] No one thought the price excessive or reason for caution. That year, Novoselov pursued Viatka's former revolutionaries to submit their memoirs for publication in the main volume. By year's end, he had gathered more than five hundred pages of such material.[51] His Istpart also encouraged submission for possible publication of multiple essays on Viatka's economic and social conditions following the October Revolution and of memoirs and documents on Viatka's Red Guards, chiefly in 1918.[52] On December 22, 1926, Novoselov convened a meeting of authors of all the works in question. Taking measure of the great amount of work planned, he worried only that it would not be finished on time. Novoselov said nothing about any need to reduce the number of volumes or abridge their content.[53] That would soon change.

On January 27, 1927, just back from Istpart's Fourth Conference, Novoselov addressed a session of the Commission for Celebrating the October Revolution. Five days later, he spoke at a meeting of authors whose works were designated for publication to honor the jubilee. He had bad news. Grand plans for the printing of multiple items would have to be scaled back or scrapped altogether. "It is necessary," Novoselov declared, "to fight against an onslaught of paper, which is threatening to drown our tenth anniversary." Reminding his listeners of unsold items on 1905, Novoselov declared that "we cannot have any such sort of scandal surrounding literature for the upcoming tenth anniversary of the October Revolution." He then announced the abandonment of several projects and a contraction of the number of pages of others. Financial responsibility for still others would shift to other agencies such as the Young Communist League or labor unions, in effect, putting their publication in doubt. The commission would fund only five items in addition to the major work *October and the Civil War*.[54]

Novoselov's audience was not pleased. Sponsors and authors of books now rejected or designated for major abridgement strenuously objected. At the commission's session of January 27, representatives of the Young Communist League and of labor unions objected to the likely extinction of their projects.[55] At the meeting of February 2, Tokarev—an author of the aforementioned essay, "The Prerequisites of October," which would soon arouse the ire of Kuchkin and Kapustin—spoke out forcefully. He opposed a sharp contraction in the size of his planned contribution. "My work has already been written," he declared, "I have spent a lot of time and energy on it."[56] Equally offended, his colleagues said much the same thing.

Novoselov understood, as he put it, his audience's "bewilderment" and "discomfort."[57] But he sternly instructed Tokarev and others like him that the regional party committee, Istpart's central office, and Istpart's Fourth Conference demanded the cuts. The center was concerned, Novoselov continued, about overly ambitious and expensive programs adopted by many of its locals. Novoselov then added that Moscow was also equally if not more concerned that many items previously printed had not adhered to the party line (a point of considerable discussion in the next chapter). Nevertheless, authors whose books had been targeted managed to achieve a measure of success, albeit, as it turned out, cosmetic. The meeting adopted resolutions limiting the abbreviation of works already written to the removal of unnecessary facts and excess verbiage.[58]

The major item, *October and the Civil War*, survived the cut but just barely. The commission and Istpart had initially planned for an "exhaustive account," a volume of eight hundred pages in a print run of five thousand copies.[59] Novoselov still hoped for a substantial if smaller volume. In late March, he wrote Savel'ev in Moscow asking for financial support for its publication even if in an abridged format. He also wanted Savelev's permission to seek additional funds locally for it and several other books planned to commemorate 1917. Viatka's Istpart, Novoselov wrote, "awaits your clear and precise response. We wait for your directives without which our work cannot proceed."[60] If he heard from Savel'ev, the response was not what Novoselov and his Istpart preferred. That May, Viatka's commission had no choice but to reduce the volume's size to an unspecified number of pages and to limit its print run to one thousand five hundred copies. Authors whose contributions were now rejected were encouraged to submit their work to the journals *Sputnik bol'shevika* and *Viatsko-Vetluzhskii krai*.[61]

That August, the volume appeared in a print run of three thousand copies but with a mere 188 pages.[62] Its editors had slashed the entry on 1917 by Favorov from 150 typed pages to a mere twenty. And it reduced a contribution on the civil war in Viatka province's rural areas and towns from more than a hundred typed pages to a mere thirteen.[63] Even Novoselov experienced the sting of rejection, if only by his own hand. To be sure, *October and the Civil War* reproduced much of his material on the Bolshevik party in 1917 and 1918. But his short essay on February in Viatka, as mentioned previously, appeared not in the book but in the journal *Sputnik bol'shevika*.[64]

NOTES

1. See sessions of the regional party committee's secretariat in 1926 in GASPI KO, f. P-1, op. 4, d. 34, ll. 107, 116, and f. P-1, op. 4, d. 17, l. 16, and of the regional committee's bureau that year in GASPI KO, f. P-1, op. 4, d. 15, ll. 160–161 ob., f. P-1, op. 5, d. 15, l. 113.

2. See decisions by the school's soviet in October and November 1926 in GASPI KO, f. P-1262, op. 8, d. 3, ll. 3, 10, and f. P-1262, op. 9, d. 3, l. 23. See also the school's annual report for the 1927/28 academic year in GASPI KO, f. P-1262, op. 10, d. 20, l. 5.

3. See decisions by the secretariat in March and the bureau in April in GASPI KO, f. P-1, op. 4, d. 34, l. 108, and d. 15, l. 152.

4. For the decision, see GASPI KO, f. P-1, op. 6, d. 21, ll. 113, 131. Krupskaya's telegram in GASPI KO, f. P-1, op. 6, d. 32, l. 190.

5. For the bureau's decision on December 31, 1926: GASPI KO. f. P-1, op. 4, d. 19, l. 132. On May 7, 1926, the bureau had called on the party's fraction in the regional soviet's executive committee to seek an allotment of 16,500 rubles for the purpose: GASPI KO, f. P-1, op. 4, d. 15, l. 174. In mid-1928, the regional party committee targeted its department for agitation and propaganda for retrenchment. It called on the department to replace paid propagandists with volunteers and limit the amount of literature it distributed free of charge. See sessions of the provincial party committee's bureau, July 23, 1928, in GASPI KO, f. P-1, op. 6, d. 19, ll. 56–57, 62–63, and of the committee's secretariat, August 21, 1928, in GASPI KO, f. P-1, op. 6, d. 37, l. 42.

6. See a session of the committee's secretariat, July 1925, in GASPI KO, f. P-1, op. 3, d. 37, ll. 81, 85; on February 1, 1926, in GASPI KO, f. P-1, op. 4, d. 34, l. 40; and on March 22, 1926, in GASPI KO, f. P-1, op. 4, d. 34, l. 103. See also a discussion by the committee's bureau, April 9, 1926, in GASPI KO, f. P-1, op. 4, d. 15, l. 157 ob. and of May 28, 1926, in GASPI KO, f. P-1, op. 4, d. 15, ll. 181, 184. The regional party committee required other newspapers to undertake similar cost-saving measures. It also complained of unspecified poor ideological direction at *Viatskaia pravda*.

7. GASPI KO, f. P-1, op. 3, d. 33, ll. 5, 36, f. P-1, op. 4, d. 34, l. 25, f. P-1 op. 4, d. 15, l. 114.

8. See the demand for closing Truzhenik by the party committee's bureau, April 2, 1926, in GASPI KO, f. P-1, op. 4, d. 15, l. 152, a decision confirmed by the secretariat on June 7, 1926, in GASPI KO, f. P-1, op. 4, d. 34, l. 151 ob.

9. On Truzhenik's publication activity, see its report in GASPI KO, f. P-6864, op. 2, d. 672, ll. 114-117 ob.

10. On its debts, see GASPI KO, f. P-6864, op. 1, d. 72, ll. 252, 299. On the post office, GASPI KO, f. P-6864, op. 1, d. 286, l. 73.

11. For problems with individual factories and the Pedagogical Institute as well as with regional departments for agriculture, labor unions, and the International Organization for Aid to Revolutionary Fighters, see GASPI KO, f. P-6864, op. 1, d. 286, ll. 86, 98 and op. 2, d. 652, ll. 38, 41, 77, 88.

12. See the report in GASPI KO, f. P-6864, op. 2, d. 511, l. 5.

13. See the report in 1925 on Truzhenik's activity, GASPI KO, f. P-6864, op. 2, d. 672, l. 116 ob.

14. *1905 god v Viatskoi gubernii* (Viatka: Truzhenik, 1925). Istpart also sponsored a more popular work of sixty-six pages: N. Solonitsyn, *Viatskaia guberniia v Revoliutsii 1905 g.* (Viatka: Truzhenik, 1925) in a press run of ten thousand. It focused more on events in Petrograd and in the Black Sea Fleet than in Viatka. Also: N. Solonitsyn, *Kholunitskaia zabastovka 1871 g. (Istoricheskii ocherk)* (Viatka: Truzhenik, 1925) with an introduction from Viatka's Istpart; *Viatskaia politicheskaia ssylka* (Viatka: Truzhenik, 1925); S. Semakov, *Iz revoliutsionnogo*

proshlogo molodezhi Viatskoi gubernii (1905–1908 g.g.) (Viatka: Truzhenik, 1926) with an introduction by A. Novoselev (I-V).

15. *1905 v Viatskoi gubernii (Sbornik statei, vospominanii i materialov)*, ed. S. N. Poroshin (Viatka: Truzhenik, 1925). In its introduction, Novoselov pointed out that many of the essays had been written hastily in order to release the book in 1925.

16. See information presented by the regional party committee's secretariat, August 10, 1925, in GASPI KO, f. P-1, op. 3, d. 33, l. 36. See also a session of the Commission for Celebrating the 1905 Revolution, November 26, 1925, in GASPI KO, f. P-1, op. 4, d. 281, l. 25 and a session of Istpart's collegium on December 7, 1925, in GASPI KO, f. P-45, op. 1, d. 222, l. 36.

17. See their response in December 1925 in GASPI KO, f. P-6864, op. 2, d. 762, ll. 39–40.

18. GASPI KO, f. P-45, op. 1, d. 235, l. 22. Even at one ruble, the book, *1905 in the Viatka Province*, was sold at a loss. The book cost 1.20 rubles to produce. See Novoselov's report to the Commission for Celebrating the 1905 Revolution, November 16, 1925, in GASPI KO, f. P-1, op. 4, d. 281, ll. 12–13.

19. See Novoselov's inquiries in September and November 1926 in GASPI KO, f. P-45, op. 1, d. 212, ll. 88, 104.

20. RGASPI, f. 70, op. 1, d. 46, l. 46. It returned a number of copies of *PR*: no. 3 (15) (1923), published in a press run of eleven thousand; no. 4 (16) (1923), ten thousand copies; no. 5 (17) (1923), ten thousand copies; and no. 6–7 (18–19) (1923), eight thousand copies. Hardback copies cost 1.50 rubles. A subscription in 1926, whether for twelve, six, or three issues, cost one ruble for each. On subscription, see the insert to *PR*, no. 11 (46) (November 1925), between pages 328 and 329.

21. On the number of subscriptions and purchase by libraries, see Elizarova's comments at Istpart's Third Conference, May 1924, *PR*, no. 8–9 (31–32) (August–September 1924), 412.

22. See Istpart's report on its activity from April 1923 to April 1924 in RGASPI, f. 70, op. 1, d. 46, l. 174. Ol'minsky complained at some point in 1927: RGASPI, f. 91, op. 1, d. 129, ll. 4–5, 10.

23. *PR*, no. 8–9 (31–32) (August–September 1924), 429, 436.

24. See Istpart's report on its activity from late 1924 to October 1925 in *PR*, no. 12 (47) (December 1925), 269.

25. Information in E. N. Gorodetsky, *Sovetskaia istoriografiia Velikogo Oktiabria* (Moscow: Izdatel'stvo "Nauka," 1981), 219. For the plan to publish collections of documents under Pokrovsky's general direction, see an undated list in RGASPI, f. 147, op. 1, d. 40, ll. 10–11.

26. "Vsem Istpartotdelam," *PR*, no. 3 (50) (March 1926), 268.

27. See the report on problems with paper production: "Proizvodstvo—na pevyi plan," *Viatskaia pravda*, February 11, 1925, 4.

28. Brian Kassof, "Glavlit, Ideological Censorship, and Russian-Language Books Publishing, 1922–38," *Russian Review* 74, no. 1 (January 2015): 84, 86.

29. For the full membership, see RGASPI, f. 147, op. 1, d. 40, l. 1. In late November 1925, the Presidium of the USSR's Central Executive Committee created a similar commission with Kalinin as the chair. It included some of the same people in the Central Committee's commission: Bubnov, Gusev, Molotov, and Pokrovsky, among others. It also included from Istpart Ol'minsky and Savel'ev. For this state commission, see RGASPI, f. 147, op. 1, d. 40, l. 13.

30. RGASPI, f. 70, op. 4, d. 310, l. 50.

31. RGASPI, f. 70, op. 4, d. 310, l. 49.

32. The undated circular in RGASPI, f. 70, op. 1, d. 33, l. 1a.

33. RGASPI, f. 70, op. 4, d. 310, l. 5.

34. Gusev's remarks were later published in *Pravda*: S. Gusev, "O iubileinoi literature," *Pravda*, February 26, 1927, 5. See also similar comments at the Fourth Conference: RGASPI, f. 70, op. 1, d. 33, l. 47.

35. M. Essen, "O gotovliashchemsia bumazhnom potoke k desiatiletiiu Oktiabria," RGASPI, f. 70, op. 3, d. 960, l. 5. The item is undated. I am using what seems to be the final copy (among many drafts in this folder).

36. Essen, "O gotovliashchemsia bumazhnom potoke," l. 5.

37. RGASPI, f. 70, op. 1, d. 33, l. 30. (Also in GASPI KO, f. P-45, op. 1, d. 236, l. 43.)

38. GASPI KO, f. P-45, op. 1, d. 236, l. 10. Savel'ev's remarks at the conference are in RGASPI, f. 70, op. 1, d. 33, ll. 41–55. In addition, the republics of Ukraine, Belorussia, Transcaucasia, Uzbekistan, and Turkmenistan were allotted 3,440 pages, almost half of that amount assigned to Ukraine: GASPI KO, f. P-45, op. 1, d. 236, l. 10. For Istpart outside of the Russian Republic, see the list of locals, especially those for the Ukraine, in *PR*, no. 11–12 (November–December 1928), 362–363.

39. RGASPI, f. 70, op. 1, d. 33, l. 25 and op. 4, d. 310, l. 6. Quote on l. 6.

40. RGASPI, f. 70, op. 1, d. 33, l. 87.

41. RGASPI, f. 70, op. 4, d. 324, l. 47 ob.

42. RGASPI, f. 70, op. 4, d. 324, l. 84.

43. Information on Pokrovsky provided by Savel'ev at the conference on January 6; RGASPI, f. 70, op. 1, d. 34, l. 49.

44. *PR*, no. 1 (60) (January 1927), 273. In his remarks, Savel'ev did allow that local branches might publish more items than allowed under the general plan if they could find local financing. (GASPI KO, f. P-45, op. 1, d. 236, l. 10.) Delegates may well have convinced their leaders to increase by a specific amount the number of pages allowed for publication by locals with the financial support of the center from 2,000 to 2,960. See a list of material allowed and handwritten revisions in GASPI KO, f. P-45, op. 1, d. 236, ll. 47–48.

45. RGASPI, f. 70, op. 1, d. 5, l. 1.

46. Gusev, "O iubileinoi literature," 5.
47. GASPI KO, f. P-45, op. 1, d. 242, l. 106.
48. RGASPI, f. 147, op. 1, d. 40, ll. 8–9.
49. RGASPI, f. 72, op. 1, d. 16, l. 148. I do not have the specific month. It recommended a reduction in the number of pages.
50. GASPI KO, f. P-1, op. 4, d. 50, l. 38. The cost for each item varied significantly, depending on the number of pages (from 64 to 250 pages) and print run (from one hundred to five thousand copies).
51. See Novoselov's requests for submissions in March, April, and September 1926 in GASPI KO, f. P-45, op. 1, d. 212, ll. 29, 31, 42–42 ob., 87. See also Novoselov's role in encouraging the compilation of memoirs at meetings of Istpart's Group of Assistance in 1926 in GASPI KO, f. P-45, op. 1, d. 146, ll. 1–1 ob., 4–5 ob., 8–8 ob. For items submitted, see handwritten and typed memoirs and documents considered for possible publication in GASPI KO, f. P-45, op. 1, d. 100, 225 ll.
52. See more than 250 typed pages of such material on social and economic conditions in GASPI KO, f. P-45, op. 1, d. 37, 246 ll. On the Red Guards, see items in GASPI KO, f. P-45, op. 1, d. 38, 88 ll. Novoselov was especially active in this latter project.
53. GASPI KO, f. P-45, op. 1, d. 106, l. 22.
54. Novoselov's remarks of February 2, 1927: GASPI KO, f. P-1, op. 5, d. 235, l. 72. For Novoselov's oral comments and written suggestions on January 27, 1927, see GASPI KO, f. P-45, op. 1, d. 106, ll. 1–3, 27–27 ob.
55. GASPI KO, f. P-45, op. 1, d. 106, ll. 1–2. See more than 200 pages of handwritten material for a volume on labor unions in the Viatka province in GASPI KO, f. P-45, op. 1, d. 228, ll. 20–127.
56. GASPI KO, f. P-1, op. 5, d. 235, l. 73.
57. GASPI KO, f. P-45, op. 1, d. 106, ll. 2–3.
58. GASPI KO, f. P-1, op. 5, d. 235, l. 74.
59. Novoselov mentioned initial plans for the total number of pages in the introduction of the volume that eventually was published: *Oktiabr' i Grazhdanskaia voina v Viatskoi gubernii*, IV. I am presuming that the total print run was originally set at a number no less than that for the major publication on 1905.
60. GASPI KO, f. P-45, op.1, d. 242, l. 37.
61. See Novoselov's report, May 7, 1927, in GASPI KO, f. P-1, op. 5, d. 235, l. 49. The suggestion to submit such efforts to the two journals had been made earlier by Novoselov at a session of the commission's publication subcommission, April 15; GASPI KO, f. P-1, op. 5, d. 235, l 42 ob.
62. See a report in GASPI KO, f. P-1, op. 4, d. 50, l. 170. It was published at a total cost of 2,870 rubles. Plans for most other books were abandoned.

Nevertheless, at year's end, Viatka's Istpart still harbored hopes to reprint this particular work with a number of items added. See the report to Moscow from the head of Viatka's Istpart, Liubovikov, on its activity in 1927: RGASPI, f. 70, op. 2, d. 101, l. 7. It would soon be disabused of any such fantasy.

63. Compare Favorov's typescript in GASPI KO, f. P-45, op. 1, d. 103, 149 ll. and his article in *Oktiabr' i Grazhdanskaia voina v Viatskoi gubernii*, 1–19. Compare the lengthy manuscript and typescripts by N. Gorodilova on the civil war in the province in GASPI KO, f. P-45, op. 1, d. 95, 361 ll, d. 141, ll. 1–100, d. 142, 170 ll. with her item in *Oktiabr' i Grazhdanskaia voina v Viatskoi gubernii*, 20–32. Both Favorov and Gorodilova attended the session of authors on February 2, 1927. Along with Tokarev, they objected to such retrenchment: GASPI KO, f. P-45, op. 1, d. 237, l. 22.

64. See typescripts of Novoselov's essays in GASPI KO, f. P-45, op. 1, d. 106, ll. 51–158, and of his "February in Viatka," ll. 159–164.

SIX

Moscow's Embrace of the Political

MORE THAN FINANCIAL CONSTRAINTS AND overly ambitious plans threatened Istpart's future at the center and in the provinces. By the mid-1920s, an escalating politicization of historical scholarship challenged the integrity of Istpart's mission and thus the agency's very existence. As noted in this book's introduction, this process was not a matter of any explicit dictate by party leaders. It occurred, as John Barber has described it, from "the largely spontaneous activity of militants" in the profession itself.[1] A highly partisan version for 1917 emerged as a result. Not everyone in Viatka, however, was in step with the center's grand narrative for the great year.

POKROVSKY AND PIONTKOVSKY MILITANT

Two of Istpart's founders, Pokrovsky and Piontkovsky, contributed to the onrushing politicization of scholarship and the infighting among party historians that accompanied it. In the mid- and late 1920s, Pokrovsky revised his pronouncements regarding historical methodology and the party's past to secure, as Enteen has written, his considerable administrative authority as chair of the Presidium of Communist Academy, rector of the Institute of Red Professors, head of the Society of Marxist Historians, and leader of the History Institute of the Communist Academy.[2] Litvin concurred: "Having become a bureaucrat, Pokrovsky was forced to aggressively attack his rivals in the realm of scholarship and in the administrative control of it."[3]

An intolerant Pokrovsky emerged. In 1927, he wrote that the Communist Academy, a collection of research institutes, should not be a "parliament of opinions." To permit an open exchange of views was not the business of a

"Bolshevik scholarly center."[4] In so doing, Pokrovsky became, as his own supporters put it, a warrior not subject to "academic decorum."[5]

Piontkovsky followed Pokrovsky's example. "Proletarian Marxist scholarship was first of all a revolutionary science," he declared in 1927 in the literary journal *Pechat' i revoliutsiia*. As such, it would contribute to the inevitable destruction of an aristocratic and bourgeois society and the conquest of power by the proletariat: "In the hands of the proletariat, history becomes a militant weapon."[6] That year, Piontkovsky confided in his diary: "Uniformity of thought and uniformity of action are necessary for waging a political struggle."[7]

Pokrovsky and Piontkovsky were not alone. In June 1925, politicization of the historical profession had taken on an organized, if not yet wholly intemperate, form with the formation of the Society of Marxist Historians. The new organization's constitution called for a struggle against "idealism disguised as Marxist."[8] As of January 1927, the society numbered seventy-two full and thirty-eight corresponding members. At the beginning of 1929, it had 169 and 176 respectively.[9]

In 1926, young historians associated with that society's Methodology Section sought to use their discipline for the politicization of the school curriculum. Earlier in the decade, the Russian Republic's Commissariat of Enlightenment had replaced traditional subjects, including history, with the so-called complex method—a study of "complex themes" under the rubrics of nature, labor, and society. As an official at Narkompros, Pokrovsky had reluctantly approved the new scheme. Now a new cohort of party historians, many of them his past or present students, demanded the return of history as an independent subject precisely because of its political utility. It could be employed, they said, to expose the treachery and deviations of all opponents of the Bolshevik regime, past and present.[10]

POLITICS TRUMPS SCHOLARSHIP: ISTPART'S FOURTH CONFERENCE

In early January 1927, Moscow hosted Istpart's Fourth Conference. As previously mentioned, delegates focused on the large number of publications scheduled for the tenth anniversary of the October Revolution. In so doing, they also discussed the very issue confronting Istpart from the outset—the proper relationship between scholarly and political criteria. Heretofore, Istpart had hoped to find a mutually supportive balance. At this conference, the agency's leaders and delegates displayed a loss of faith in the possibility of a symbiosis. Some conferees still spoke fetchingly of the scholarly canon, but they now thought of it in a figurative sense, as something distinct from the imperative to produce work of immediate political utility. Politics trumped scholarship, although the result was, its advocates insisted, all the more vociferously, "scholarly" or "academic," or "scientific."[11]

In his opening address Gusev demanded a thoroughgoing politicization of Istpart's mission.[12] After noting the possibility of war with the USSR's capitalist neighbors and the dangers posed by intraparty opposition, Gusev thundered, "We are Bolsheviks not academics. . . . We must cast aside the academicism which takes place in much of the work of Istpart's center and of its locals." Monographs had "suffered from academicism" by distancing party history from current tasks. Corrective efforts were underway, Gusev announced, "to change the physiognomy of the journal *Proletarskaia revoliutsiia*" in order to end its isolation from life.[13]

Delegates agreed. Finkel'shtein declared that the conference "must establish a definite border between our Istpart's past and future."[14] In the past, rather than helping the party in its struggle against hostile groups Istpart's personnel had "sat around and had gotten lost in paper."[15] The head of Saratov's Istpart, Zakhar Semenovich Petrov, a party member since 1924, expressed similar sentiments: "We believe it necessary to avoid academicism" and thereby achieve, as he would have it, "scholarship."[16] Only a single modest voice dissented. Mikhail Abramovich Rubach, head of the USSR's Central Archive, thought his colleagues inappropriately juxtaposed politically useful history, on one hand, with scholarly work, on the other. "Such a sharp and unadorned formulation of the question is incorrect." He called for both types of history.[17]

Savel'ev (fig. 6.1), Gusev's deputy at Istpart and the editor of *Proletarskaia revoliutsiia*, followed with a major address on Istpart's preparations for celebrating October's tenth anniversary. Perhaps because of his post at the journal, he briefly allowed for something of a coexistence between scholarly research and political propaganda. While Istpart should sponsor highly politicized and agitational literature, it should also promote work that went beyond "apologies for Soviet institutions and organs."[18] Then Savel'ev turned more comfortably strident. Istpart's political mission was of utmost importance. All publications should take "a class and party approach toward evaluation of events." Many works on the period from 1917 to 1918 had failed to do so. They contained "an excessive amount of factual material" about bourgeois parties and other political groups but "with extraordinarily scant information about our party."[19]

On the evening of January 5, Isidor Vladimirovich Volkovicher addressed those assembled on the proper use of various sources for a history of the October Revolution.[20] He had the credentials to speak authoritatively about the subject.

Figure 6.1. M. A. Savel'ev in the Museum of the Revolution, 1928. Courtesy of the Russian State Documentary Film and Photo Archive.

Four years earlier, in 1923, he had compiled and edited an Istpart publication on the history of the Bolshevik party with a large section on 1917. The work conformed at the time with the agency's effort to combine scholarly standards and politicized history. The portion of the volume on 1917 contained multiple illustrations and portraits of revolutionary heroes as well as excerpts from the publications of both Lenin and Trotsky.[21] Its most interesting item, however, was the memoir by V. Iakovlev, a Bolshevik official in the Moscow region in 1917. Iakovlev presented the advance of Bolshevik influence during the second half of the year as a somewhat spontaneous affair. The "growth of revolutionary sentiment," he wrote, led to a "process of the general bolshevization of the masses." In October, Iakovlev acknowledged, a majority of Bolsheviks in the party's Moscow municipal and provincial committees questioned the wisdom of an armed uprising.[22] That same year, Volkovicher reviewed for *Proletarskaia revoliutsiia* a book by Lelevich, *October at Military Headquarters*, in which he praised the author for "a correct methodological approach" that had relied on all manner of documents, memoirs, and newspapers that represented differing points of view.[23] Yet two years later, Volkovicher, now more the politician, expressed a different opinion about his craft. In 1925, as discussed previously, he harshly reviewed Novoselov's draft for a book on Viatka in 1905 because of its insufficient attention to the activity of Bolsheviks. The following year, in comments on the first issue of the journal *Istorik-Marksist*, published by the Society of Marxist Historians, he wanted far more criticism of idealism in history "concealed under various 'Marxist' guises."[24] Now at the conference, Volkovicher represented the duality in his own (and Istpart's) professional life as he played, simultaneously, the roles of the scholar and the politician.

In his address, Volkovicher stressed the importance of the traditional canons of scholarship. Historical research was for professionals who possessed the technical skills necessary to analyze a source's origin and content. Writing history was not a "spontaneous process" in which its practitioners might use information in any way they saw fit. Otherwise, would-be scholars might drown themselves and their readers in extraneous detail. Many of Istpart's publications, Volkovicher noted, demonstrated the point well. Then Volkovicher turned relentlessly political. He criticized much of the literature published in the provinces on the 1905 revolution for a failure to adhere to the grand narrative. Istpart's locals had neglected to show how party organizations responded to developments in St. Petersburg throughout the year and to the armed revolt in Moscow in December. Turning his attention to 1917, Volkovicher insisted that present and future work present local events in the context of what happened at the center. Moreover, it should focus squarely on the activity of the Bolshevik party and cite only Bolshevik sources.[25]

Pavel Osipovich Gorin, recent graduate in history from the Institute of Red Professors and a representative at the conference from the Society of Marxist Historians, thought Volkovicher was too cautious. He wanted an explicitly politicized methodology, one without concessions to any traditional notions of historical research. Gorin demanded adherence to what he called a "Marxist-scientific method" that would lead, whatever the author's intent, to an objective truth. In effect, the method determined the historian's consciousness. The result would be "a history of the party that is scientific," Gorin asserted, because its authors "have the method, which not one bourgeois historian possesses."[26]

Draft theses in response to Volkovicher's address were in keeping with Gorin's shrill posture. "Only a Marxist history, a Leninist history, can be a scholarly history."[27] In the end, however, Volkovicher's own ambivalence and objections from a few delegates to such strong language moved the conference's organizers to withdraw the draft. Final resolutions called on Istpart's central office to craft a statement on historical methodology within the foreseeable future.[28]

The conference's overall concluding resolutions mimicked Gusev's and Savel'ev's harsh rhetoric. Istpart must "in the future coordinate all of its research work with the party's current political struggle and use our revolutionary past for the revolutionary present."[29] An article that followed in *Proletarskaia revoliutsiia* praised delegates for ending Istpart's "academic isolation." They had done so by making their agency's work relevant to the party's struggle against petty bourgeois and bourgeois influence and all forms of deviation.[30]

FIXED IMAGES

From its inception, Istpart planned to display the party's history and the story of 1917 in a national network of museums. In late 1926, Sergei Ivanovich Mitskevich, head of Moscow's Museum of the Revolution and a member of Istpart's collegium, and his assistant Nadezhda Vasil'evna Romanovskaia drafted resolutions on regional museums of revolution for Istpart's Fourth Conference. They both emphasized that most exhibits give priority to local history. At first, Romanovskaia seemed to waver. She wanted a display of material in the context of national events, even if the latter were, she admitted, "chosen schematically." But Romanovskaia hastened to insist that "the regional principle (*kraevedcheskii printsip*) determine the arrangement" of exhibits.[31] The Fourth Conference that followed, however, was not so solicitous of a locality's preferences. Resolutions required that museums reinforce the emerging grand narrative for party history generally and 1917 in particular by assembling their exhibits in such a way as to demonstrate the party's domination of events, real and alleged, at the center and elsewhere. Accordingly, displays were to "link local history with the all-Russian and all-union history of the revolutionary movement and party."[32] Shortly thereafter, Moscow demanded that in celebrating the tenth anniversary of the October Revolution local museums should rely heavily on materials of national and international significance. They could thereby "provide a fuller and more correct portrayal of events."[33]

That July, Istpart's center repeated the point in instructions for any and all exhibits. It insisted that Moscow's Central Museum show the "fundamental

Figure 6.2. Istpart Exhibit, 1928. Courtesy of the Russian State Documentary Film and Photo Archive.

direction of the revolutionary process" in the country without any "detailed presentation of local particularities." Regional museums were to do much the same thing. Moscow disallowed any display there of material "isolated from the national and international movement." Events at the center, it insisted, were "necessary explanatory moments" for an understanding of local history.[34]

No less than museums, archives were now subject to thoroughgoing politicization. Istpart's Third Conference in May 1924 had instructed the agency's branches to ensure the placement of such important (and sensitive) material as the party's documents in an archive's special "political section" under the direct control, as mentioned previously, of the head of Istpart's local. The effort might antagonize the older generation of archivists but, as one delegate put it, "it is necessary to be freed from the dictatorship of specialists."[35]

Three years later, within days after the closing of Istpart's Fourth Conference, Pokrovsky had recovered well enough to address the Second Conference of Archivists of the Russian Republic, held from January 11–15, 1927. Archives, he declared, were an "arsenal from which weapons are drawn."[36] Within weeks, on February 7, the Central Committee issued a secret directive, signed by Molotov as the committee's secretary and Savel'ev as Istpart's deputy director, that was sent to all party organs and local Istparts. The party's archives henceforth would be accessible only to party members who had been thoroughly vetted.[37] The special depository for sensitive party documents in Viatka, and presumably elsewhere, was relabeled as the "secret archive."[38] There followed throughout the country what the historian Mikhail Zelenov has called a "bacchanalia of purges" to destroy politically harmful documents.[39] The campaign was justified, at least publicly, as an effort to overcome a shortage of raw material at the country's paper mills by the surrender of so-called junk for purposes of recycling. By October 1929, archives had relinquished twenty-five thousand tons of documents.[40]

1917 MADE SIMPLE

The occasion of the tenth anniversary of the October Revolution prompted greater pressure for a useful rendering of 1917 to accompany a grand celebration of the event, extending from Moscow to the far ends of the USSR. Moscow prepared a menu of delights: an amnesty of convicts (including some political prisoners); a special stipend for students; awards for participants in the revolution and civil war; mass demonstrations and spectacles; release of films, most notably Sergei Eisenstein's *October*; proposals for new housing; and the promise of a seven-hour workday.[41]

In its own proposals to duly mark the great year, Istpart's leadership demanded an overarching narrative. The request had begun modestly enough when, three years earlier in November 1924, *Proletarskaia revoliutsiia* featured an article by the Old Bolshevik and journalist Ivan Petrovich Flerovsky, "We Must Be Ready for the Tenth Anniversary of the October Revolution." He called on Istpart's central office to issue its locals appropriate instructions on how to collect and publish materials that would demonstrate implementation throughout the country of the party's directives in 1917.[42]

A year later, in December 1925, Istpart convened a conference to plan for a proper celebration of 1917 in print. Kanatchikov chaired the session attended by, among others, Flerovsky, Pokrovsky, Volkovicher, Shteinman, and Drabkina.[43] It required of Istpart's branches a presentation of events in their regions structured around developments in Petrograd and Moscow. They would show how Bolsheviks rushed forward to stage their own "local October."[44] Framers of the plan did allow, if reluctantly, for the importance of spontaneity. "If in your locality," they suggested, "the October revolt was the result of the spontaneous movement of the masses, then study this movement."[45]

As previously discussed, in 1926 and 1927, the party's Press Department and Istpart slashed the volume of printed work on 1917, much to the consternation of Istpart's branches. Moscow repeatedly insisted that it did so to preclude the appearance of items of poor quality and of little or no public interest, material destined to rot in stores and warehouses before the inevitable pulping. But the Press Department and Istpart's leadership intended that fewer publications would allow for rigorous vetting to ensure their adherence to a grand narrative. At Istpart's Fourth Conference, Gusev, when demanding cutbacks, disingenuously rushed to say that his insistence on fewer publications was a matter of economizing rather than a ban on ideologically unacceptable work.[46] That November, Savel'ev more honestly assessed Istpart's purpose in his draft of a report to the party's Central Committee. He admitted that his agency sought to prevent "the release of trashy and ideologically irresolute publications."[47]

In 1927 and 1928, Istpart's central office plunged ahead to erase the distinction between the historical past and the political present. *Proletarskaia revoliutsiia* published articles denouncing Stalin's political rivals Trotsky, Kamenev, and Zinoviev.[48] One jeremiad called for a suspension of disbelief by equating the positions in 1917 of Kamenev and Trotsky. Kamenev's noted opposition to the staging of the October revolt made him "a more consistent Trotskyist than Trotsky himself."[49] The October 1927 issue of *Proletarskaia revoliutsiia* featured Iaroslavsky's polemical attack on Kamenev, Zinoviev, and Trotsky for their alleged failure to understand Lenin's insistence on an armed revolt in October. In contrast, Stalin fully supported Lenin.[50] In the same issue, Piontkovsky reported that Stalin, among others, played a critical role in the purportedly detailed planning and implementation of the armed revolt.[51]

Trotsky understood well his victimization and his inability to do much about it. In October 1927, he responded to a questionnaire sent by Istpart to him and 1,500 other participants in the October Revolution. He began, appropriately enough, with his own doubts about the efficacy of any response. Why, he wondered, had Istpart asked him to write about his activity in 1917, "when the entire official apparatus, including yours, works to conceal, destroy, and distort all traces of my involvement."[52] Nevertheless, Trotsky proceeded to counter, in detail, "a conscious and evil distortion of the past."[53] As he had earlier in his "Lessons of October," Trotsky emphasized his revolutionary credentials from 1917. While in "Lessons," he had avoided mention of Stalin, he now wrote extensively of Stalin's conditional support in early 1917 of the Provisional Government and of Russia's participation in the war. Trotsky then departed from the subject at hand to discuss Lenin's criticism of Stalin during the last years of Lenin's life.

Even as Istpart went through the motions of gathering information from Trotsky and other participants in the events of 1917, its historians denounced memoirs for their "wretched philosophy of history" and distortion of facts.[54] Reviewers dismissed Shliapnikov's account precisely because of its heavy reliance on his own recollections rather than on a "materialist philosophy of history."[55] He had failed to portray the Bolshevik party as the major dynamic throughout the year of revolution. His response further antagonized his critics. They would have him, he said in May 1927, "falsify the authentic history and events of which I was a participant and eyewitness."[56] Pokrovsky responded with an apology for his own prior "shameful" encouragement of Shliapnikov's writing.[57] It did not seem to bother him that at that moment his students published articles (as discussed in chap. 3) that relied heavily on Shliapnikov's work in a volume edited by none other than Pokrovsky. And curiously, on March 14, 1928, Istpart's collegium calmly discussed Shliapnikov's fourth volume of *1917*, yet to be published. It agreed to tell the State Publishing House that it did not object to its future release but without Istpart's imprimatur.[58]

On May 24, 1927, Istpart convened a meeting in Moscow of representatives from its auxiliaries, the Groups of Assistance. Over three days, delegates discussed the relative worth of reminiscences that their units had encouraged and transcribed. Fishkin from Ekaterinoslav insisted that the material was useful, whatever the embarrassing problems it dredged up from the past: "Earlier sins were nothing to be ashamed of or to conceal."[59] But his was a minority view. Reminiscences of former Mensheviks, SRs, and Bundists (members of the Bund, a Jewish socialist political party) were regarded as too personal to be of value, and, worse, their narrators justified their past activity, which was now at odds with the master narrative for 1917.[60] As one detractor put it, their tales contained "considerable individualism and lyrical expressions."[61]

These critics got their way. The conference's resolutions put it somewhat antiseptically: auxiliaries failed to establish the "necessary organizational and ideological liaison" with local Istparts.[62] Days later under Savel'ev's signature, Istpart informed locals of the meeting's conclusions. For good measure, he added that in their discussion of the past, some comrades in Groups of Assistance, implicitly, nonparty people for the most part, "had willy-nilly concealed or justified their own mistakes and those of whole groups." It was time to reject what Savel'ev called such "unhealthy deviations."[63] Less than a year later, on January 28, 1928, Istpart's collegium castigated auxiliaries for an "unscholarly and non-objective" evaluation of events.[64] Some might be allowed to continue, the collegium affirmed, but in a radically different, implicitly politically conformist form. Thereafter, the number of auxiliaries declined, and in May 1928, they ceased to exist altogether.

Piontkovsky and other historians hastened to revise their own renditions of the past. Spontaneity no longer dominated their narrative of 1917. Rather, a purportedly strong and disciplined Bolshevik party under Lenin's firm leadership shaped both people and events to its liking.[65] In so doing, the party overwhelmed a wealthy and well-organized bourgeoisie bent on the creation of a right-wing military dictatorship. It simultaneously shattered efforts by SRs and Mensheviks to betray socialism and the people, the petty bourgeoisie, they allegedly represented.[66] Such a narrative elegantly reinforced the contemporary polemic about the party's and the country's need for iron discipline and for Stalin's firm leadership when confronted with the twin threats of domestic counterrevolution and foreign intervention.

In January 1928, first Essen then Savel'ev scolded Istpart's locals for their politically poor work. The former declared that they had published "some kind of castrated history" by failing to focus on past deviations within the party's ranks.[67] Savel'ev followed with a letter to all branches. With few exceptions, their publications for the tenth anniversary of the October Revolution inappropriately avoided a thorough condemnation of deviations within the party while underestimating the party's role in 1917.[68]

A PROLETARIAN REVOLUTION

Historians now learned and repeated that the October revolt had been, plain and simple, a proletarian revolution. Previous acknowledgement of the significance of waves of peasant spontaneity or of the dual character of the great event began to give way to a preoccupation with the role of the party and proletariat.

Stalin contributed to the rewrite in late 1926 and on several occasions in 1927, albeit without the fanfare that accompanied his letter in 1931 to *Proletarskaia revoliutsiia*. While continuing to insist on the importance of the Soviet state's contemporary alliance (*smychka*) with the peasantry, Stalin hastened to present events in October exclusively as a proletarian revolution carried out under the leadership of the Bolshevik party. In so doing, Stalin doubtlessly hoped to legitimize the dictatorship of the proletariat and underscore the possibility of the creation by it of socialism in one country. He made the point in an address on December 13, 1926, to the Seventh Expanded Plenary Session of the Comintern's Executive Committee and then in correspondence published in *Bol'shevik*, the Central Committee's biweekly publication, in spring 1927. The October revolution's main task was not the completion of a bourgeois revolution that had begun the previous February but rather the establishment of a dictatorship of the proletariat and poorest peasantry.[69] Any step to finish the bourgeois revolution, such as granting land to the peasantry, was a "derivative phenomenon" (*proizvodnoe iavlenie*).[70]

On June 23, 1927, Stalin took up the subject in a letter to Pokrovsky. As mentioned previously, in 1925, Pokrovsky had written that the October Revolution combined two revolutions, the first "the last act of the bourgeois revolution" and the second "the first act of the proletarian revolution."[71] Stalin informed Pokrovsky that the historian had grievously erred. Among Lenin's several renditions of 1917, Stalin deftly selected an article published in *Pravda* on the occasion of October's fourth anniversary. Citing Lenin, Stalin insisted that a full-fledged proletarian revolution had occurred, one that completed the bourgeois revolution only "in passing" (*mimokhodom*), its completion a "by-product" (*pobochnyi produkt*) of the establishment of Bolshevik rule.[72]

Stalin's letter remained private, published for the first time in the ninth volume of his *Works* in 1948. Nevertheless, Pokrovsky quickly modified his interpretation of October to suit Stalin's tastes. He did so that fall in remarks at courses for teachers of social studies in higher educational institutions. Implicitly following Stalin's directions, Pokrovsky duly highlighted Lenin's 1921 description of October as his, Pokrovsky's, own. A proletarian revolution had resolved the issues of the bourgeois-democratic revolution only "in passing, as a by-product" of the proletarian, socialist revolution.[73]

NOT SO SIMPLE IN VIATKA

The emerging master narrative demanded a tale of events appropriate for a history of 1917 at the center and in all other parts of the country. Local or regional history might provide a few discrete details but no more than that when describing their own "October revolution." "It was still 'October in the provinces,'" as Yanni Kotsonis has put it, "even if the calendar read December, January, or February."[74] In a well-researched article, Hickey found a compliant local Istpart that helped Smolensk get its "October."[75]

Yet, as Corney has noted, many regions "failed to produce the story leaders were expecting." Local publications emphasized Bolshevik party's numerical weakness, an absence of an independent Bolshevik organization, and the considerable influence of Mensheviks and SRs well into 1918. By the mid-1920s, "the coherent integrated story of revolution and party had not materialized."[76]

Viatka's Istpart was one of the agencies that refused to cooperate. It had not seemed so stubborn in early 1927. Following Istpart's Fourth Conference in January, Viatka's local declared its readiness to politicize and crudely, if need be, its work. It declared that "sometimes Istpart's workers had become too absorbed in research." Now every Istpart worker must "apply the past to the revolutionary tasks of the present day."[77] Days later, on February 6, Novoselov set forth similar sentiments in an article in *Viatskaia pravda*, subtitled "We Will Overcome the Academic Deviation in Our Work." He promised to end Istpart's "disengagement from the party's current political work" and liquidate its "abnormal and harmful 'academic deviation.'"[78] Henceforth, Viatka's Istpart would concentrate on the party's past struggle with all forms of opposition and political deviation. To that end, it would work more closely with the party's department of agitation and propaganda. Moreover, Viatka's local joined the national effort to purge its archive of so-called junk. In Viatka alone in 1927 and 1928, more than twenty-four people, untrained and working in cold, damp, and poorly lit quarters, sent over 101 tons of material to paper mills.[79]

Despite the shrill rhetoric and ongoing purge of the archive, Novoselov and his Istpart resisted efforts to grossly falsify and exaggerate the party's role in Viatka in 1917. In July 1927, Novoselov told the center just how different things had been in Viatka as opposed to Petrograd and other major urban areas in 1917. The Red Army's Military-Political Academy in Moscow had asked Viatka's Istpart for archival materials about the work in 1917 of the Bolshevik party's military organization, a unit for spreading the party's message among troops. Novoselov responded that Viatka had no such material because the party there had formed no such unit.[80]

One month later, his Istpart released its major publication, *October and the Civil War in the Viatka Province*. At first glance, Moscow had reason to be pleased with the result. The volume did not include the essay by Tokarev and Tsaregorodtsev. Limited space played a role in its absence, but so did, no doubt, its controversial depiction of Viatka in 1917 with the Bolshevik party largely absent. Tsaregorodtsev understood it well. In June 1927, he had written in hand on the title page of one of the typescripts prepared for publication: "My work is unsatisfactory. The party's role is not evident or its presence felt (as if it didn't exist)."[81] Moreover, Viatka used Moscow's template by including "October" in the its title. Authors acknowledged the "lateness" of October in Viatka but only to underscore the inevitable, albeit tardy, nature of the Bolsheviks' seizure of power there.

And yet the volume failed the center's political test. In his introduction, Novoselov advised his readers that they should read the book while keeping in mind the province's "own conditions and peculiarities." Workers and the village poor took up revolutionary struggle "sometimes late and sometimes in their own way."[82] In his contribution that followed (as discussed previously in chap. 4), Novoselov underscored the Bolshevik party's numerical weakness and limited influence throughout 1917. In spring 1917, Viatka's Bolsheviks had cooperated extensively with Mensheviks. Later that year, the party seized power only in the city of Viatka and that thanks largely to armed detachments sent to the city by the party's leadership in Petrograd.[83]

Other contributors to the volume also promoted Viatka's own version of 1917. In his article, "October in Viatka," Favorov largely ignored the Bolsheviks. Instead, he focused on the bourgeoisie and on the Menshevik and SR parties, who, he admitted, dominated events. Favorov turned his attention to Bolshevik activity only after mid-November.[84] In his article, Solonitsyn acknowledged the party's tenuous hold on power well into 1918. Highlighting the importance of Trotsky's trip to Viatka early that year, Solonitsyn quoted at length from the now disgraced leader's fiery appeal to resist any further incursion of Kolchak's army into the province.[85]

In late 1927 and early 1928, reviews of *October and the Civil War in the Viatka Province* in *Proletarskaia revoliutsiia* limited their assessment of the book to a largely uncritical summary of its content.[86] Nevertheless, a piece published locally underscored its heresy. It came from none other than the pen of Tokarev in the September 1927 issue of *Viatsko-Vetluzhskii krai*. Perhaps he was angry that his article, jointly written with Tsaregorodtsev, had not been accepted for the work under review, a volume considerably smaller in size than originally planned. At any rate, he took up the sword for the new orthodoxy. He complained that contributors had exaggerated the significance of Mensheviks and SRs, underestimated Bolshevik influence among workers and soldiers, and failed to portray the proletariat as the class hegemon of the revolution.[87] Although Tokarev believed Novoselov's contribution to be useful, he thought that its many details—implicitly, about events beyond Bolshevik control—distracted from the "orderly progression of the party's history."[88]

Tokarev and like-minded colleagues had more than just the book to worry about. The preceding year and throughout much of 1927, Viatka's own distinct story was pursued by Novoselov, prior to his departure for the North Caucasus, and then by Liubovikov, Novoselov's replacement at Istpart, in preparations for the opening of Viatka's branch of the Museum of the Revolution. As we have seen, Istpart's Fourth Conference and Istpart's central office demanded that all such institutions present local material in the context of a grand narrative. In Viatka, Liubovikov and Novoselov failed to get the message. They wanted an emphasis on Viatka's history "with an insertion of items of national significance only for clarifying local phenomena."[89] Shortly after its grand opening on October 30, 1927, attended by 270 guests, Liubovikov, now also the museum's director, insisted that it "adhere strictly to maintaining a regional character (*kraevedcheskii kharakter*)."[90]

The museum arranged its content to conform to the national template with exhibits on the revolutionary movement of the nineteenth century, the 1905 revolution, the imperialist war, the October Revolution, and the civil war.[91] Yet whatever this prejudicial structure for a presentation of the past in broad strokes, visitors in 1927 and 1928 preferred displays with a discrete local flair. They wrote in the museum's guest book of their admiration for exhibits prepared by Viatka's local of the International Organization for Aid to Revolutionary Fighters (MOPR in abbreviated Russian).[92] They were likely drawn to an emotional appeal to defend and spread the communist faith abroad. But visitors also made it clear that they welcomed the effort precisely because it came from their own local MOPR branch, one of the first, if not the first of its kind, in Soviet Russia and already famous as one of the most active.[93] They also appreciated exhibits on the prerevolutionary past that highlighted the presence in exile in their own region of such future Bolshevik luminaries as Dzerzhinsky and Vorovsky. Some guests thought the museum should add more local material. They wanted a display of items on the area's radical youth in the past and on the region's industry in the present.[94] Visitors had nothing to say about the presentation of the 1917 period. Neither the museum's staff nor its guests found the year's "little history" particularly noteworthy.

The exhibits have not survived the intervening years. However, multiple photographs from the museum's early history have, and they amply reinforce those first visitors' impressions. They make evident that displays captured for all to see and feel the pathos of revolutionaries in a Viatka prison, the intensity of the civil war in the region, and the ardor of the local MOPR.[95] In striking contrast, the exhibit under the banner "The Revolution in Viatka" (*Perevorot v Viatke*) lacked objects, portraits, or photographs from 1917 that might elicit an emotional response. It included a snapshot of the "counterrevolutionary" Supreme Soviet that might have attracted attention for all the wrong reasons, from the official point of view.[96]

Three years after the museum's founding, much remained the same. In 1930, an inspector, S. Sitnikova, from the museum for the Nizhnii Novgorod province (an administrative unit recently expanded to include Viatka) was not altogether pleased with her subject. In faint and twisted praise, she found "the absence of a significant disproportion between material of all-Russian and local significance."[97] Unadorned criticism followed in comments about the presentation of the October Revolution. "October's banners," Sitnikova declared, "should occupy a central place in the section on October rather than decorate the staircase" leading to the museum on the second floor.[98] No doubt such banners, even if authentic, had been set aside by the staff as being of foreign provenance, coming from other locales besides Viatka. The city had not, as Novoselov had pointed out, experienced its own "October."

A few years later, however, the museum presented a different tale. By 1933, its staff had altered "The Revolution in Viatka" display to present, they hoped, a more inspiring story, one attuned to a larger narrative (fig. 6.3). At the exhibit's apex, the photograph of the Supreme Soviet gave way to portraits of Soviet leaders of national rather than local import: Ia. M. Sverdlov, V. Volodarsky, V. V. Vorovsky, and L. B. Krasin (although Vorovsky had spent time in exile in the province). A second row featured photographs of Viatka's own from 1917. They were (from left to right) Antselovich, M. Popov, and—old quarrels set aside with Moscow's flattened version of events, now triumphant—Kapustin and Kuchkin. A painting, *The Year 1917*, by Viatka's artist M. A. Demidov separated the two rows. It featured an unknown orator striking a Lenin-like pose while addressing his audience at Viatka's Municipal Theater.[99] Nevertheless, the effort hardly encouraged visitors to stop, look, and ponder the year. The exhibit still lacked fiery banners, belligerent placards, and frightening weapons. They were all appropriately absent from a "history that wasn't."

Earlier, in 1927, Viatka's Istpart and its museum had not been alone in their allegiance to a region's distinct past. That year, the grand narrative for 1917 remained elusive in essays, monographs, memoirs, and collections of documents published by other locals. Although Viatka's history of 1917 avoided Moscow's harshest criticism, the published work by other branches did not. *Proletarskaia revoliutsiia* repeatedly castigated locals in Vladimir, Kiev, Orlov, Ekaterinburg, Samara, Stavropol, Ul'ianovsk and Briansk, among others, for

Figure 6.3. Exhibit, "The Revolution in Viatka," 1933. Courtesy of Kirov's Regional Museum of Local History.

a litany of predictable errors: exaggeration of the influence of Mensheviks and SRs, depredation of the importance of class struggle, and disparagement of the activity and significance of the Bolsheviks and their party in 1917.[100] Shteinman dismissed a chronicle of the revolutionary movement in 1917 in Kiev because its "information on the party drowns in a mass of unnecessary minutiae."[101] "It is self-evident," she concluded "that the party organization's life must be accorded eminent pride of place."[102] For similar reasons, Shteinman condemned a chronicle of events in Saratov. In that work, "the party and the workers movement literally drown in a sea of most detailed reportage" about other organizations and political parties.[103]

Proletarskaia revoliutsiia tolerated an obvious departure from the grand narrative primarily in areas once part of the Russian Empire in 1917 but now beyond the USSR's reach. Thus it reported that preparation of "October" in Latvia proceeded "in its own way" (*svoeobraziem*), hindered by an evacuation of industry and the disintegration of the economy.[104] In Finland, "October occurred neither in the literal nor figurative sense." Throughout 1917, the Finnish proletariat demanded not power but only economic concessions.[105]

A region's own version of its history, however, was only a sideshow at best. Istpart at the center had "made 1917 simple."

NOTES

1. Barber, *Soviet Historians*, 11.
2. Enteen, *Soviet Scholar-Bureaucrat*.
3. Aleksei Litvin, *Bez prava na mysl': Istoriki v epokhu Bol'shego Terrora. Ocherki sudeb* (Kazan: Tatarskoe knizhnoe izdatel'stvo, 1994), 12.
4. M. Pokrovsky, "O deiatel'nosti Kommunisticheskoi akademii," *Vestnik Kommunisticheskoi akademii* 22 (1927), 18.
5. Ts. (Grigorii Samoilovich) Fridliand, "Voinstvuiushchii istorik-marksist," *Pod znamenem marksizma*, no. 9–10 (September–October 1928), 14.
6. S. Piontkovsky, "Oktiabr' i russkaia istoricheskaia nauka," *Pechat' i revoliutsiia*," no. 2 (March 1927), 114.
7. *Dnevnik istorika S. A. Piontkovskogo (1927–1934)* (Kazan: Kazanskii gosudarstvennyi universitet, 2009), 82.
8. "Ustav obshchestva istorikov-marksistov," *IM*, no. 1 (1926), 320; M. Pokrovsky, "Zadachi Obshchestva istorikov-marksistov," *IM*, no. 1 (1926), 3; I. Volkovicher, "Istorik-Marksist," *PR*, no. 7 (54) (July 1926), 260–262.
9. M. N. Naidenov, "O leninskom etape v istoricheskoi nauke," *Voprosy istorii*, no. 2 (February 1966), 34. The vast majority of the society's members were party members and based in Moscow.

10. See Larry E. Holmes, "Two Ideologies: Controversy over Social Studies and History in the Soviet Schools, 1921 to 1928," *Slavic and European Education Review*, no. 1–2 (1985), 1–28. This effort peaked at sessions of the Methodology Section at the First Conference of Marxist Historians, December 28, 1928, to January 4, 1929. See *Trudy Pervoi Vsesoiuznoi konferentsii istorikov-marksistov*, vol. 2 (Moscow: Izdatel'stvo Kommunisticheskoi akademii, 1930), 453–608; "Vsesoiuznaia konferentsiia istorikov-marksistov," *IM*, no. 12 (1929), 300–333.

11. References below to this conference are from a verbatim report and other materials sent to local Istparts. The item sent to the Viatka organization is in GASPI KO, f. P-45, op. 1, d. 236, ll. 1–67. Gusev's major address is also at RGASPI, f. 70, op. 1, d. 33, ll. 5–33 and Savel'ev's, ll. 41–55.

12. Perhaps Gusev's address, at least as an opening speech, took delegates by surprise. See comments to that effect by the delegate Rubach: GASPI KO, f. P-45, op. 1, d. 236, l. 31. Pokrovsky was scheduled to give the opening address. He was ill, however, and organizers understood at the last moment, a day before the conference's opening on January 4, that he could not attend. See Savel'ev's remarks at the conference's morning session, January 6, in RGASPI, f. 70, op. 1, d. 34, l. 49.

13. GASPI KO, f. P-45, op. 1, d. 236, ll. 22, 26.

14. GASPI KO, f. P-45, op. 1, d. 236, l. 29. Finkel'shtein had been a Zionist from 1900 to 1914 and a party member since 1917. See information on her in RGASPI, f. 70, op. 4, d. 310, l. 24.

15. GASPI KO, f. P-45, op. 1, d. 236, l. 29.

16. GASPI KO, f. P-45, op. 1, d. 236, l. 33. On Petrov, see RGASPI, f. 70, op. 4, d. 310, l. 25.

17. Rubach did so in the discussion following Gusev's presentation: RGASPI, f. 70, op. 1, d. 33, l. 20. See also the conference's report in GASPI KO, f. P-45, op. 1, d. 236, ll. 31–32.

18. GASPI KO, f. P-45, op. 1, d. 236, l. 12.

19. GASPI KO, f. P-45, op. 1, d. 236, ll. 4, 6.

20. RGASPI, f. 70, op. 1, d. 33, ll. 148–172.

21. I. V. Volkovicher, *25 let R.K.P. (bol'shevikov), 1898–1923: Illiustrirovannyi iubileinyi sbornik* (Moscow: Gosudarstvennoe izdatel'stvo, 1923). On 1917, see 223–273. Two years later, Istpart sponsored Volkovicher's amply illustrated monograph on Polish socialism in the 1870s: I. Volkovicher, *Nachalo sotsialisticheskogo rabochego dvizheniia v byvshei russkoi Pol'she: Podgotovitel'nyi period partii "Proletariat"* (Moscow-Leningrad: Gosudarstvennoe izdatel'stvo, 1925).

22. *25 let R.K.P.*, 264, 269, quote on 264.

23. Volkovicher's review of G. Lelevich, *Oktiabr' v stavke* (Gomel: Gomel'skii rabochii, 1922), in *PR*, no. 5 (17) (1923), 345–346, quote on 346.

24. *PR*, no. 7 (54) (July 1926), 262.

25. RGASPI, f. 70, op. 1, d. 33, ll. 148,157, 162–163, 168, quote on l. 157.

26. RGASPI, f. 70, op. 1, d. 34, ll. 22–23, quote on l. 22. Gorin would soon become the deputy editor of Istpart's *Proletarskaia revoliutsiia*.

27. RGASPI, f. 70, op. 4, d. 327, l. 154. See draft theses in RGASPI, f. 70, op. 1, d. 36, ll. 52–53.

28. RGASPI, f. 70, op. 4, d. 327, l. 56; *PR*, no. 1 (60) (January 1927), 274.

29. GASPI KO, f. P-45, op. 1, d. 236, l. 52. These resolutions repeated in "Rezoliutsii i postanovleniia IV soveshchaniia zaveduiushchikh istpartotdelami 4–8 ianvaria 1927 g., utverzhdennye istpartom TsK VKP(b)," *PR*, no. 1 (60) (January 1927), 265.

30. A. Stanchinsky, "IV Vsesoiuznoe soveshchanie zaveduiushchikh istpartotdelami," *PR*, no. 1 (60) (January 1927), 265.

31. Mitskevich's theses are in Gosudarstvennyi arkhiv Kirovskoi oblasti [hereafter GAKO], R-2221, op. 1, d. 1, ll. 9–14 and Romanovskaia's in ll. 17–20, quotes on l. 18.

32. *PR*, no. 1 (60) (January 1927), 277.

33. See undated instructions in GAKO, f. R-2221, op. 1, d. 1, l. 26.

34. *PR*, no. 7 (66) (July 1927), 282, 283.

35. *PR*, no. 8–9 (31–32) (August–September 1924), 450.

36. V. E. Korneev and O. N. Kopylova, "Arkhivist v totalitarnom obshchestve: Bor'ba za 'chistotu' arkhivnykh kadrov (1920–1930-e gody)," *Otechestvennye arkhivy*, no. 5 (1993), 129.

37. G. Mosolov, *IMEL—Tsitadel' partiinoi ortodoksii. Iz istorii Instituta Marksizma-Leninizma pri TsK KPSS, 1921–1955* (Moscow: Novyi khronograf, 2010), 152.

38. *O sud'bakh i mgnoven'iakh proletevshikh ... Ocherki istorii Gosudarstvennoi arkhivnoi sluzhby Kirovskoi oblasti* (Kirov: "O-Kratkoe," 2008), 22.

39. M. V. Zelenov, *Apparat TsK RKP(b)-VKP(b), tsenzura i istoricheskaia nauka v 1920-e gody* (Nizhnii Novgorod: Volgo-Viatskaia akademiia gosudarstvennoi sluzhby, 2000), 220.

40. Zelenov, *Apparat TsK*, 220.

41. For a discussion of the jubilee, see Vitalii Tikhonov, "Revoliutsiia 1917 g. v kommemorativnykh praktikakh i istoricheskoi politike sovetskoi epokhi," *Rossiiskaia istoriia*, no. 2 (March–April 2017), 92–112. Many of these plans bore fruit; see Corney, *Telling October*, 175–199. See esp. Corney's discussion of Eisenstein's *October*, 188–191, 193–197.

42. I. Flerovsky, "Nado byt' gotovym (K desiatiletnemu iubileiu Oktiabr'skoi revoliutsii)," *PR*, no. 11 (34) (November 1924), 109–122, esp. 118–119.

43. RGASPI, f. 147, op. 1, d. 26, l. 9.

44. See the plan in RGASPI, f. 147, op. 1, d. 26, ll. 18–26. The prospectus began with a section, "The Prerequisites of a Local October," 18.

45. RGASPI, f. 147, op. 1, d. 26, l. 20. On January 28, 1926, Kanatchikov issued an invitation to a number of people, Pokrovsky included, to attend a meeting at Istpart headquarters to coordinate the work of organizations and institutions preparing historical literature for the tenth anniversary. It would discuss the plan just set forth. See RGASPI, f. 147, op. 1, d. 26, l. 8. I have not seen any indication that it met.

46. RGASPI, f. 70, op. 1, d, 33, l. 30.

47. RGASPI, f. 70, op. 1, d. 38, l. 11.

48. O. Varentsova, "Dve taktiki," *PR*, no. 4 (63) (April 1927), 3–10; F. Drabkina, "Priezd tov. Lenina i martovskoe soveshchanie predstavitelei bol'shevistskikh organizatsii," *PR*, no. 4 (63) (April 1927), 150–163 (an attack on Kamenev); N. Maiorsky and N. El'vov, "K voprosu o kharaktere i dvizhushchikh silakh Oktiabr'skoi revoliutsii," *PR*, no. 11 (70) (November 1927), 34–73 (an assault on Kamenev, Zinoviev, and Trotsky); D. Baevsky, "Leninskaia i kamenevskaia otsenka revoliutsii 1917 g.," *PR*, no. 12 (71) (December 1927), 3–52. M. Savel'ev, "Lenin i Oktiabr'skoe vooruzhennoe vosstanie," *PR*, no. 11 (70) (November 1927), 3–33. See articles on Stalin in the December 1929 issue of *PR* that celebrated his fiftieth birthday.

49. Baevsky, "Leninskaia i kamenevskaia otsenka," 11.

50. Em. Iaroslavsky, "Bolsheviki v Oktiabre," *PR*, no. 10 (69) (October 1927), 26–90.

51. S. Piontkovsky, "Voenno-revoliutsionnyi komitet v oktiabr'skie dni," *PR*, no. 10 (69) (October 1927), 110–137.

52. "Pis'mo v Istpart TsK VKP(b). O podelke istorii Oktiabr'skogo perevorota, istorii revoliutsii i istorii partii," in L. Trotsky, *Stalinskaia shkola fal'sifikatsii. Popravki i dopolneniia k literature epigonov* (Berlin: Izdavel'stvo "Granat," 1932), 13. This is a reprint by the USSR's Academy of Sciences (Moscow: "Nauka," 1990).

53. "Pis'mo v Istpart," 13. Istpart sent the questionnaire to 1,500 people and received 350 back: V. A. Peresvetov, "Deiatel'nost' Istparta po sobiraniiu vospominanii ob Oktiabr'skoi revoliutsii i Grazhdanoskoi voine," *Voprosy istorii*, no. 5 (May 1981), 119.

54. See the condemnation of memoirs as of little or no value that had been written by Miliukov, Sukhanov, Chernov, and others in I. Tatarov, "Kratkii obzor literatury ob Oktiabr'skom perevorote," *PR*, 10 (69) (October 1927), 299–300; S. G. Tomsinsky, "Oktiabr' v belogvardeiskom osveshchenii," *IM*, no. 5 (1927), 184–190.

55. D. Kin, "Semnadtsatyi god v izobrazhenii t. Shliapnikova," *IM*, no. 3 (1927), 40–55; Ark. Lomakin, "O novoi knige tov. Shliapnikova," *Bol'shevik*, no. 5 (March 1, 1927), 91–96; A. Divil'kovsky, review in *Pechat' i revoliutsiia*, no. 2 (1927), 164–166.

56. A. Shliapnikov, "Otvet kritikam," *Bol'shevik*, no. 10 (May 31, 1927), 84. For a discussion of the harsh criticism of Shliapnikov's work, see Barbara

C. Allen, *Alexander Shliapnikov, 1885–1937: Life of an Old Bolshevik* (Chicago: Haymarket Books, 2016), 309–312. In February and March 1932, the Orgburo, in Shliapnikov's presence, then the Politburo, condemned his work and prohibited its publication and distribution.

57. M. Pokrovsky, "Neskol'ko malen'kikh popravok," *Bol'shevik*, no. 14 (July 31, 1927), 88. Some time before September 1927, Shliapnikov submitted to *Proletarskaia revoliutsiia* an article, "Soldiers' Mutinies During the War," RGASPI, f. 72, op. 3, d. 494, 52 ll. The staff began editing it for publication. It was not published. Someone wrote in the upper-left hand corner of the first page: "Typical of spies!"

58. RGASPI, f. 70, op. 1, d. 7, l. 55. The fourth volume miraculously appeared in October 1931 in a press run of five thousand copies: A. Shliapnikov, *Semnadtsatyi god* (Moscow-Leningrad: Gosudarstvennoe sotsial'no-ekonomicheskoe izdatel'stvo, 1931). As in his earlier volumes, Shliapnikov relied on a wide range of documents, avoided caricatures, emphasized the material rather than political objectives of the Russian populace, and acknowledged the significance of spontaneity. He did not embellish Stalin's role and treated Martov, Trotsky, and, after March, Kamenev and Zinoviev as influential antagonists of the Provisional Government and war. Perhaps the book was published because much of it had already appeared in print. In a letter sent to Stalin and other Soviet leaders in February 1932, Shliapnikov responded to a recent grilling by the party's Orgburo in part by noting that the volume's important chapters had already been printed in *Proletarskaia revoliutsiia* in 1926. See M. V. Zelenov, ed., *I. V. Stalin: Istoricheskaia ideologiia v SSSR v 1920–1930-e gody: Perepiska s istorikami, stat'i i zametki po istorii, stenogrammy vystuplenii. Sbornik dokumentov i materialov*, pt. 1, *1920–1930- gody* (Sankt-Peterburg: "Nauka-Piter," 2006), 181.

59. RGASPI, f. 70, op. 3, d. 1, l. 90. See also Fishkin's remarks on ll. 125, 133.

60. See for example, remarks in RGASPI, f. 70, op. 3, d. 1, l. 34.

61. RGASPI, f. 70, op. 3, d. 1, l. 14.

62. RGASPI, f. 70, op. 3, d. 1, l. 125.

63. GASPI KO, f. P-45, op. 1, d. 231, ll. 6–7.

64. See resolutions of the collegium in GASPI KO, f. P-45, op. 1, d. 246, ll. 5–6, quote on l. 5.

65. Piontkovsky, "Voenno-revoliutsionnyi komitet," 110–137.

66. V. Rakhmetov, "Ob odnom neudachnom uchebnike po istorii Rossii," *IM*, no. 7 (1928), 227–228; Z. Serebriansky, *Ot Kerenshchiny k proletarskoi diktature* (Moscow-Leningrad: Moskovskii rabochii, 1928), 101, 105–137.

67. M. Essen, "O blizhaishikh perspektivakh raboty mestnykh istpartov," *PR*, no. 1 (January 1928), 193.

68. RGASPI, f. 70, op. 1, d. 42, l. 39.

69. I. V. Stalin, *Sochineniia*, vol. 9 (Moscow: Gosudarstvennoe izdatel'stvo politicheskoi literatury, 1948), 82, 188–190, 206–211, 217–218.

70. Stalin, *Sochineniia*, vol. 9, 209.

71. M. Pokrovsky, "Dva Oktiabria," in *Oktiabr'skaia revoliutsiia: Sbornik statei, 1917–1927* (Moscow: Izdatel'stvo Kommunisticheskoi akademii, 1929), 95–96 (first published in *Sputnik agitatora*, no. 18, 1925).

72. Stalin, *Sochineniia*, vol. 9, 269–281, quotes on 277. Lenin's article is in V. I. Lenin, *Polnoe sobranie sochinenii*, 5th ed., vol. 44 (Moscow: Izdatel'stvo politicheskoi literatury, 1970), 144–152, see especially 144, 145, 147. Lenin's piece was published in *Pravda*, October 18, 1921.

73. M. N. Pokrovsky, "Oktiabr'skaia revoliutsiia v izobrazheniiakh sovremennikov," in *Oktiabr'skaia revoliutsiia: Sbornik statei, 1917–1927* (Moscow: Izdatel'stvo Kommunisticheskoi akademii, 1929), 182. Pokrovsky's speech was first published in revised form in *IM*, no. 5 (1927), the journal's third of four issues that year. Pokrovsky completed a draft of the speech on August 30, 1927. See the entry for the year 1927, reference n. 155 in http://pokrovsky.newgod.su/research/bibliografiya/bibliografiya (accessed January 23, 2018). And yet two years later, in a foreword to a volume of his collected essays on the October revolution, Pokrovsky returned somewhat to his initial viewpoint. He wrote that in October 1917 elements of the bourgeois-democratic and proletarian revolutions intertwined, the latter completing the former "not by a little." See Pokrovsky's forward in *Oktiabr'skaia revoliutsiia: Sbornik statei, 1917–1927* (Moscow: Izdatel'stvo Kommunisticheskoi akademii, 1929), 5.

74. Yanni Kotsonis, "Ordinary People in Russian and Soviet History," *Kritika* 12, no. 3 (Summer 2011): 736. During the 1920s, Moscow, albeit often condescendingly, encouraged regional studies (*kraevedenie*). Centralization of authority doomed the discipline and many of its specialists. See Emily D. Johnson, *How St. Petersburg Learned to Study Itself: The Russia Idea of Kraevedenie* (University Park: Pennsylvania State University Press, 2006), 155–176. The Viatka Historical Society was closed in 1930, but its Research Institute for Regional Studies endured until 1941. Aware of its exceptional status, it maintained a low profile as part of the local pedagogical institute. See M. S. Sudovikov, "Viatskii NII kraevedeniia v pervye gody svoei raboty," in *Viatskii istoricheskii sbornik. God 2013-i* (Kirov: "Loban'," 2013), 33–46.

75. Hickey, "Paper, Memory and a Good Story."

76. Corney, *Telling October*, 125, 149.

77. GASPI KO, f. P-45, op. 1, d. 235, l. 1.

78. A. Novoselov, "Ocherednye zadachi Istparta. Otzhivem 'akademicheskii uklon' v etoi rabote," *Viatskaia pravda*, February 6, 1927, 2.

79. *O sud'bakh i mgnoven'iakh proletevshikh*, 23.

80. GASPI KO, f. P-45, op. 1, d. 242, l. 108.

81. GASPI KO, f. P-45, op. 1, d. 94, l. 8. Political considerations also contributed to Viatka Istpart's decision not to publish an extended piece, once

also designated for *Oktiabr' i Grazhdanskaia voina*, by Fedor Aleksandrovich Khorobrykh, an instructor at the local Pedagogical Institute, "Agrarnaia revoliutsiia v Viatskoi gubernii (1917–1921)". The manuscript is in GASPI KO, f. P-45, op. 1, d. 93, ll. 114–222. In early 1927, Viatka sent it to Istpart's central office for vetting. On May 24, Moscow rejected it as a poorly written essay that ignored the activity of the Bolshevik party in the countryside and spoke of the completion of the socialist revolution there only in 1919. See the negative review of Khorobrykh's work in GASPI KO, f. P-45, op. 1, d. 93, ll. 111–113 and the decision by Istpart's office, May 24, l. 110.

82. *Oktiabr' i Grazhdanskaia voina v Viatskoi gubernii* (Viatka: Istpart, 1927), IV.

83. A. Novoselov, "Viatskaia organizatsiia VKP (bol'shevikov) v 1917–18 g.g.," in *Oktiabr' i Grazhdanskaia voina*, 67–139. From his initial typescript, Novoselov removed several comments about Kuchkin's activity in Kirov in early 1917. See comments in the typescript in GASPI KO, f. P-45, op. 1, d. 91, ll. 63, 66.

84. M. Favorov, "Oktiabr' v Viatke," in *Oktiabr' i Grazhdanskaia voina*, 1–19. After graduating with a degree in history from Moscow University in 1911, Favorov taught the subject in several schools before and after 1917. From 1923 to 1926, he headed Viatka's workers faculty (*rabfak*) and from 1926 to 1930 served as rector of Viatka's Pedagogical Institute. In 1932, he departed Viatka for Nizhnii Novgorod. For biographical information, albeit incomplete, see *Rektory ViatGGU, 1914–2004* (Kirov: Izdatel'stvo ViatGGU, 2004), 46–56. In two polemical tracts on 1917, published in 1927 in the periodical of Viatka's Pedagogical Institute, Favorov chose not to exaggerate the Bolshevik party's significance but rather to attack Viatka's teachers union and, more generally, the city's bourgeoisie. See M. Favorov, "Uchitel'stvo i uchashchaiasia molodezh' g. Viatki v 'Oktiabre'1917 g.," *Student-leninets*, no. 3–4 (1927), 6–12 and M. Favorov, "Viatskaia burzhuaziia v Oktiabre," *Student-leninets*, no. 5–6 (1927), 12–17.

85. N. Solonitsyn, "Iz istorii Grazhdanskoi voiny v gubernii. Sobytiia 1918 goda," in *Oktiabr' i Grazhdanskaia voina*, 33–66; on Trotsky, 57–58.

86. *PR*, no. 10 (69) (October 1927), 314 and *PR*, no. 1 (72) (January 1928), 180–183.

87. Review in *Viatsko-Vetluzhskii krai*, no. 9 (September 1927), 46–47. See also Tokarev's highly politicized account of the October revolution, an event that launched, as he put it, a new epoch in human history: S. Tokarev, "Znachenie Oktiabra," *Student-leninets*, no. 3–4 (1927), 3–5.

88. *Viatsko-Vetluzhskii krai*, no. 9 (September 1927), 47.

89. See instructions from Liubovikov and Novoselov for celebrating the tenth anniversary of the October revolution in GAKO, f. R-2221, op. 1, d. 1, ll. 3–8, quote on l. 3.

90. GAKO, f. R-2221, op. 1, d. 2, l. 8 ob. For a history of Viatka's Museum of the Revolution, see V. S. Zharavin, "Muzei revoliutsii v Viatke: Iz istorii muzeinogo dela kraia," *Gertsenka: Viatskie zapiski*, vol. 5 (Kirov: "Viatka," 2003), 151–155.

91. See the report by Liubovikov in February 1930, in GAKO, f. R-2221, op. 1, d. 1, l. 147. At first, the museum had two rooms, in 1928 it had four.

92. See multiple comments in 1927 and 1928 in the guest book (*Kniga zapisei*), GAKO, f. R-2221, op. 1, d. 4. An inventory of the many items in the museum's MOPR section is in GAKO, f. R-2221, op. 1, d. 1, ll. 102–114.

93. After the formation of MOPR in November 1922, Viatka created its own branch in January 1923 with cells soon to follow in many of the region's towns and villages. They collected money, clothing, and other items to support workers and political prisoners abroad. Members also corresponded with jailed revolutionaries and with governments to request their release. See V. Kalininchenko, "'Viatka izvestna vsei Evrope'," in *Viatka: Kraevedcheskii sbornik*, vol. 3 (Kirov: Volgo-Viatksoe knizhnoe izdatel'stvo, Kirovskoe otdelenie, 1977), 70–80. Although less frequently, visitors commented on exhibits arranged by the local chapter of the Society for Air and Chemical Defense (*Osoviakhim*, in abbreviated Russian).

94. GAKO, f. R-2221, op. 1, d. 4, ll. 27 ob., 28, 60, 73.

95. The Collections Department of Kirov's Regional Museum of Local History possesses a folder of about 150 photographs of Viatka's Museum of the Revolution from 1927 to 1930 and a few photographs from successive years up to 1933. See photographs of the museum's initial displays of jailed political prisoners and prisoners in exile (KOMK 31115 and KOMK 31126/2); on the civil war (KOMK 16485/211V); and by MOPR (KOMK 16485/54V).

96. KOMK 31120/3. The display was part of a larger exhibit, "The October Revolution and Civil War in the Viatka Province."

97. GAKO, f. R-2221, op. 1, d. 1, l. 148.

98. GAKO, f. R-2221, op. 1, d. 1, l. 148. Sitnikova also complained that "the bombs and other weapons of the participants of the revolutionary struggle did not occupy a central place" (l. 148). In 1935, the Museum of the Revolution merged with Kirov's Regional Museum. In 1964, a catalog of memoirs on the 1917 revolution and civil war in Viatka contained exclusively, except for one possible exception, items on the latter topic. See P. I. Sokhrannyi, *Katalog vospominanii ob Oktiabr'skoi revoliutsii i Grazhdanskoi voine (fondy muzeia)* (Kirov: Knizhnoe izdatel'stvo, 1964). The museum may well have made relatively little of October until 1977. That year, it opened a separate building, the Diorama, that featured a smartly illuminated huge canvas 35 m wide and 8 m high, "The Formation of Soviet Power in Viatka." That work reimagined a single day, December 1, 1917, when workers and soldiers demonstrated in the city for soviet power. It was, in fact, but one of many events that contributed to the establishment of Bolshevik rule in the city and province. See an account of the relative insignificance of the events of this day in Iu. N. Timkin, *Smutnoe vremia na Viatke: Obshchestvenno-politicheskoe razvitie Viatskoi gubernii vesnoi 1917-osen'iu 1918 gg.* (Kirov: Izdatel'stvo VGPU, 1998), 33.

99. Collections Department, Kirov's Regional Museum of Local History (KOMK 31137). Compare it with the display in a photograph taken earlier (KOMK 31120/3). Kuchkin here bears a striking resemblance to the Soviet poet Vladimir Mayakovsky. The painting is "1917 god. V Viatskom gorodskom teatre." Its author, Demidov, born in the province, worked in Viatka from 1917 until his death in 1929. The painting now hangs in Kirov's Diorama. A second painting below is also probably by Demidov. As best as I can tell, it depicts an event that did not occur in 1917. Perhaps the author confused the demonstration portrayed here with another that transpired farther north in the city on December 1 and discussed in n. 98. The museum's guest book inexplicably contains no entries from late 1928 to early 1933.

100. See reviews in *PR*, no. 2–3 (61–62) (February–March 1927), 397–401; *PR*, no. 6 (65) (June 1927), 311; *PR*, no. 11 (70) (November 1927), 221–236; *PR*, no. 12 (71) (December 1927), 263; *PR*, no. 5 (76) (May 1928), 187–189. See also Klopikhina's discussion of the condemnation of several volumes on the North Caucasus by Nikolai Leonardovich Ianchevsky: Vasilina Sergeevna Klopikhina, "Deiatel'nost' istpartov na Severnom Kavkaze (1920–1939 gody)" (diss., Stavropol State University, Stavropol, 2011), 171. The works in question: N. L. Ianchevsky, *Grazhdanskaia bor'ba na Severnom Kavkaze*, vol. 1 (Rostov-na-Donu: Sevkavkniga, 1927) and N. L. Ianchevsky, *Grazhdanskaia bor'ba na Severnom Kavkaze*, vol. 2 (Rostov-na-Donu: Sevkavkniga, 1927).

101. *PR*, no. 2–3 (61–62) (February–March 1927), 397.

102. Shteinman, *PR*, no. 2–3 (61–62) (February–March 1927), 397.

103. *PR*, no. 2–3 (61–62) (February–March 1927), 398.

104. V. Mishke, "Podgotovka Oktiabria v Latvii," *PR*, no. 1 (72) (January 1928), 37.

105. V. Smirnov, "K desiatiletiiu proletarskoi revoliutsii v Finliandii," *PR*, no. 2 (73) (February 1928), 40.

SEVEN

The Passing of Istpart and Professional Civility

THE DEMISE OF ISTPART'S DUAL mission preceded the agency's own disappearance into the Lenin Institute. Some locals remained, but for the most part, they resembled what they had been, a mere shadow of the center's grand plans. Many, including Viatka's local, ceased to exist. Their end signified the mortality of scholarly standards and professional civility throughout Soviet academic life. The fragile nature of both was already apparent. At Istpart, the traditional canon of scholarship and professional decorum were threatened from the agency's founding. Ol'minsky and Nevsky had an antagonistic relationship, some historians behaved badly in the spat over Trotsky's "Lessons of October," and Novoselov and Kuchkin disliked each other. But none of those disputes compared with the incivility that came to dominate exchanges among competing groups of party historians and the toxic attitude toward their colleagues beyond the party's pale.

ISTPART'S DEATH THROES

Most regional Istparts lacked the funds and the personnel to justify their mission, however modestly designed. In April 1927, the Central Committee ordered the reduction of Istpart's branches from eighty-six to fifty-nine.[1] Additional retrenchment followed. On May 26, 1928, Istpart's collegium found that only sixteen of the fifty-three locals still in existence functioned normally. Familiar ailments continued: a small and poorly qualified cadre and a catastrophic condition of the archives, where they existed at all.[2] By October 1928, only thirty-eight locals remained, twenty-five of which had a staff of one.

Viatka's Istpart was one of those that survived with a single employee.³ Within months, it reverted to what it had been at the start—an agency that existed largely on paper. On May 27, 1927, Novoselov asked the regional party committee to send him to a warmer climate in the Soviet Union's south.⁴ On August 12, 1927, the committee assigned him to the North Caucasus regional party committee,⁵ and appointed Liubovikov in his stead. Liubovikov had little time, or perhaps inclination, to maintain his predecessor's level of activity. As he had previously, Liubovikov devoted his energy to fulfilling his duties as director to Viatka's Museum of the Revolution. In early 1928, the regional party committee did not consider his position there and the nominal post at Istpart sufficiently worthy to grant his request for an increase in salary to a modest 183 rubles a month.⁶

When the regional party committee drew up its agenda for the first quarter of 1928, it failed to mention Istpart.⁷ That year's Commission for Celebrating the October Revolution did not include Liubovikov or anyone else claiming to represent Istpart.⁸ In mid-1928, when Moscow's Istpart asked its locals for their publishing plans, Liubovikov responded that his unit had no funds to print anything. He hoped it might sponsor a collection of documents and encourage research, but he was not certain just how it might do so.⁹ He did not have the time to contribute to any such effort. Students at the local pedagogical institute might, he mused, volunteer their services.¹⁰ Liubovikov was on surer ground that year when he sought to improve Istpart's physical accommodations. He asked the regional soviet to donate carpets recently expropriated from local churches,¹¹ and he managed to purchase a life-sized statue of Lenin from Moscow for 125 rubles.¹²

In 1929, Viatka's Istpart ceased to exist. On January 14, the Presidium of the All-Russian Central Executive Committee placed Viatka in the newly enlarged Nizhnii Novgorod region. Viatka's regional party committee and its Istpart were formally disbanded in June.¹³

The national Istpart lingered for a time but largely on paper. In 1927 and 1928, Istpart and the Lenin Institute negotiated about how best to "save" Istpart in its merger with the institute. In those discussions, the institute repeatedly demonstrated a condescending reluctance to take over Istpart. Its leaders suggested that the institute did not have space for any new people. Moreover, they insisted that that Istpart's presence would divert time and resources away from the institute's focus on the publication of Lenin's collected works.¹⁴ In May 1928, the Central Committee ordered Istpart's absorption by the Lenin Institute.¹⁵ In a compromise of sorts, Ol'minsky, Pokrovsky, and Savel'ev were appointed to the institute's Directorate, with Savel'ev as its deputy director.

Istpart had ceased to exist at the national level. The situation was not much better farther afield. After 1928, a few locals limped on but with little to do. On January 7, 1929, representatives from twenty-five branches gathered for a conference in Moscow.[16] The official in charge, Essen, announced that the major task was to assist with the publication of new editions of Lenin's collected works. The study of party history and of 1917 remained important but only for the "exposure of various deviations from the correct Leninist line."[17] Essen wanted particular emphasis on the Bolshevik party's multiple successes throughout its history to refute, she said, memoirs that denied it.[18] Istpart's original mission, like the Istpart organization, was now a dead letter.

BEYOND ISTPART: POLITICIZATION ALONG THE HISTORICAL FRONT

In the late 1920s, party historians denounced each other and their previously respected nonparty colleagues on a variety of topics. They did so in heated, heavily politicized disputes about the role of patrimonial capitalism in medieval society, the importance of commercial capitalism in Russian history, the existence of socioeconomic formations (in particular the so-called Asiatic mode of production), the relationship between Bolshevism and Populism, the meaning of the 1905 revolution, and the place of foreign capital in Russian banking and economic development before 1917. These conflicts involved still more exchanges of personal insults and denunciations that were so common, as we have seen, in the Soviet historical profession. An extremely nasty conflict erupted between Pokrovsky and Iaroslavsky and their disciples over the 1905 revolution.[19] Those disputes have been discussed well and at length by historians, John Barber in particular.[20] What follows in this and the next chapter is a focus on issues of pivotal importance to this study of Istpart—historical methodology and a history of 1917.

INSTITUTIONS ON THE WARPATH

In 1921, Narkompros formed an Association of Research Institutes at Moscow State University to supervise the activity of faculties of social sciences in higher educational institutions. Renamed the Russian Association of Research Institutes of the Social Sciences (RANION), it became an independent entity in 1926, free of the university. The following year, an orchestrated campaign criticized its members for undertaking work purportedly irrelevant to the Soviet

Union's contemporary tasks.[21] In 1929 and 1930, the Communist Academy absorbed many of RANION's agencies, the History Institute among them. At the opening of the Communist Academy's own History Institute in 1929, Pokrovsky denounced RANION for its failure to present the past in conformity with Marxism.[22] Its so-called bourgeois specialists had avoided, in particular, the history of revolution. The History Institute would retain only those historians from RANION who could not be replaced by Marxists. By 1930, RANION had ceased to exist.

Participants at the First Conference of Marxist Historians, held in late December 1928 and early January 1929, equated the Bolshevik historian with a militant propagandist. In advance of the conference's opening, the Society's chair Pokrovsky and its academic secretary Gorin declared the new organization's primary objective to be the exposure of "anti-Marxist and pseudo-Marxist tendencies" in contemporary Marxist historical scholarship.[23] In his opening address on December 28, Pokrovsky proclaimed: "Marxist historians comprise one of the detachments of Lenin's army."[24] Delegates agreed. The party's historians, they resolved, must cast aside "old professorial habits and academic inclinations." They should study history as scholar-revolutionaries at the ideological front.[25]

In February 1930, the society and the Communist Academy convened a Conference of Teachers of Leninism, Party History, and the History of the Comintern. Delegates equated crude partisanship with scholarship. A major address called "Party History as a Science" was given by Kin, who had written in 1927 an article (as previously discussed) that acknowledged cooperation of Mensheviks and Bolsheviks in 1917. Kin now declared that progressive natural laws governed the party in the past and in the present; therefore, the party could only pursue an "objective course." In short, it could never err.[26] Conferees agreed: "The severest adherence to the party line in research guarantees genuine scholarship."[27]

In 1929, a commission of the Lenin Institute investigated museums of the revolution throughout the country. It recommended the destruction of what it called "iconostases" supposedly representing the revolutionary movement before 1917 but in which the class struggle and Bolshevism all but disappeared in a fetish for petty details and "objectivism." All exhibits "must be permeated with [the party's] contemporary needs."[28]

DISMISSAL OF MEMOIRS

Only certain sources measured up to the new standards. A continuing campaign against memoirs as a useful source led to a denunciation in 1929 and 1930 of the journal *Katorga i ssylka* (Penal Servitude and Exile). The periodical had long published memoirs of non-Bolshevik revolutionaries who dominated the journal's sponsor, the Society of Political Prisoniia and Exiles. The society was founded in 1921 and headed by none other than Iaroslavsky. The journal had mistakenly, its detractors now insisted, printed memoirs by people not supportive in the past (and, implicitly, in the present) of the Bolshevik party. It hardly helped matters that many people, including party members in good standing, had found memoirs in *Katorga i ssylka* more interesting than those in *Proletarskaia revoliutsiia*. At Istpart's Fourth Conference, Mitskevich, a member of Istpart's collegium and director of the Museum of the Revolution, put it well: *Katorga i ssylka* printed reminiscences of considerable interest, whereas almost no one read such material in Istpart's publication, its issues shelved with their pages still uncut.[29]

Ol'minsky led the charge in late 1929 against *Katorga i ssylka*. He complained that it printed uncritical obituaries of non-Bolsheviks. He reinforced his point by placing the journal alongside books, if only slightly less malodorous, that contained memoirs of a counterrevolutionary nature that remained harmful despite the forewords and commentary added by Bolsheviks. To make his point, Ol'minsky ventured farther afield with a condemnation of the diary of the "crowned half-idiot Nikolai Romanov" that had been published in Berlin. It and other such memoirs were "a heap of trash."[30] When reviewing Krupskaya's reminiscences on Lenin the following year, Ol'minsky was complimentary but felt compelled to characterize memory as "frail and subjective."[31]

The September 1930 issue of *Proletarskaia revoliutsiia* criticized *Katorga i ssylka* for publishing memoirs by individuals who had opposed the Bolshevik party in 1917 and in the civil war that followed.[32] Ol'minsky added his influential voice to the assault.[33] Iaroslavsky leaped to the defense of the journal and its sponsoring society. His biographer Sandra Dahlke has insisted that Iaroslavsky did so not as a defender of scholarship but rather as a patron protecting his people.[34] Be that as it may, in *Proletarskaia revoliutsiia*'s November issue, Iaroslavsky defended the principle of a heterogeneity of opinions. He spoke, he said, for the society's presidium and the editorial board of its journal. Although *Katorga i ssylka* had published memoirs that were incorrect "from the point of view of a revolutionary study of Marxism-Leninism," it had a right to publish them.[35] *Proletarskaia revoliutsiia*'s editorial board disagreed, and so did Ol'minsky. Iaroslavsky had called for "various points of view," Ol'minsky declared, whereas *Proletarskaia revoliutsiia* correctly demanded "a *party* point of view." Ol'minsky proclaimed: "That which yesterday was revolutionary, today can take on a different meaning."[36]

AN ASSAULT ON BOURGEOIS HISTORIANS

Warfare at the historical front extended to the imprisonment of so-called bourgeois historians. From 1929 to 1931, the Soviet state arrested many specialists, among them about 130 historians.[37] Pokrovsky turned a deaf ear to their pleas for help.[38] In January 1932, he went further. He sent the Secret Department of the State Political Administration (OGPU) letters that he had received over previous months from several arrested historians asking him to intervene on their behalf. Perhaps Pokrovsky forwarded them to the OGPU only to protect himself. Surely he knew the police had already read them.[39] Be that as it may, he had been and remained in no mood to help.

On September 8, 1931, Evgenii Viktorovich Tarle asked Pokrovsky's to assist him in restoring his good name and career. He had previously been a highly respected historian of the French revolution and European imperialism and a full member of the USSR's Academy of Sciences since 1927. Tarle had been arrested in January 1930 for alleged involvement in a conspiracy to overthrow the Soviet government. In the regime that would have followed, he allegedly was to have served as minister of foreign affairs. Tarle wrote Pokrovsky from Alma-Ata in Kazakhstan, where he had been in exile since August 1931. He hoped Pokrovsky might help despite a history between them of heated disagreements about their respective interpretations of Napoleon, World War I, and current Soviet policy toward Turkey.[40] An insulting reply followed. Pokrovsky had read Tarle's confession, he wrote, and thought Tarle fortunate to be comparatively safe and sound in Kazakhstan. If he had committed such heinous crimes in Tarle's beloved France, the apostate would have found himself in the infamous penal colony of Devil's Island. Tarle's name had become too toxic for any future publication of his work. Pokrovsky condescendingly suggested that he might nevertheless find it possible to intervene on Tarle's behalf. Pokrovsky was ill and bedridden, but when his health improved, he would try "to negotiate with whom it is necessary," a thinly veiled reference to Stalin.[41] Before Pokrovsky could do anything, in the unlikely event he was so inclined, he died of bladder cancer on April 10, 1932. No thanks to Pokrovsky, Tarle returned to Moscow later that year.

On November 12, 1931, Vladimir Ivanovich Picheta wrote Pokrovsky. Like Pokrovsky, he had studied history under Kliuchevsky at Moscow State University. After the 1917 revolution, Picheta became the first rector of Belorussian State University. While there, he continued his career as an author of well-received economic histories of Russia and Belorussia from the eighteenth to the twentieth centuries. Arrested in 1930, Picheta spent time in solitary confinement in Leningrad, where his health deteriorated. In August 1931, he was sent to Viatka, where he penned his appeal.[42] He told Pokrovsky he had been forced to sign a confession in Leningrad. In desperation, "I even hanged myself, but the rope broke."[43] "Look into my fate and save me from death. *I am a true and honorable son of Soviet power* [his emphasis]. I live with the hope that you will help me."[44] There is no record of Pokrovsky's response. He likely preferred to ignore his disgraced colleague's plea. Picheta remained in Viatka until 1934, when he was transferred to the Voronezh Pedagogical Institute for a post teaching history.

Piontkovsky kept pace with Pokrovsky's broadsides at anyone outside the contracting ideological pale—historians and other specialists alike. In mid-June 1930, he dismissed the suicide of the Bolshevik poet Vladimir Mayakovsky as evidence of an "extreme individualist who could not identify with the collective."[45] At the same time, Piontkovsky condemned bourgeois historians who had been arrested or who were facing imminent arrest. "Our task is to help them die off without a trace," Piontkovsky told his fellow historians in a speech before the Society of Marxist Historians in October 1930.[46] On November 1, he wrote in his diary that the recently imprisoned historians Sergei Fedorovich Platonov and Sergei Vladimirovich Bakhrushin belonged to a right-wing group of nationalist-monarchists who had planned a revolt to restore the Russian monarchy.[47] In his book published the following year, *Bourgeois Historical Scholarship in Russia*, Piontkovsky used brutal, although perhaps figurative language by calling for the annihilation of bourgeois historians along with the bourgeoisie and kulaks. "It is necessary," he declared, "to finish bourgeois historiography off forever."[48]

NOTES

1. M. V. Zelenov, *Apparat TsK RKP(b)-VKP(b), tsenzura i istoricheskaia nauka v 1920-e gody* (Nizhnii Novgorod: Volgo-Viatskaia akademiia gosudarstvennoi sluzhby, 2000), 211–212, 216. Istpart's Fourth Conference in January 1927 called for a reduction of the number of regional Istparts from eighty-six (or eighty-seven) to fifty-nine: GASPI KO, f. P-45, op. 1, d. 236, l. 55. Zelenov reports that at first the plan was to leave fifty-eight in place but it was changed to fifty-nine when it was decided to keep the Voronezh Istpart: Zelenov, *Apparat TsK*, 213.

2. RGASPI f. 70, op. 1, d. 42, ll. 62–63. Viatka's Istpart was not among those functioning normally. It was only "partially developed." Nineteen others performed poorly. The center had no contact with four others (l. 62).

3. See numbers in *PR*, no. 11–12 (82–83) (November–December 1928), 362–363.

4. GASPI KO, f. P-1, op. 1, op. 5, d. 31, l. 210.

5. GASPI KO, f. P-1, op. 5, d. 14, l. 129.
6. See the session of the party committee's secretariat, April 20, 1928, GASPI KO, f. P-1, op. 6, d. 36, l. 103 ob.
7. GASPI KO, f. P-1, op. 5, d. 15, ll. 160–162.
8. See a proposal from the subcommission for agitation and propaganda to the regional party committee's secretariat, October 5, 1918, GASPI KO, f. P-1, op. 6, d. 37, l. 86 ob. The commission would include representatives from, among others, the Young Communist League (*Komsomol*), Zhenotdel, the Main Administration for Political Enlightenment (*Glavpolitprosvet*), the regional trade unions council, and the party fraction of the regional soviet's executive committee.
9. See the request of June 5, 1928, by the Central Committee's Istpart in GASPI KO, f. P-45, op. 1, d. 246, l. 13 and Liubovikov's response in June, l. 12.
10. See Liubovikov's suggestion to Viatka Istpart's collegium, April 24, 1928, in GASPI KO, f. P-45, op. 1, d. 248, l. 1.
11. See Liubovikov's request submitted to the regional soviet's executive committee, GASPI KO, f. P-45, op. 1, d. 232, l. 56.
12. See the correspondence in GAKO, f. R-2221, op. 1, d. 1, ll. 131, 145–146.
13. GASPI KO, f. P-45, op. 1, d. 234, l. 9.
14. See an entire folder on the merger: RGASPI, f. 70, op. 1, d. 40, 110 ll. On the Lenin Institute's reluctance, see especially RGASPI, f. 70, op. 1, d. 42, l. 23. The merger is discussed well in V. G. Mosolov, *IMEL—Tsitadel' partiinoi ortodoksii. Iz istorii Instituta Marksizma-Leninizma pri TsK KPSS, 1921–1955* (Moscow: Novyi khronograf, 2010), 153–155. Both institutions looked at merger from "their own vantage point" (153) and "institutional points of view" (155).
15. *Nauchnyi rabotnik*, no. 10 (October 1928), 84.
16. GASPI KO, f. P-45, op. 1, d. 246, ll. 21–24. On the number, *PR*, no. 1 (84) (January 1929), 275. Istpart's Fourth Conference in January 1927 had been attended by forty-seven heads of locals and three other representatives from the provinces. In 1939, the party's Central Committee disbanded all Istpart locals.
17. GASPI KO, f. P-45, op. 1, d. 246, l. 22. Essen also declared that Istpart's locals, especially those in the USSR's national republics, should oppose all efforts to idealize petty-bourgeois national parties (the Bund and others) (l. 22). See also Essen's comments in M. Essen, "O 5-m vsesoiuznom istpartovskom soveshchanii," *PR*, 1 (84) (January 1929), 275. At this conference, Savel'ev gave a separate report on the work of the Lenin Institute.
18. GASPI KO, f. P-45, op. 1, d. 246, l. 22. Essen repeated this demand the following year; M. Essen, "Ob institutakh po istorii partii," *PR*, no. 5 (100) (May 1930), 287–288.
19. See the commentary and documents in M. V. Zelenov, ed., *I. V. Stalin: Istoricheskaia ideologiia v SSSR v 1920–1930-e gody: Perepiska s istorikami, stat'i i zametki po istorii, stenogrammy vystuplenii. Sbornik dokumentov i materialov*, pt.

1, *1920–1930-gody* (Sankt-Peterburg: "Nauka-Piter," 2006), 71–73, 91–112. Years later in January 1936, Iaroslavsky, with no more than a school education and sensitive to a fault, recalled in a letter to Stalin his lingering bitterness over the clash with Pokrovsky. "I prepared," he wrote, "an enormous amount of material on the 1905 revolution. I planned for a serious and detailed work in which the role of Comrade Stalin would be demonstrated throughout our party's history. In this work, I received no support. I ran up against a wall of opposition. Why so? Because I had not graduated from the Institute of Red Professors or had not studied under Pokrovsky? or because, unlike others, I without a state examination and without any scholarly awards had not received an advanced degree.?" Zelenov, *I. V. Stalin*, 216.

20. Barber devotes most of his book to these controversies; Barber, *Soviet Historians*. See also, Enteen, *Soviet Scholar-Bureaucrat*, 84–86, 122–128; Jonathan Frankel, "Party Genealogy and the Soviet Historians," *Slavic Review* 25, no. 4 (December 1966): 590–591; A. N. Artizov, "Nikolai Nikolaevich Vanag (1899–1937 gg.)," *Otechestvennaia istoriia*, no. 6 (November–December 1992), 95–109; and George M. Enteen, Tatiana Gorn, and Cheryl Kern, *Soviet Historians and the Study of Russian Imperialism* (University Park: Pennsylvania State University Press, 1979). See also Aleksei Litvin, *Bez prava na mysl': Istoriki v epokhu Bol'shego Terrora. Ocherki sudeb* (Kazan: Tatarskoe knizhnoe izdatel'stvo, 1994). Litvin noted that in 1931 Pokrovsky wrote multiple letters to the Central Committee's secretariat, denouncing fellow Marxist historians (including Mints, Vanag, Iaroslavsky) for alleged political heresy (15). For more on the conflict between Iaroslavsky and Pokrovsky, see A. A. Chernobaev, *"Professor s pikoi", ili Tri zhizni istorika M. N. Pokrovskogo* (Moscow: Izdatel'stvo "Lit," 1992), 192–198.

21. S. Sapozhnikov, "O zadachakh i postanovke raboty nauchno-issledovatel'skikh institutov obshchestvennykh nauk," *Kommunisticheskaia revoliutsiia*, no. 10 (May 1927), 50.

22. M. N. Pokrovsky, "Institut istorii i zadacha istorikov-marksistov," *IM*, no. 14 (1929), 3–5.

23. *PR*, no. 6–7 (77–78) (June–July 1928), 380–381, *IM*, no. 8 (1928), 261–262, *Pod znamenem marksizma*, no. 6 (June 1928), 230. It is difficult to determine the number of people in attendance. Artizov points out that more people than expected were at the first session: four hundred delegates, two hundred guests: A. N. Artizov, "M. N. Pokrovskii: final kar'ery—uspekh ili porazhenie?" *Otechestvennaia istoriia*, no. 1 (January–February 1998), 85. Artizov acknowledged that in opening remarks Pokrovsky emphasized the importance of research (85).

24. "Vsesoiuznaia konferentsiia istorikov-marksistov," *IM*, no. 11 (1929), 218.

25. "Vsesoiuznaia konferentsiia istorikov-marksistov," *IM*, no. 11 (1929), 291, 224, 231, 248, 250; "Vsesoiuznaia konferentsiia," *IM*, no. 12 (1929), 300–301.

26. "Materialy soveshchanii prepodavatelei leninizma, istorii partii i istorii Kominterna," *PR*, 4 (99) (May 1930), 168–171; "Otchet o soveshchanii prepodavatelei po istorii partii, leninizma i istorii Kominterna," *PR*, 2–3 (97–98) (February–March 1930), 174, 176.

27. "Materialy soveshchanii prepodavatelei leninizma," 313.

28. M. Essen, "O Muzee Revoliutsii SSSR," *PR*, no. 6 (89) (June 1929), 244–245, quote on 245.

29. RGASPI, f. 70, op. 1, d. 33, l. 24.

30. M. Ol'minsky, "Pis'mo v redaktsiiu," *PR*, no. 12 (95) (December 1929), 223. Ol'minsky is probably referring to *Dnevnik Imperatora Nikolaia II, 1890–1906 g.g.* (Berlin: Slovo, 1923). In fact, the introductory notes in that book are quite critical of the tsar's personality and his political nearsightedness (7–9).

31. M. Ol'minsky, "Po povodu vospominanii o Lenine N. K. Krupskoi i A. Lunacharskogo," *PR*, no. 2–3 (97–98) (February–March 1930), 194. Klopikhina found that in 1927 in a draft of a review, Ol'minsky denounced such memoirs as "mass insensible fantasy" and "nonsensical lies." Klopikhina, "Deiatel'nost' istpartov," 131. And yet in 1931, the State Social and Economic Publishing House reissued a second edition of a book of memoirs by White Army generals, first issued in 1927; *Denikin. Iudenich. Vrangel': Memuary*, 2nd ed. (Moscow-Leningrad: Gosudarstvennoe sotsial'no-ekonomicheskoe izdatel'stvo, 1931).

32. A. Bur on *Katorga i ssylka*'s issues no. 8–9, 10, 11, and 12 for 1929 and no. 1, 2, 3, 4, and 5 for 1930, in *PR*, no. 9 (104) (September 1930), 168–173.

33. Ol'minsky, "Otvet t. Iaroslavskomu," *PR*, no. 11 (106) (November 1930), 188.

34. Sandra Dahlke, *Individuum und Herrschaft im Stalinismus: Emel'jan Jaroslavskij (1878–1943)* (Munich: R. Oldenbourg Verlag, 2010), 258. Dahlke argues that Iaroslavsky had no interest whatsoever in defending or rejecting traditional canons of historical scholarship. For him, history was a means to remind his audience of his own credentials as an Old Bolshevik and to promote and protect the considerable number of his clients in the profession. Otherwise, historical writing "had no autonomous worth." (270). George Enteen expressed much the same opinion in an article on Iaroslavsky. It was "loyalty to an old friend," Enteen observed, that occasionally led Iaroslavsky to take what appeared to be a principled stand. George M. Enteen, "Writing Party History in the USSR: The Case of E. M. Iaroslavsky," *Journal of Contemporary History* 21, no. 2 (April 1986): 326. John Barber assessed Iaroslavsky similarly. Iaroslavsky "protested strongly against unjustified criticism and political labeling . . . but only when he or his own associates were involved": Barber, *Soviet Historians*, 143.

35. E. Iaroslavsky, "Kakim dolzhen byt' i kakov est' zhurnal 'Katorga i ssylka'," *PR*, no. 11 (106) (November 1930), 183–187.

36. Ol'minsky, "Otvet," 188.

37. Both Barber and Litvin refer to the number 130: Barber, *Soviet Historians*, 41; Litvin, *Bez prava na mysl'*, 16.

38. Litvin, *Bez prava na mysl'*, 13, 23, 24. Chernobaev reported on rumors, undocumented, that Pokrovsky was one of the chief informers (*donoschik*, in the Russian singular) regarding Platonov's alleged crimes: Chernobaev, *"Professor s pikoi"*, 176. Years earlier, in 1919, Pokrovsky had intervened after Platonov's arrest and helped limit his imprisonment to a single day: Vera Kaplan, "Weathering the Revolution: Patronage as a Strategy of Survival," *Revolutionary Russia* 26, no. 2 (2013): 109.

39. Pokrovsky's letter in RGASPI, f. 147, op. 2, d. 11, l. 3. The letters were from Evgenii Tarle, Vladimir Picheta, and Aleksei Ivanovich Iakovlev.

40. See a discussion of the relationship between the two historians in Stuart R. Tompkins, "Trends in Communist Historical Thought," *Slavonic Review* 13, no. 38 (January 1935), 307–309; Enteen, *Soviet Scholar-Bureaucrat*, 86–88; and Konstantin F. Shteppa, *Russian Historians and the Soviet State* (New Brunswick, NJ: Rutgers University Press, 1962), 58–63. On Tarle, see E. I. Chapkevich, *Poka iz ruk ne vypalo pero: Zhizn' i deiatel'nost' E. V. Tarle* (Orel: "Orel," 1994) and B. S. Kaganovich, *Evgenii Viktorovich Tarle: Istorik i vremia* (Sankt-Peterburg: Izdatel'stvo Evropeiskogo universiteta, 2014). Tompkins points out that Pokrovsky took issue with Tarle's assertion that Germany had been the aggressor launching World War I. Pokrovsky blamed monopolistic capital. Pokrovsky also disputed Tarle's assertion that Napoleon wished to create a European economic community rather than mere despotic rule. Moreover, Tarle had regarded the Soviet Union's policy toward Turkey as a continuation of the efforts of its tsarist predecessor.

41. RGASPI, f. 147, op. 2, d. 11, l. 5.

42. Picheta's four-page handwritten letter of November 12, 1931 is in RGASPI, f. 147, op. 2, d. 11, ll. 15–16 ob. Along with his letter, Picheta sent an essay, "My Social and Political Credo," written while he was in prison in Leningrad, dated October 22, 1930. For the credo, see RGASPI, f. 147, op. 2, d. 11, ll. 17–25.

43. RGASPI, f. 147, op. 2, d. 11, l. 15 ob. He wrote that he had been interrogated in Leningrad for a month.

44. RGASPI, f. 147, op. 2, d. 11, l. 16.

45. *Dnevnik istorika S. A. Piontkovskogo (1927–1934)* (Kazan: Kazanskii gosudarstvennyi universitet, 2009), 326.

46. S. Piontkovsky, "Velikorusskaia burzhuaznaia istoriografiia poslednego desiatiletiia," *IM*, no. 18/19 (1930), 170. Piontkovsky addressed a session on industrial capitalism sponsored jointly by the History Institute of the Communist Academy and by the Society of Marxist Historians.

47. *Dnevnik istorika*, 362.

48. S. A. Piontkovsky, *Burzhuaznaia istoricheskaia nauka v Rossii* (Moscow: Molodaia gvardiia, 1931), 102.

EIGHT

Methodology Ex Cathedra
Stalin Speaks and Istpart's Legacy

DURING THE 1920S, STALIN HAD little to say about the writing of party history except for his public denunciation of Trotsky's "Lessons of October" in 1924, a few public pronouncements in 1926 and 1927, and private correspondence with Pokrovsky in 1927.[1] That changed in October 1931 when Stalin responded in an imperious and dramatic fashion to a flicker of Istpart's old self. As we have seen, the agency had undergone an uncelebrated death at the center and in Viatka, among other provinces. An original faith in a partisan yet scholarly rendition of 1917 had given way to a highly politicized narrative. And yet in 1929, a volume edited by Iaroslavsky recalled Istpart's earlier approach to the writing of history. Relying on documents and memoirs, the book challenged cardinal tenets of the grand narrative for 1917. Stalin was not pleased. This chapter discusses that challenge, Stalin's response, and the effort by Iaroslavsky and several historians to parry the Soviet leader's criticism. It then summarizes the tortuous efforts that followed by party historians to write an acceptable history of their party and of Stalin's direct involvement in it.[2] That grand venture ended in 1938 with the publication of a *History of the Communist Party: The Short Course*. The volume caricatured Istpart's earlier abandonment of the scholarly canon and a reasonably objective rendition of 1917.[3]

In mid-1930, *Proletarskaia revoliutsiia* published an article by Anatolii Grigor'evich Slutsky, head of a group in the Communist Academy's History Institute formed to study German Social Democracy before World War I. Slutsky mentioned that before 1914, not Lenin but Rosa Luxemburg, member of the left wing of the German Social Democratic Party, had best understood the so-called opportunism of Karl Kautsky.[4] Slutsky wrote that Luxemburg better grasped that Kautsky had inappropriately supported the electoral process and cooperation with liberal "bourgeois" groups. Kautsky had done so in the belief that a proletarian revolution would occur only in the distant future.[5] Well aware of the controversial nature of the Slutsky's remarks, the journal's editorial staff approved the article's publication "for discussion purposes."

Slutsky and the editorial board got more than they bargained for. The following year, sometime between October 20 and 27, Stalin submitted a sharp rebuke.[6] He denounced the journal's editorial board for accepting an article that portrayed Lenin as less than resolute in the struggle against opportunism. The board was guilty of rotten liberalism and aiding Trotskyism. "The question whether Lenin *was* or *was not* a real Bolshevik," Stalin declared, "cannot become a subject of discussion."[7] History was not primarily an exercise in the use of historical records. "Who else besides hopeless bureaucrats would rely only on paper documents?" asked Stalin rhetorically. "Why did he [Slutsky] prefer digging into randomly selected papers?"[8] Stalin's letter rapidly metastasized. In reappeared in multiple journals and was printed that December as a sixteen-page brochure in a massive press run of three hundred thousand copies on sale for five kopecks each.[9]

The letter set off a firestorm among historians and party propagandists. Much of that discussion is beyond the confines of this work, which focuses on the historical writing on 1917.[10] However, Stalin's comments at the letter's close were of particular importance. As if parenthetically, he wrote that in addition to Slutsky, other "Bolshevik historians are not free of mistakes." Their number included "unfortunately c. [comrade] Iaroslavsky whose books on party history, despite their worth, contain a number of errors of principle and historical character."[11] Stalin had in mind the four-volume *History of the Communist Party* published under Iaroslavsky's direction from 1926 to 1929 (with a fifth planned for the future). As subsequent developments revealed, Stalin objected in particular to the fifty or so pages in the fourth volume, printed in 1929 in an ample press run of ten thousand copies, that covered the party's activity from February through April 1917.[12]

At one time, Istpart came close to validating, if not sponsoring, the entire enterprise. In early 1928, Iaroslavsky asked it to relieve him of the responsibility of editing the work. Ol'minsky suggested that his people could help but that Iaroslavsky should remain as chief editor, a position assigned to him by the party's Central Committee. Savel'ev agreed. Lepeshinsky, who had remained at Istpart, albeit in a diminished capacity since his dispute with Ol'minsky over Nevsky's book, was more accommodating. He thought the agency might find the most "vulnerable places and mistakes," but he too insisted that the final editing and responsibility remain with Iaroslavsky.[13] On March 13, Istpart's soviet offered to undertake only what it called a preliminary examination of the four volumes.[14]

Whatever Istpart's distance from the overall project, the fourth volume—the one that Stalin found especially objectionable—presented a version of 1917 hauntingly reminiscent of that set forth by Istpart in the early and mid-1920s. Its journal, *Proletarskaia revoliutsiia*, which had survived Istpart's own closing in 1928, printed a largely positive review of the fourth volume in its November 1929 issue.[15] For the coverage of the year 1917, it wanted more attention to the activity of the Bolshevik party and of the Red Guards. Otherwise, young readers might get the impression that the revolution "was a walk in the park" (*khoroshaia progulka*).[16] Stalin's evaluation was of a different genre.

In the introduction to volume 4, Iaroslavsky had proclaimed that he and his team of contributors, many of them students at the Institute of Red Professors, sought to address key issues "with maximum historical objectivity." In apparent contrary fashion, he then hastened to take note of the relevance of the past to current political disputes within the party. "We consider our work," Iaroslavsky wrote, "as the fulfillment first of all of a militant party mission."[17] The author of the section in question by Stalin was none other than the young historian Kin, who had equated scholarship with adherence to the party line in 1930. In his contribution to this fourth volume, published a year earlier, he and his editor, Iaroslavsky, had badly misread what that political mission meant. With frequent reliance on Shliapnikov's work, Kin repeated much of what Istpart's historians had said previously about the first few months of 1917. The February revolt had occurred without the leadership of any one party. For weeks thereafter, a weak and disorganized Bolshevik party failed to understand the importance of the newly created soviets. Everywhere its members joined Mensheviks in "an ecstasy of unification." The party's leaders in Petrograd expressed conditional support of the Provisional Government and of Russia's involvement in the war. Kin mentioned by name Stalin, "who took a mistaken position regarding these fundamental issues." Kin then rushed to note that Stalin "rather quickly corrected his position."[18] But, Kin continued, many other Bolsheviks opposed Lenin's condemnation of the Provisional Government and the war, even after Lenin's return to the capital in early April.[19]

On October 28, 1931, Iaroslavsky wrote Stalin regarding the latter's critical comments. It was an impertinent response, minimizing the gravity of Stalin's objections and placing blame on others. Iaroslavsky began sensibly enough: "I consider your reproach of me as correct." And then, as if Stalin had nothing original to say, Iaroslavsky insisted that he had previously recognized his own errors and had asked his comrades to help correct them. Iaroslavsky then addressed what he knew to be Stalin's main objections, even as he, Iaroslavsky, minimized his own alleged mistakes. "It is especially painful for me to acknowledge that by an oversight I allowed in the fourth volume such a description of your views upon your return from exile in the spring of 1917." Iaroslavsky admitted that he should have examined Kin's piece more carefully, because it relied on the memoirs of Shliapnikov, "not at all an objective or dispassionate historian and observer."[20] Any item that used Shliapnikov's work, Iaroslavsky acknowledged, was unacceptable.

Iaroslavsky was at his disingenuous best. In his article on the Bolshevik party in February and March of 1917 published by *Proletarskaia revoliutsiia* in early 1927, Iaroslavsky cited Shliapnikov's *The Eve of 1917* to demonstrate the party's weakness and disorganization.[21] Moreover, in his letter to Stalin, Iaroslavsky hoped to justify his failure as editor of the fourth volume to recognize what, he now admitted, was the heretical nature of Shliapnikov's work. He emphasized for a purportedly uninformed leader that Shliapnikov's *1917* had previously enjoyed official sanction: "It had been published with the Central Committee's imprimatur. On its cover appeared 'Istpart,' and Istpart was a department of the Central Committee." And then, as if he did not understand the core of Stalin's objections and his own admission of Kin's errors, Iaroslavsky ended his letter with an insulting display of willful ignorance: "Show me the 'series of mistakes of principle and of historical character' about which you speak at your letter's close."[22]

Iaroslavsky knew very well the reasons for Stalin's displeasure, but he had a right to be bewildered by it. As discussed previously, in his book published in 1927, *The Party of Bolsheviks in 1917*, Iaroslavsky had praised (as he understood it) Stalin's modesty and self-deprecatory honesty when Stalin had acknowledged his own support of the Provisional Government before Lenin's arrival. Kin too had reason for puzzlement. According to Piontkovsky, Kin drafted a letter to Stalin in which he underscored that Iaroslavsky himself had written such an account of the spring of 1917 for which he, Kin, was considered culpable. It was never sent.[23] But Kin would soon send two ill-advised letters to Stalin.

Meanwhile, Stalin and Kaganovich, a member of the Central Committee's Politburo, spoke with Iaroslavsky to set him straight. According to Piontkovsky, who was in close contact with Iaroslavsky at the time, both Soviet leaders told their victim that they were surprised that he could allow even a hint that "in March, Stalin held a position analogous to that of Kamenev's" for conditional support of the war and of the Provisional Government. Iaroslavsky admitted his error but again blamed Kin.[24]

Iaroslavsky then distanced himself farther from the errors of the fourth volume. He did so on November 11, 1931, in a letter to *Pravda*. He had received an advanced copy of a review of the volume that would appear in the newspaper on November 18.[25] Signed by G. Petrov, this authoritative piece was perhaps written by Fedor Nikolaevich Petrov, an Old Bolshevik and one of the associate editors of the ongoing project *The Great Soviet Encyclopedia*. The author demonstrably struck all the right notes. A Leninist presentation of the October Revolution, Petrov began, required a portrayal "of our party's role in all of its grandeur and magnificence." He attacked Kin (and thereby Iaroslavsky) for equating Kamenev's so-called right opportunism of February and March with the party line. Kin's depiction of the party in February and March had mistakenly relied on Shliapnikov "as the supreme judge and authority." Petrov then broadened the discussion to include Piontkovsky's description of October in the same volume. Piontkovsky had presented a version that, years earlier, had been his own and the standard one but that was now unacceptable. As Piontkovsky would still have it in this volume, in October there occurred "two revolutions, the proletarian socialist revolution and a bourgeois-democratic revolution."[26] Petrov now declared that "this theory of the duality, of the double-face of October," had nothing in common with Leninism. A glorious proletarian revolution occurred in October that achieved bourgeois-democratic objectives only in passing.

Iaroslavsky responded angrily. He did not deny responsibility for the volume's mistakes, but he was "only the editor." He continued: "It is necessary to keep perspective and consider *my actual* work in this matter" (original emphasis).[27] On November 18, *Pravda* published Petrov's review. Away from the capital in the city of Batum in the Georgian republic, Iaroslavsky received a copy only on November 24. He immediately wrote *Pravda*: "The review left me with a heavy heart."[28]

In the meantime, on November 14, Kin wrote Stalin first to apologize for his blunder and then to provide a tortured explanation that only made matters worse. Much like Iaroslavsky in his letter to Stalin of October 28, Kin blamed Istpart. For the tenth anniversary of the October Revolution, Istpart had published, as Kin put it, a huge number of brochures and books that had discussed the errors committed in March 1917 of a majority of the party's members including, implicitly, Stalin. He had brought the matter up in his contribution to the fourth volume to demonstrate that, unlike many others (again, implicitly,

Figure 8.1. Happier times. Iaroslavsky and Stalin at the Fifteenth Party Congress, Moscow, December 1927. In the first row, right to left: Iaroslavsky and Stalin. Courtesy of the Russian State Documentary Film and Photo Archive.

Stalin), Kamenev had persisted in his erroneous ways. Kin promised henceforth to regain Stalin's "complete trust."[29]

The next day, Iaroslavsky's confession of errors appeared in *Bol'shevik*. He began with due praise of Stalin's letter and a denunciation of the crude and "Trotskyist" interpretations in the fourth volume. After condemning the work's portrayal of the party in early 1917, Iaroslavsky confessed to his own "rotten liberalism" that had led him to select Kin, among others, to write the volume.[30] The confession, although calculated, nevertheless exacerbated Iaroslavsky's foul mood. Piontkovsky recalled that his colleague "had reached such a state that he created the impression of a person suffering from a major psychic trauma, almost something like insanity. He sat in an empty office at the Central Control Commission, propping up his head on his hand, blankly staring out of the window."[31]

On November 25, Iaroslavsky, who was now in Batum, sent Stalin another impertinent remark, one inconsistent with his confession in *Bol'shevik* ten days earlier. As previously on October 28, Iaroslavsky displayed condescending ignorance when asking Stalin to show him his "mistakes of principle."[32] Iaroslavsky then took up the "thankless task" of defending Kin. He admitted his own guilt in allowing publication of Kin's error but insisted that detractors unfairly accused the young historian of all manner of imagined heresies. Iaroslavsky then proceeded to defend the entire work in question. "I am now re-examining still again, with pencil in hand, line by line 'The History of the Communist Party.' I see especially clearly what a great responsibility I took upon myself to render a fully developed scholarly history of the Communist party. And without false modesty, I have come to the conclusion that it is the most significant and the most *creative* work in the field." On reading that comment, Stalin wrote an abrupt "No" in the letter's left-hand margin.[33]

On December 1, Kaganovich spoke at the Institute of Red Professors in celebration of its tenth anniversary. In his remarks, "For the Bolshevik Study of Party History," he denounced the four volumes in their entirety.[34] Unmoved by Iaroslavsky's confession of the fifteenth, *Bol'shevik* published in its November 30 issue a harsh editorial and devastating review by a brigade at the Institute of Red Professors. Both items condemned the fourth volume for a multitude of heresies.[35] Its authors had advanced "Trotskyist libel" about events in February and March 1917. They had presented "a conscious falsification of the history of 1917 in a Menshevik spirit."[36] Piontkovsky mistakenly interpreted the October revolt as a merger of bourgeois-democratic and socialist revolutions. The revolt was, in fact, primarily socialist and completed the bourgeois-democratic phase only in passing. Moreover, the volume systematically ignored Stalin's contributions during 1917 and the civil war that followed.[37]

That same issue of *Bol'shevik* also printed another confession of a sort by Iaroslavsky. Albeit tardy in the minds of many, it featured his denunciation of the journal *Katorga i ssylka* for "rotten liberalism." Iaroslavsky demanded that it and all other journals restructure their work to conform to the "instructions in comrade Stalin's letter."[38]

On December 6, Kin wrote yet another letter to Stalin. Once again, he attempted to explain his reference to Stalin's position in March by saying he had done so only to show that Kamenev—and not, implicitly, Stalin—had continued to adhere to it. Kin then deflected any blame from himself to the entire collective of authors of the fourth volume. They had discussed how best to deal with the matter. In a barely concealed reference to Istpart's previous publications, Kin added that many other historians, when writing about events in March, "had gotten it all wrong," but their work had not become a cause célèbre for self-criticism.[39]

Unlike Kin, Iaroslavsky now grasped the need for a servile mea culpa, whatever the facts of the party's past and his own, as Iaroslavsky put it, limited role in the work in question. In a letter published in *Pravda* on December 10, he acknowledged "a series of the most crude errors" on his part that included Trotskyist interpretations that deviated from an objective presentation of the party's history. Volume 4, he confessed, repeated the Trotskyist slander about the Bolshevik party in February and March 1917. It also failed to acknowledge that in October, the revolution completed the bourgeois-democratic revolution only as an "auxiliary result" of the grand socialist revolution. And yet Iaroslavsky still hoped to wriggle free of much of the blame. He was guilty only in so far as he had chosen his authors badly. No longer in a mood to protect Kin, Iaroslavsky insisted that the young historian had not served him well. Iaroslavsky added that his poor choices and careless editing of the volumes in question resulted in part "from my excessive burden of work and inordinate trust in those members of the authors' collective who are not thoroughly imbued with party loyalty."[40]

Nevertheless, the assault on Iaroslavsky and his work continued. On December 29, Iaroslavsky wrote Lev Zakharovich Mekhlis, editor of *Pravda*, that he had not been given, as promised, an opportunity to comment on a recent sharply critical review of the four volumes that had appeared that day in *Pravda*. He had been tricked from seeing it, Iaroslavsky bitterly claimed, by the newspaper's staff.[41] Mekhlis responded that very day with a nasty but perhaps correct assessment. Iaroslavsky had imagined a conspiracy against him out of his own emotional and psychological stress. "It seems to me (excuse me if I speak too harshly)," Mekhlis wrote, "that your letter is the result of a nervous condition."[42]

On January 1, Iaroslavsky still had some fight left, notwithstanding his several public confessions of guilt. That day, he wrote *Bol'shevik* to object to its editorial of November 30. Iaroslavsky admitted that the fourth volume contained errors, but he could not agree that "supposedly the history of October is largely depicted in a Trotskyist rather than Leninist spirit."[43] On January 12, the board responded. It wanted to know just what specifically he found objectionable in its editorial.[44] The next day, obviously under great stress, Iaroslavsky wrote a furious note to one the board's editors, Aleksandr Ivanovich Krinitsky, in angry strokes replete with crossovers and additions (fig. 8.2). "I have written to you earlier about my disagreements with the editorial in *Bol'shevik* and the review of the fourth volume of a five-volume 'History of the Communist Party.' I do not see any need to repeat what I've already written. It would have made some sense *before* the appearance of the journal's issue, but I believe it now completely unnecessary." Iaroslavsky signed it "with communist greetings."[45] It was probably never sent.

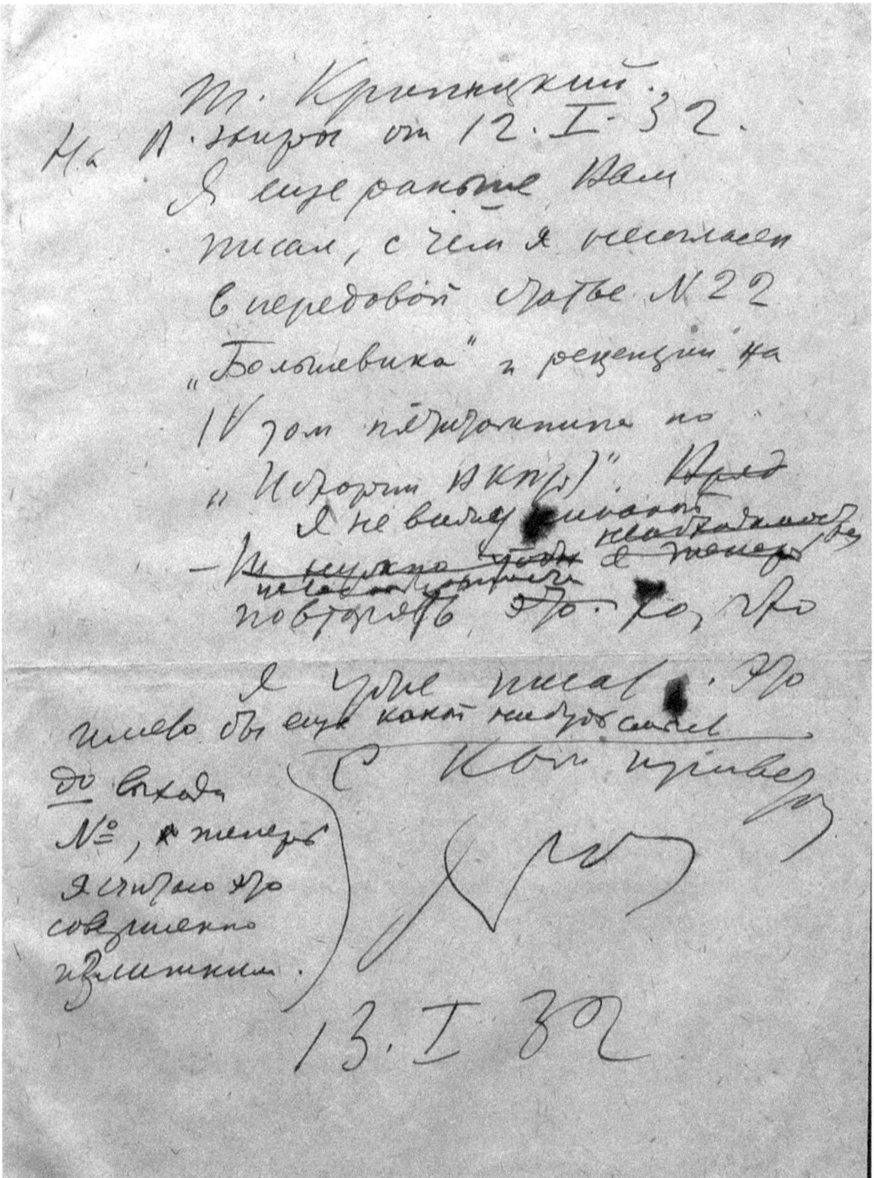
Т. Криницкий.
На В. записку от 12.I.32.
Я еще раньше Вам
писал, с чем я несогласен
в передовой статье № 22
„Большевика" и рецензии на
IV том хрестоматии по
„Истории ВКП(б)". ~~Вред~~
Я не вижу никакой необходимости
~~И нужно ... и теперь~~
повторять это. То, что
я уже писал, это
имело бы еще какой-нибудь смысл
до выхода №, а теперь
я считаю это
совершенно
излишним.
С ком. приветом
Яр
13.I.32

Figure 8.2. Iaroslavsky's response to the editorial board of *Bol'shevik*, January 13, 1932. Courtesy of the Russian State Archive of Social and Political History.

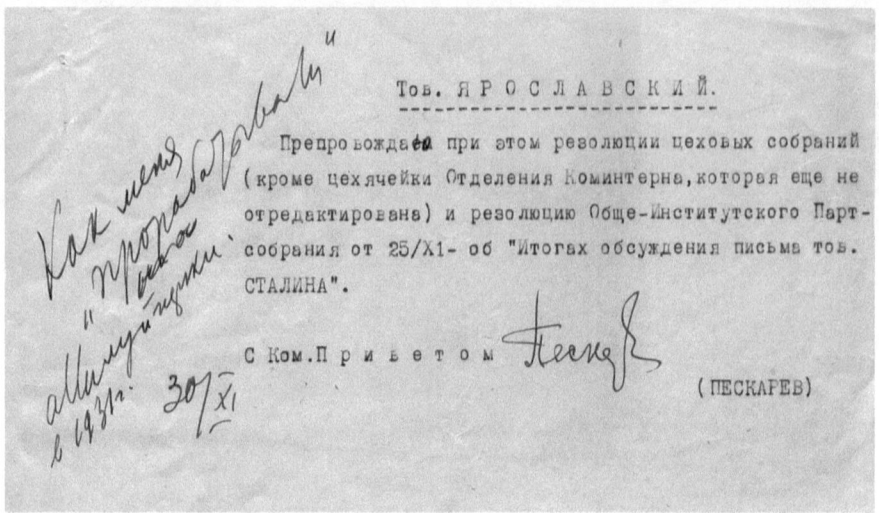

Figure 8.3. Iaroslavsky: "How the hallelujah chorus worked me over in 1931." Courtesy of the Russian State Archive of Social and Political History.

A week later, Stalin summoned Iaroslavsky to his office. As Iaroslavsky recalled the meeting the next day in correspondence with his colleagues, Stalin telephoned Mekhlis at *Pravda* with instructions to end the harsh criticism and mentioned that *Bol'shevik* should end it as well.[46] Although public censure largely ceased, Iaroslavsky's resentment lingered. Sometime later, he dashed off another angry handwritten comment. He did so on a note sent to him earlier, in late November, that informed him of resolutions on Stalin's letter that were adopted on November 15 by the party organization at the Institute of Red Professors. Iaroslavsky recalled "how the hallelujah chorus worked me over in 1931" (fig. 8.3).[47]

Nevertheless, Iaroslavsky soon recovered nicely enough to play a prominent role over the next six years in the compilation of an official history of the party. Ironically, he had become the beneficiary of Stalin's self-appointed role as historian-in-chief.

With his letter to *Proletarskaia revoliutsiia*, Stalin launched the first of his many forays to manipulate and rewrite the party's history. He wanted, as David Brandenberger has called it, a "single, animated, evocative narrative."[48] Stalin drafted several historians, Iaroslavsky prominent among them, to the project. Its sensitivity and Stalin's meddling led to "false start after false start."[49] However, one theme emerged. In an increasingly insistent manner, Stalin demanded a story, albeit now in exaggerated form, that had dominated Istpart's eventual grand narrative for 1917. In a thorough rewrite of the final product in summer 1938, Stalin insisted (much like Istpart had by 1928) on the party's control of events from the center, the insignificance of spontaneous activity by workers and peasants (and by non-Russian nationalities), and the relative absence of a distinctive history in one or another province. Stalin and his coterie of historians thereby produced the *Short Course*, published in fall 1938.⁵⁰

Immediately after the its publication, well-meaning commentators faulted the book for neglect of the party's history in the regions. At a meeting of party propagandists on October 1, 1938, Stalin responded in his customary pedantic and didactic manner: "Some people complain that there is little said here about Moscow." "That is true," he continued. "And there is nothing here about our comrades from the Urals, Baku, or Khar'kov. But if we satisfied all these people, what would we have? It would not be a history of our party but rather a collection of essays on the revolutionary movement in various regions of the country."⁵¹

So much for Viatka. So much for history.

NOTES

1. David Brandenberger has noted that much of Stalin's commentary in the 1920s about 1917 "was *ad hoc* and fragmentary." After the dispute over Trotsky's "Lessons of October," "Stalin said little more of note about 1917 for the remainder of the decade"; Brandenberger, "Stalin's Rewriting of 1917," *Russian Review* 76, no. 4 (October 2017): 669, 672.

2. This summary relies considerably on several works: Brandenberger, "Stalin's Rewriting of 1917," 674–689; David Brandenberger, *Propaganda State in Crisis: Soviet Ideology, Political Indoctrination, and Stalinist Terror, 1927–1941* (New Haven, CT: Yale University Press, 2011), 51–66, 142–161, 198–215; and the commentary and documents in M. V. Zelenov, ed., *I. V. Stalin. Istoricheskaia ideologiia v SSSR v 1920–1950-e gody: Perepiska s istorikami, stat'i i zametki po istorii, stenogrammy vystuplenii*, pt. 1, *1920–1930-e gody* (St. Petersburg: "Nauka-Piter," 2006), especially 291–439.

3. *Istoriia Vsesoiuznoi Kommunisticheskoi Partii (bol'shevikov): Kratkii kurs* (Moscow: Gosudarstvennoe izdatel'stvo politicheskoi literatury, 1938).

4. A. Slutsky, "Bol'sheviki o germanskoi sotsial-demokratii v period ee predvoennogo krizisa," *PR*, no. 6 (June 1930), 38–73. Slutsky headed a group formed in 1929 in the Communist Academy's History Institute for the study of German Social Democracy and the Second International before 1914. On the discussion of German Social Democracy, see Barber, *Soviet Historians in Crisis*, 107–117.

5. For a discussion of the complexity of Kautsky's views, see Stanley Pierson, *Marxist Intellectuals and the Working-Class Mentality in Germany, 1887–1912* (Cambridge, MA: Harvard University Press, 1993), 229–255.

6. I. Stalin, "O nekotorykh voprosakh istorii bol'shevizma. Pis'mo v redaktsiiu zhurnala 'Proletarskoi revoliutsii'," *PR*, no. 6 (113) (1931), 3–12. On the date of submission, see V. V. Krylov, "Iz istorii zhurnala 'Proletarskaia revoliutsiia' (1921–1941)," *Sovetskie arkhivy*, no. 3 (1974), 69, reference n. 42. The issue was submitted for printing on October 28.

7. Stalin, "O nekotorykh voprosakh," 3.

8. Stalin, "O nekotorykh voprosakh," 9–10.

9. See the announcement in *Pravda*, December 7, 1931, 4. I. V. Stalin, *O nekotorykh voprosakh istorii bol'shevizma: Pis'mo v redaktsiiu zhurnala "Proletarskaia revoliutsiia"* (Moscow: Moskovskii rabochii, 1931). The issue of *PR* that initially carried Stalin's letter had an unusually high press run of eight thousand copies, three thousand more than was customary at the time.

10. For a description and analysis of controversies, see Barber, *Soviet Historians*, 126–136; Aleksei Litvin, *Bez prava na mysl': Istoriki v epokhu Bol'shego Terrora. Ocherki sudeb* (Kazan: Tatarskoe knizhnoe izdatel'stvo, 1994), 28, 51. After printing Stalin's letter, *Proletarskaia revoliutsiia* suspended publication in 1932 to reappear only in 1933 with a new editorial board. Some party historians did not for the moment regard Stalin's letter as the definitive word regarding methodology. See Robert C. Tucker, "The Rise of Stalin's Revolutionary Cult," *American Historical Review* 84, no. 2 (April 1999): 360; Robert C. Tucker, *Stalin in Power: The Revolution from Above, 1928–1941* (New York: Norton, 1990), 156–159; Barber, *Soviet Historians*, 132–133. On the controversy over Iaroslavsky's work, discussed below, see Piontkovsky's diary, *Dnevnik istorika S. A. Piontkovskogo (1927–1934)* (Kazan: Kazanskii gosudarstvennyi universitet, 2009), 375, 441–447. These same sources discuss a clumsy, if not unwitting, distinction by one of the authors of the fourth volume, I. I. Mints, between political expediency and scholarly objectivity. He was told that there was no such distinction. *Proletarskaia revoliutsiia*'s editorial board was not at first sufficiently self-critical of its publication of Slutsky's article. On October 20, 1931, in response to commentary preceding Stalin's, it had rushed to note that Slutsky's article had been labeled "for discussion purposes" and had been published before a majority of the board's members had read it. It too modestly, as it turned out, promised a reevaluation of the pre-war relationship between Bolsheviks and the Second International. Seven days later, on October 27, now aware of Stalin's objections, the board duly condemned the article's publication and its, the board's, explanation of October 20. See both responses in *PR*, no. 6 (113) (1931), 199, 13.

11. Stalin, "O nekotorykh voprosakh," 12. Stalin also criticized in passing as "anti-Leninist and Trotskyist contraband" the book, *Course on Party History* (Kurs istorii VKP(b), by Vladislav Ottonovich Volosevich. Stalin was aware of Volosevich's predicament if only because the victim himself had informed him. In a letter of March 17, 1931, Volosevich asked for Stalin's help in blunting

criticism at his place of work, Leningrad's Military-Technical Academy. See Zelenov, *I. V. Stalin*, 123.

12. Em. Iaroslavskii, ed., *Istoriia VKP(b)*, vol. 4 (Moscow-Leningrad: Gosudarstvennoe izdatel'stvo, 1929). On the compilation and authors of the work, including those of the fourth volume, see Litvin, *Bez prava*, 102–103, 169–171.

13. RGASPI, f. 70, op. 1, d. 15, ll. 45, 47.

14. RGASPI, f. 70, op. 1, d. 15, l. 1.

15. The review by K. Sidorov also covered the third volume. See *PR*, no. 11 (94) (November 1929), 264–281. On noting that Iaroslavsky edited the multivolume work, Enteen assessed that it was Iaroslavsky's "most controversial work and also the most scholarly in his entire output." Enteen, "Writing Party History," 329.

16. *PR*, no. 11 (94) (November 1929), 273.

17. *Istoriia VKP(b)*, 5–6.

18. *Istoriia VKP(b)*, 77–78.

19. *Istoriia VKP(b)*, 53, 75–78, 93, 114, 137. Kin was the author of the chapters on March and April.

20. RGASPI, f. 89, op. 7, d. 72, l. 1.

21. Em. Iaroslavsky, "Bol'sheviki v fevral'sko-martovskie dni 1917 g.," *PR*, no. 2–3 (61–62) (February–March 1927), 39–40.

22. RGASPI, f. 89, op. 7, d. 72, ll. 1–2. Shliapnikov hoped to publish even more, but the State Publishing House ruled against a repetition of a "crude anti-party falsification of party history and of the revolution." RGASPI, f. 72, op. 3, d. 1010, l. 49. In late November 1934, Shliapnikov wrote Stalin requesting that he facilitate publication of his memoir on the civil war in the Northern Caucasus (where Shliapnikov had briefly served); Allen, *Alexander Shlyapnikov*, 347.

23. *Dnevnik istorika*, 442. For doing so, Piontkovsky called Kin a "complete blockhead" (442). At a subsequent meeting, Iaroslavsky showed Piontkovsky and others where, Iaroslavsky insisted, he did not write what Kin had alleged (443). Either Iaroslavsky showed some other book rather than the one in question or pointed to pages other than those which Kin had in mind. Kin knew in 1930 of Stalin's growing sensitivity about the leader's conduct in March 1917. See the commentary and documents to follow in Zelenov, *I. V. Stalin*, 113–122, especially 121.

24. *Dnevnik istorika*, 442. This information is based on Piontkovsky's recollection of a meeting of several authors of the fourth volume, including Kin and himself, with Iaroslavsky on November 11. For an interpretation that Kamenev's and Stalin's views were not fundamentally but only tactically distinct from those held by Lenin, see the article by Lars T. Lih, "All Power to the Soviets," https://johnriddell.wordpress.com/2017/03/23/all-power-to-the-soviets-part-1-biography-of-a-slogan/, and the critical response by S. A. Smith in an interview in *Revolutionary Russia* 31, no. 2 (2018): 223–224.

25. G. Petrov, "Ob istorii Oktiabr'skoi revoliutsii (Istoriia VKP(b) t. IV. Pod obshchei redaktsiei Em. Iaroslavskogo)," *Pravda*, November 18, 1931, 4.

26. *Istoriia VKP(b)*, vol. 4., 238. Several pages later, Piontkovsky modified his prose somewhat to say that the revolution only "in passing" brought an end to the "bourgeois-democratic revolution" (240).

27. RGASPI, f. 89, op. 7, d. 73, l. 2a. Iaroslavsky brought up the related matter of 1905. He insisted that in that year Lenin spoke of "two wars" in the countryside.

28. RGASPI, f. 89, op. 7, d. 72, l. 2a.

29. Zelenov, *V. I. Stalin*, 142–143, quote on 143.

30. Em. Iaroslavsky, "V redaktsiiu 'Bol'shevik'," *Bol'shevik*, no. 21 (November 15, 1931), 84–86. Stalin had seen an earlier draft of the confession. He wrote no commentary on it. See Zelenov, *I. V. Stalin*, 140–141.

31. *Dnevnik istorika*, 451. Piontkovsky recalled this, an earlier and undated scene, in his diary entry of February 3, 1932. Many years later, another of his colleagues spoke of Iaroslavsky's despondency and fears of worse to come: M. V. Zelenov and D. Brandenberger, eds., *Kratkii kurs istorii VKP(b). Tekst i ego istorii*, pt. 1, *Istoriia teksta "Kratkogo kursa istorii VKP(b),"* 1931–1956 (Moscow: ROSSPEN, 2014), 721.

32. Zelenov, *I. V. Stalin*, 144. Iaroslavsky mentioned that at a recent plenary session of the party's Central Committee, Stalin had promised to do so.

33. Zelenov, *I. V. Stalin*, 145.

34. "Za bol'shevistskoe izuchenie istorii partii," *Pravda*, December 12, 1931, 2–3.

35. The editorial: "Postavit' delo izucheniia istorii nashei partii na nauchnye bol'shevistskie rel'sy," *Bol'shevik*, no. 22 (November 30, 1931), 1–7. The evaluation: "Protiv fal'sifikatsii istorii Oktiabria pod flagom 'ob"ektivnosti'," *Bol'shevik*, no. 22 (November 30, 1931), 68–78.

36. "Postavit' delo izucheniia istorii," 4.

37. "Protiv fal'sifikatsii istorii Oktiabria," 72, 75, 78.

38. Em. Iaroslavsky, "Ob odnoi fal'sifikatsii istorii nashei partii," *Bol'shevik*, no. 22 (November 30, 1931), 66–68, quote on 68. And yet Iaroslavsky continued in back channels to defray if not limit the damage to *Katorga i ssylka*. In early 1932, *Istorik-Marksist* published a shrill editorial, "For a Decisive Restructuring of the Historical Front." Among other inflammatory remarks, it denounced *Katorga i ssylka* for a failure to provide a "Bolshevik history of penal servitude and exile," *IM*, no. 1–2 (23–24) (1932), 10. The following issue of *Istorik-Marksist* featured an article sharply critical of an item that had recently appeared in *Katorga i ssylka*. *IM*, no. 3 (25) (1932), 142–164. According to Dahlke, Iaroslavsky agreed with the criticism of his organization's publication but not entirely. He wrote to the editorial board of *Istorik-Marksist* that *Katorga i ssylka* must undergo Bolshevik criticism. But he then added that if the board of *Istorik-Marksist*

found it necessary to change the profile of the journal, then it should put the matter before the party's Central Committee for a decision. See Sandra Dahlke, *Individuum und Herrschaft im Stalinismus: Emel'jan Jaroslavskij (1878–1943)* (Munich: R. Oldenbourg Verlag, 2010), 258.

39. Zelenov, *I. V. Stalin*, 153.

40. E. Iaroslavsky, "V redaktsiiu 'Pravdy'", *Pravda*, December 10, 1931, 4. Iaroslavsky's draft of the letter is in RGASPI, f. 89, op. 7, d. 72, ll. 9–15. There he discussed, among other subjects, the work's grievous errors regarding Populism, the period from 1905 to 1907, Rosa Luxemburg, and the national question in 1917. A meeting with Stalin on December 9 may have played a role in Iaroslavsky's most vigorous mea culpa to date.

41. RGASPI, f. 89, op. 7, d. 72, ll. 39–40. The article in question was by one of the volume's authors: N. Popov, "Ob izvrashcheniiakh vzgliadov leninskoi partii na pererastanie burzhuazno-demokraticheskoi revoliutsii v sotsialisticheskuiu," *Pravda*, December 29, 1931, 2–3.

42. RGASPI, f. 89, op. 7, d. 73, l. 41.

43. RGASPI, f. 89, op. 7, d. 73, l. 47. Iaroslavsky also expressed his dismay at Popov's harshly critical review that had appeared in *Pravda* on December 29. Iaroslavsky declared that he was not obligated to assent when "comrades pile up their own mistakes": RGASPI, f. 89, op. 7, d. 73, l. 47.

44. RGASPI, f. 89, op. 7, d. 73, l. 48.

45. RGASPI, f. 89, op. 7, d. 73, l. 49.

46. See Iaroslavsky's letter of January 21, 1932, in Zelenov and Brandenberger, *Kratkii kurs*, 113. On January 20, Iaroslavsky entered Stalin's office at 4:05 p.m. and left at 4:25. Later that day, Mekhlis entered Stalin's office at 9:20 p.m. and departed at 9:30. *Na prieme u Stalina. Tetradi (zhurnaly) zapisei lits, priniatykh I. V. Stalinym (1924–1953 gg.)* (Moscow: Novyi khronograf, 2008). This source is available at http://istmat.info/node/165 (accessed July 16, 2020).

47. RGASPI, f. 89, op. 7, d. 74, l. 1. The note was sent by Georgii Sergeevich Peskarev, a student at the Institute of Red Professors. In a letter to Stalin on August 16, 1932, Iaroslavsky referred to the "hallelujah chorus that now makes a political career of working me over." Zelenov and Brandenberger, *Kratkii kurs*, 128. Three years later, Iaroslavsky wrote a colleague of his bitterness over the earlier criticism by party historians who were, in his opinion, far less worthy than he to write about the past. "I have lived through and suffered the party's history unlike many red professors, who have experienced nothing of the sort, who only stitch together quotations." Zelenov and Brandenberger, *Kratkii kurs*, 194.

48. Brandenberger, *Propaganda State*, 38. Stalin also read and edited material submitted for a history of the Russian Civil War, published under Maxim Gorky's name in 1935, and a school textbook on the history of the USSR by Andrei Shestakov published in 1937.

49. Brandenberger, *Propaganda State*, 35. For documentation of the zigs and zags, the "false starts," see Zelenov and Brandenberger, *Kratkii kurs*, 115–420.

50. Brandenberger characterizes the product as a "textbook that was not only inaccessible, but confusing and inconsistent as well": *Propaganda State*, 215. Stalin had removed heroes from the script, including much of his own real and inflated self, and many villains. The *Short Course* appeared first in serial form in *Pravda* in September and then as a book in October. It did speak in some detail about Kamenev's treachery in March and April and Stalin's alleged opposition to it: *Istoriia Vsesoiuznoi Kommunisticheskoi partii*, 176. For drafts of the *Short Course* and Stalin's extensive editing, see David Brandenberger and Mikhail Zelenov, eds., *Stalin's Master Narrative: A Critical Edition of the History of the Communist Party of the Soviet Union (Bolsheviks), Short Course* (New Haven, CT: Yale University Press, 2019).

51. Zelenov, *I. V. Stalin*, 399. See Stalin's similar dismissive response at an earlier session, September 27, to criticism of an inadequate attention to the activity of individual people: Zelenov and Brandenberger, *Kratkii kurs*, 429–430.

NINE

Their Fate

IN 1939, *PROLETARSKAIA REVOLIUTSIIA* PUBLISHED Iaroslavsky's article, "Stalin as a Historian of the Party's History." In it, he extolled the Soviet leader's earlier letter to the journal as a "decisive blow against attempts to drag Trotskyist contraband into literature on the party's history."[1] Iaroslavsky joined the party's Central Committee in 1939 and remained there until his death in 1943 (fig. 9.1).

In 1933, Ol'minsky and Gusev died of natural causes, as did Elizarova two years later. In 1932, Savel'ev chaired the presidium of the Communist Academy. From 1936 until his death in1939, he served as the deputy director of the Marx-Engels-Lenin Institute. Shestakov led a team of historians that wrote a textbook for the elementary school on the history of Russia and the Soviet Union. It underwent multiple editions from 1937 until 1955, extending well beyond his own death in 1941. Dubrovsky survived two arrests, imprisonment, and exile to end his career at the History Institute of the Academy of Sciences. He died in 1970.

After charges of mismanagement of funds in 1933 and his purge from the party, Liubovikov was removed from his post as head of Viatka's Museum of the Revolution. He recovered soon enough with restoration of his party membership and appointment as a state arbiter in 1935 and chief arbiter for the Kirov region in 1938. After several strokes, he retired in 1944. Liubovikov died in Kirov in 1974. During the 1930s, both Tokarev and Tsaregorodtsev taught at Kirov's Pedagogical Institute and thereafter at several military academies. Their careers were not without controversy. Another of their joint efforts, a history of the Viatka party organization from 1903 to 1933 (sponsored by the

Figure 9.1. Iaroslavsky addresses the Seventh Conference of the Young Communist League, July 1932. Courtesy of the Russian State Documentary Film and Photo Archive.

regional party committee in 1936) encountered severe criticism. Their detractor claimed to have found the "grossest political mistakes" and an "extremely liberal evaluation of Trotskyism."[2] In October 1937, the party removed Tokarev from its ranks and from his position at the local pedagogical institute, only to restore him to both the following February.[3]

In late 1927, Novoselov left Viatka for the Northern Caucasus. By 1929, he served as the deputy head of the Maikop regional party committee's department that was responsible for record keeping and the assignment of the party's leading cadre. Six years later, Novoselov was in Moscow working as a party official in the Institute of Ferrous Metals and Gold. There he fell victim to an absurdity that eclipsed anything he had experienced earlier in his dispute with Kuchkin, one now fit for the caustic pen of the nineteenth-century Russian novelist Mikhail Saltykov-Shchedrin.[4]

In June 1935, the party committee for Moscow's Lenin district (an area that included Novoselov's institute) examined the past and present status of all of its members. Its verification commission reported that the party in Viatka had removed Novoselov in 1921 and readmitted him only in 1925.[5] It was a sloppy investigation that neglected to assess the party's own records. That material would have indicated, as discussed previously, that after joining the party in Viatka's Urzhum district in August 1920, Novoselov had diligently carried out his duties as head of the local agitprop. He had not been purged.[6] That post and Novoselov's subsequent appointment as head of Viatka's Istpart were hardly positions accessible to anyone expelled at that time from the party's ranks. A report from the party organization in the city of Viatka in late 1924 indicated that Novoselov had never been a member of any other political party and made no mention of any purge from the party's ranks.[7]

Nevertheless, in 1935, the verification commission insisted on Novoselov's earlier expulsion. He had allegedly made matters worse by a refusal to reveal it in subsequent reviews (and purges) of the party's membership in 1929 and 1933. The commission thought it had sufficient proof of Novoselov's treachery in his own hand. In an application (*otchetnaia kartochka*) for a new party card during an exchange of the items in March 1927, he had written "1925" (not 1920) as the year of his admission into the party (fig. 9.2). The document had been sent, as was customary, to Moscow for safekeeping. A member of the verification commission summoned the item and demonstrably circled "1925." It was apparent proof that until that year Novoselov had been beyond the party's pale since his purported expulsion in 1921.

To write "1925" was a terrible, if understandable, clerical error on Novoselov's part. Perhaps he had in mind his entry into a "new" party that had been

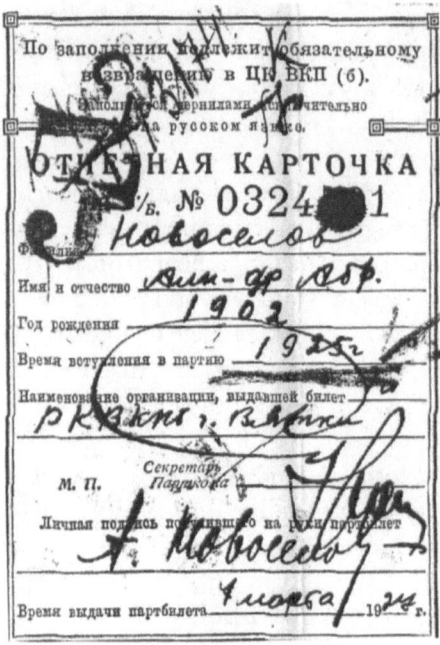

Figure 9.2. Novoselov's application for a party card, 1927. Courtesy of the Russian State Archive of Social and Political History.

renamed in December 1925. Previously, it had been the "Russian Communist Party" but now became the "All-Union Communist Party." In early 1927, that rechristening triggered the exchange of older party cards, including Novoselov's, for ones that displayed the party's new title.

Two years later, on June 25, 1929, Novoselov corrected his error. He had lost or spoiled his party card and applied to the Maikop party organization for a replacement (fig. 9.3). He correctly wrote August 1920 (not 1925) as his date of entry into the party. But the commission concluded that the maneuver was evidence of Novoselov's deception—one repeated in 1933, it said in a subsequent review of party records. The local party committee purged Novoselov. One of its officials took Novoselov's application in 1929 for a new card and scrawled in bold letters across its top "canceled" and, in smaller hand along its edge, "purged."

Novoselov's fate following this turn of events is unknown. His name does not appear in any published registers that catalog victims of the terror from 1936 to 1938. Admittedly, however, that record is incomplete; new names are added on a frequent basis. Anyone such as Novoselov purged from the party in 1935 was likely a candidate for far worse.

Figure 9.3. Novoselov's application for a party card, 1929. Courtesy of the Russian State Archive of Social and Political History.

We know for certain the terrible fate of many other people who were prominent in Istpart's history. On October 16, 1937, the police arrested Kapustin (fig. 9.4), head of the Central Committee's Press Department. The following year, on April 21, the Military Collegium of the USSR's Supreme Court sentenced him to death for participation in an alleged counterrevolutionary terrorist organization. His execution followed that very day. He shared the fate of Shliapnikov, who was arrested September 2, 1936, sentenced to death by the same collegium on September 2, 1937, and shot the next day. In August 1937, Soviet police arrested Kin, among others, at the History Institute of the Academy of Sciences. On February 8, 1937, the collegium sentenced him to death for membership in a counterrevolutionary terrorist organization. He was executed the same day. Months later, on May 25, the collegium sentenced Nevsky; his execution followed the next day. Kanatchikov was probably executed that same year. Arrested October 7, 1937, Piontkovsky was shot March 8, 1938.[8]

After a long struggle with cancer, Pokrovsky died April 10, 1932. Almost a month later, on May 4, Piontkovsky uncharitably wrote in his diary: "The historian in him spoiled the politician, and the politician spoiled the historian and, in fact, he died having been neither a historian nor a politician."[9] An assault

Figure 9.4. P. P. Kapustin, St. Mark's Square, Venice, 1936. Courtesy of the State Archive of the Social and Political History of the Kirov Region.

already underway on Pokrovsky's alleged exaggeration of economics in history and opposition to a systematic study of the past intensified in his absence. In 1939 and 1940, the Academy of Sciences sponsored the publication of two large and spiteful volumes denouncing the former dean of party historians.[10] His student, Pankratova, contributed the lead article in the initial volume.[11]

Years earlier, in 1936, the party had expelled Pankratova from its ranks and dismissed her the following year from her position at Moscow State University, exiling her to Saratov. Restored to party membership and back in Moscow in 1938, Pankratova turned with a vengeance not just on Pokrovsky but also on Piontkovsky, an allegedly Trotskyist pseudo-historian.[12] In fall 1941, Pankratova and a group of historians from the History Institute of the Academy of Sciences left Moscow, then under threat of German occupation, for Alma-Ata, the capital of the Soviet republic of Kazakhstan. Under her direction, they wrote a *History of the Kazakh Republic from the Earliest Times to the Present*, published in 1943 and nominated for the Stalin prize.[13] The volume soon encountered a negative response for an alleged anti-Russian glorification of Kazakh resistance to tsarist colonial conquest. Pankratova responded with a stern defense of the work.[14] Its nomination for the Stalin Prize was nevertheless withdrawn, and a revised edition followed in 1949 with less admiration for Kazakh defiance. Following Stalin's death in 1953, as editor of the Academy of Sciences journal *Voprosy istorii*, Pankratova played a key role in the relaxation of administrative and political control over the historical profession. Her efforts in the journal led to a controversial reevaluation of the party's activity in 1917, one much in keeping with that made by historians during the early and mid-1920s.[15]

More so than anyone else in this story, Viatka's Kuchkin enjoyed a long career with only a whiff of disgrace. After responding in 1928 to Novoselov, he remained in Moscow to graduate from the Institute of Red Professors. He continued his self-promotion and his heavy-handed criticism of historians and memoirists. In the pages of *Proletarskaia revoliutsiia* in late 1928, Kuchkin reviewed a book on the activity during the civil war of the Red Army's Twenty-Seventh Division, in which he had served as a political commissar. Kuchkin accused the author of "military illiteracy" and for writing what amounted to "muddle."[16] Several months later in the same journal, Kuchkin spoke of his own heroic activity before 1917 as a Bolshevik agitator among soldiers and workers in Beloretsk and Ufa.[17] After the publication of Stalin's letter in *Proletarskaia revoliutsiia*, Kuchkin submitted a savage attack to the journal in December 1931, "Against a Trotskyist Distortion of History," on a collection of articles, *The History of the Bolshevik Party*, published that year. Kuchkin denounced any hint that Stalin belonged to a Bolshevik right wing in early 1917 and said such a notion was "Trotskyist slander."[18] The journal did not print it.

From 1934 to 1940, Kuchkin worked at the Marx-Engels-Lenin Institute and from 1940 in the History Institute of the Academy of Sciences.[19] During the 1930s, he was one of many historians working on an official party history. He was chiefly responsible for writing the section on 1917. Kuchkin acknowledged it was a difficult task. In 1936, he shared with several colleagues his anxiety over the political sensitivity of the subject. He had spent "a great deal of time" on the period before Lenin's arrival in Petrograd in April. In particular, he had been working diligently to show how Stalin's positions had "fully coincided" with Lenin's. Moreover, Kuchkin was "troubled" by the issue at the heart of his earlier conflict with Viatka's Istpart. Kuchkin wondered whether he should show the extent, if at all, of the presence of local organizations that united Mensheviks and Bolsheviks in 1917. "Is this necessary?" he asked.[20]

Two years later, more sure of himself, Kuchkin ably demonstrated how to extol Stalin. In *The Great October Socialist Revolution*, he insisted that in February 1917, the Bolsheviks failed to seize leadership of the Petrograd Soviet because Stalin and Lenin were absent from the city. Stalin remained in exile at the moment. That April, Stalin rallied the party to seek the overthrow of the bourgeois government. Soon thereafter, he formulated plans for the October uprising and, as the head of the party's Central Committee, alongside Lenin, led the successful revolt that followed.[21]

In 1941, Kuchkin accompanied Pankratova's group to Alma-Ata, where he joined its effort to prepare a history of Kazakhstan. When the work encountered censure, Kuchkin embraced the latest nuance of official orthodoxy. Pankratova complained privately in May 1945 that her colleague too readily confessed to alleged errors of "nationalism."[22] In 1946, however, Kuchkin invited controversy with an article, "The Sovietization of the Kazakh Countryside (1926–1929)," published in *Voprosy istorii*.[23] He portrayed the Soviet Kazakh republic during the early and mid-1920s as a backward, patriarchal, and feudal society in which the Communist Party and national government had little influence. State power was firmly established only with the elections of local soviets in 1928 and 1929, when Kazakhstan's peasantry finally overthrew the dominance of wealthy landowners. "The Kazakh people," Kuchkin concluded, "at last exercised self-determination in creating an independent nation." Kazakhs thereby skipped the capitalist stage of development, moving directly from a semifeudal to a socialist society.[24]

With his article, Kuchkin stirred up a hornet's nest. The historian Lowell Tillett has ably described the environment in which Kuchkin then worked. Discussions in the immediate postwar period among Soviet historians about the non-Russian republics were difficult for all involved. The party's views,

Tillett noted, "were expressed in such piecemeal fashion and with so many apparent contradictions that even the most attentive and compliant historians could not make sense of them." In particular, "in the tortured rewriting of the history of the non-Russian peoples, the case of Kazakhstan had no rival."[25] Kuchkin's article became a case in point. Harsh criticism followed, especially from party and state officials in Kazakhstan and from historians, many of them Kazakhs. Kuchkin had committed "flagrant political mistakes" by underestimating the party's and state's influence. He had also erred grievously by allowing Kazakhs with, implicitly, only limited help from Russians to create a "nation" in an exercise of "self-determination." Characteristically, Kuchkin held fast to his argument, often resorting, as was his wont, to tough and sarcastic language. However, he admitted to an excessively gloomy assessment of the party's influence in the republic during the 1920s.[26] Years later, in a large book that exceeded four hundred pages on exactly the same subject, Kuchkin repeated his main arguments, although he replaced his comment about Kazakh "self-determination" with mention of "a transformation of the Kazakh people into a socialist nation."[27] Nevertheless, sharp criticism followed again of his portrayal of the party's and state's alleged weakness there during the 1920s. He responded in kind.[28]

Kuchkin avoided further controversy when contributing to a magisterial multivolume history of Russia and the Soviet Union.[29] He served as the chief editor of the ninth volume, *The Formation of Socialism in the USSR, 1933–1941*.[30] In its conclusion, Kuchkin echoed its authors' main theses. In the face of numerous internal and external enemies, he wrote, the Soviet government under Stalin had greatly enhanced the country's defensive and industrial capacity.[31]

Notwithstanding his status as a prominent historian, Kuchkin remained sensitive to a fault over the earlier dispute surrounding his activity in Viatka. In 1957, he reissued his article published in the May 1927 issue of *Proletarskaia revoliutsiia*, one that had prompted harsh criticism from Novoselov and Viatka's Istpart.[32] It appeared in a book of memoirs, *For the Power of Soviets*, sponsored by Kirov's regional party committee to mark the fortieth anniversary of the October Revolution. Kuchkin repeated his embellished version of his role in 1917. He also self-consciously brought up, again, his controversial signature on the Menshevik declaration inviting all of the city's social democrats, Mensheviks and Bolsheviks alike, to a meeting. An experienced warrior against Menshevism, he explained, he had vacillated, but he signed the item in hope, as he had argued earlier in his dispute with Novoselov, of attracting Bolsheviks unknown to him to the meeting. They would then demonstrably exit the hall to create their own organization. Kuchkin now hastened to add to his earlier account in *Proletarskaia revoliutsiia* what Novoselov had eventually forced him to say: "I regretted that I had signed a Menshevik declaration." Kuchkin then added that in Ufa, before 1917, he had conducted a decisive struggle with Mensheviks.[33] He ended his essay with a flourish. In early 1917, Viatka's Bolsheviks, implicitly under his guidance, aggressively fought with Mensheviks and with SRs. His signature on the Menshevik proclamation should in no way serve as an occasion to conclude that Viatka's Bolshevik organization "hatched from a Menshevik egg."[34]

A year later, in 1958, Kuchkin remained aggressive but less forthcoming in his ninety-page memoir devoted entirely to his activity in Viatka in 1917. At great length, he insisted that in the face of vigorous opposition from Mensheviks and SRs, he had successfully agitated for the Bolshevik cause before and after February 1917. In his purportedly successful effort to create a Bolshevik organization in Viatka, at no time did he cooperate with the Mensheviks. In this extended version of events, Kuchkin made nary a mention of his signature on any proclamation.[35] Eleven years later, in an account of his role as a political commissar in the Red Army in 1918 and 1919, Kuchkin interrupted his narrative to burnish his earlier credentials as an uncompromising Bolshevik in Viatka. He had addressed a local soviet dominated by SRs and Mensheviks expressly to denounce their betrayal of the revolution.[36]

For his loyal service to his party, Kuchkin received two Orders of Lenin. He died in 1973.

NOTES

1. Em. Iaroslavsky, "Stalin kak istorik VKP(b)," *PR*, no. 4 (1939), 97. Iaroslavsky experienced difficulties, as so many others did, in 1936. See Enteen, "Writing Party History," 327.

2. GASPI KO, f. P-45, op. 1, d. 195, ll. 86–93, quotes on l. 86.

3. For a biographical sketch of Tokarev's professional life, see I. A. Solov'eva, "Pervyi dekan istoricheskogo fakul'teta Kirovskogo gosudarstvennogo pedagogicheskogo instituta," in *Viatskaia zemlia v proshlom i nastoiashchem: Sbornik materialov*, vol. 1 (Kirov: Izdatel'stvo ViatGGU, 2014), 28–33.

4. For a discussion of Novoselov's subsequent fate, I rely on documents sent on October 11, 2017, by RGASPI. They include copies of Novoselov's application for a party card in Viatka on March 7, 1927, and in Maikop on June 25, 1929. RGASPI also sent a report of the findings of a verification commission of the party committee of the Moscow Institute of Ferrous Metals and Gold and a record of Novoselov's subsequent purge from the party.

5. In 1921, the party expelled about 30% of its ranks: Leonard Schapiro, *The Communist Party of the Soviet Union* (New York: Random House, 1959), 233. In Viatka province, it removed 65% of its total membership: *Kirovskaia oblastnaia organizatsiia v tsifrakh, 1917–1985* (Kirov: Volgo-Volzhskoe knizhnoe izdatel'stvo, Kirovskoe otdelenie, 1986), 18. The number of full members in the province declined from 6,727 to 2,636, a drop of 61%; candidate members from 1,929 to 410, a decline of 79%.

6. For the date of Novoselov's party membership, see the record of the Urzhum district's party committee in 1921 in GASPI KO, f. 4112, op. 19, d. 4452, l. 119 and of the Viatka district's party committee, August 1927, in GASPI KO, f. 4412, op. 17, d. 9279, ll. 5–5 ob. I have scoured the records of the party's Urzhum district committee for 1921 and 1922, the years Novoselov served there. They contain a string of reports from him to the regional agitprop in Viatka. Lists of individuals purged from the party in Urzhum for those years do not contain Novoselov's name. See lists in GASPI KO, f. P-12, op. 3, d. 77, 8 ll. and d. 78, 302 ll. The latter folder does list a Nikolai Pavlovich Novoselov as purged upon discovery of his earlier alleged desertion from the Red Army: ll.11 ob.-12. Moreover, Novoselov is not listed among those expelled from the party in the city of Viatka from 1922 to 1924: GASPI KO, f. P-3, op. 1, d. 144, 9 ll.

7. See the report from the party organization of the first district of the city of Viatka.: GASPI KO, f. P-3, op. 1, d. 338, ll. 68 ob-69. It indicated that Novoselov had been Istpart's secretary since March 1924.

8. For Piontkovsky's growing sense of doom, see *Dnevnik istorika S. A. Piontkovskogo (1927–1934)* (Kazan: Kazanskii gosudarstvennyi universitet, 2009), 18–21, 285, 287, 318–319, 359, 456, 485. Piontkovsky did manage to publish in 1935 *Ocherki istorii SSSR XIX i XX vv.* (Moscow-Leningrad: Gosudarstvennoe sotsial'no-ekonomicheskoe izdatel'stvo, 1935). A slashing review followed the next year by an editor of *Istorik-Marksist*, condemning Piontkovsky as an anti-Marxist and anti-Leninist historian: I. Frolov, "Bezotvetstvennaia kniga," *IM*, 3 (55) (1936), 119–137.

9. *Dnevnik istorika*, 464.

10. *Protiv istoricheskoi kontseptsii M. N. Pokrovskogo: Sbornik statei* (Moscow: Izdatel'stvo Akademii nauk SSSR, 1939–1940).

11. A. M. Pankratova, "Razvitie istoricheskikh vzgliadov M. N. Pokrovskogo," *Protiv istoricheskoi kontseptsii M. N. Pokrovskogo: Sbornik statei* (Moscow: Izdatel'stvo Akademii nauk SSSR, 1939), 5–69.

12. For Pankratova's attack on Piontkovsky and other historians, see A. Pankratova, "Stalin i istoricheskii front," *IM*, no. 3 (77) (1940), 14–24.

13. *Istoriia Kazakhskoi SSR s drevneishikh vremen do nashikh dnei*, ed. M. Abdykalykov and A. Pankratova (Alma-Ata: Kazogiz, 1943).

14. See Reginald Zelnik, *Perils of Pankratova: Some Stories from the Annals of Soviet Historiography* (Seattle: Herbert J. Ellison Center for Russian, East

European, and Central Asian Studies, University of Washington, 2005), 36–39. See also David Brandenberger, *National Bolshevism: Stalinist Mass Culture and the Formation of Modern Russian National Identity, 1931–1956* (Cambridge, MA: Harvard University Press, 2002), 123–129. For Pankratova's vigorous response, see her letters in 1944 to Zhdanov and to the Communist Party's Central Committee in *Istorik i vremia: 20–50-e gody XX veka. A. M. Pankratova* (Moscow: Izdatel'stvo ob"edineniia "MOSGORARKHIV," 2000), 223–236. At the same time, Pankratova tangled with Tarle over the latter's favorable rendition of tsarist foreign and colonial policy: see B. S. Kaganovich, *Evgenii Viktorovich Tarle: Istorik i vremia* (Sankt-Peterburg: Izdatel'stvo Evropeiskogo universiteta, 2014), 242–263. See also Aleksandr Dubrovsky, *Vlast' i istoricheskaia mysl' v SSSR (1930–1950-e gg.)* (Moscow: ROSSPEN, 2017), 339–370.

15. For a discussion of these developments, see Donald Raleigh's introduction to E. N. Burdzhalov, *Russia's Second Revolution: The February 1917 Uprising in Petrograd*, ed. and trans. Donald J. Raleigh (Bloomington: Indiana University Press, 1987), xiii-xiv; *Soviet Historians and Perestroika: The First Phase*, ed. Donald J. Raleigh (Armonk, NY: M. E. Sharpe, 1989); Roger D. Markwick, *Rewriting History in Soviet Russia: The Politics of Revisionist Historiography, 1956–1974* (New York: Palgrave, 2001), 51–62; and Kathleen E. Smith, *Moscow 1956: The Silenced Spring* (Cambridge, MA: Harvard University Press, 2017), 311–315. Zelnik concludes: "I think we should imagine her as neither devil nor angel, but as someone who did some harm and also much good as she tried to steer a course through the rough seas of Soviet life." Zelnik, *Perils of Pankratova*, 66.

16. A. Kuchkin, review of P. Fedorov, *Pod krasnoi zvezdoi* (Moscow-Leningrad: Gosudarstvennoe izdatel'stvo. Otdel voennoi literatury, 1928), *PR*, no. 8 (79) (August 1928), 201–202. On Kuchkin's service in the division, see E. S. Sadyrina, *Andrei Kuchkin, 1888–1973* (Kirov: Volgo-Viatskoe knizhnoe izdatel'stvo, Kirovskoe otdelenie, 1982), 80 and A. P. Kuchkin, *V boiakh i podkhodakh ot Volgi do Eniseia: Zapiski voennogo komissara* (Moscow: Izdatel'stvo "Nauka," 1969), 5.

17. A. Kuchkin, "V podpole v Ufe v 1911–1915 gg.," *PR*, no. 1 (84) (January 1929), 221–242. Uncharacteristically, Kuchkin did not glorify himself in an article published in late 1929 in *Proletarskaia revoliutsiia* about the Bolshevik party organization in Beloretsk in 1917 and 1918. A. Kuchkin, "Beloretskaia organizatsiia v 1917–1918 gg.," *PR*, no. 12 (95) (December 1929), 120–137. However, as he knew but did not say, he had spent little time there. Kuchkin confessed that the Bolsheviks should have been more accommodating of Bashkirs' quest for autonomy (129–130). To his credit, Kuchkin managed to criticize his own behavior in 1918 in A. Kuchkin, "K istorii Izhevskogo vosstaniia," *PR*, no. 6 (89) (June 1929), 153–162. He admitted that he and his comrades behaved too

aggressively when they tried to recruit workers in Izhevsk and Votkinsk to join the military campaign to retake Ufa. Their behavior contributed to a revolt in both cities against the Bolshevik regime.

18. See a copy of Kuchkin's review in RGASPI, f. 72, op. 3, d. 953, ll. 2–18. A handwritten copy is dated December 10, 1931.

19. As these and the comments to follow indicate, Kuchkin's work would make for a most interesting full-scale biography. Records for his career after 1934 are at the Russian State Archive for Contemporary History and at the Archive of the Academy of Sciences.

20. M. V. Zelenov and D. Brandenberger, eds., *Kratkii kurs istorii VKP(b). Tekst i ego istorii*, pt. 1, *Istoriia teksta "Kratkogo kursa istorii VKP(b),"* 1931–1956 (Moscow: ROSSPEN, 2014), 204.

21. Andrei Kuchkin, *Velikaia Oktiabr'skaia sotsialisticheskaia revoliutsiia* (Moscow: Gosudarstvennnoe sotsial'no-ekonomicheskoe izdatel'stvo, 1938), esp. 6–8, 27–30, 71–75, 78–82.

22. See *Istorik i vremia*, 304.

23. A. Kuchkin, "Sovetizatsiia kazakhskogo aula (1926–1929 gg.)," *Voprosy istorii*, no. 10 (1946), 3–23. The journal's editorial board included Pankratova.

24. Kuchkin, "Sovetizatsiia kazakhskogo aula," 22–23.

25. Lowell Tillett, *The Great Friendship: Soviet Historians on the Non-Russian Nationalities* (Chapel Hill: University of North Carolina Press, 1969), 84, 110.

26. For a discussion of the critical assessment of Kuchkin's work on Kazakhstan, see V. V. Tikhonov, "Diskussiia o sovetizatsiii kazakhskogo aula 1946–47," in *Istoriohrafichni doslidzhennia v Ukraïni*, vol. 24 (Kiev: Institute of the History of Ukraine, 2014), 267–280. In a sharp exchange in early 1948 over Kazakh resistance in the nineteenth century to Russian domination, Kuchkin argued that such defiance had a national-liberation character: Tillett, *Great Friendship*, 119.

27. A. P. Kuchkin, *Sovetizatsiia Kazakhskogo aula, 1926–1929 gg.* (Moscow: Izdatel'stvo Akademii nauk SSSR, 1962), 430.

28. Kuchkin's response: A. P. Kuchkin, "Vosstanovit' istinu," *Voprosy istorii*, no. 12 (December 1966), 197–199.

29. *Istoriia SSSR ot Velikoi Oktiabr'skoi sotsialisticheskoi revoliutsii do nashikh dnei*, 11 vols. (Moscow: Izdatel'stvo "Nauka," 1966–1980).

30. *Istoriia SSSR ot Velikoi Oktiabr'skoi sotsialisticheskoi revoliutsii do nashikh dnei*, vol. 9, *Postroenie sotsializma v SSSR 1933–1941 gg.* (Moscow: Izdatel'stvo "Nauka," 1971).

31. Kuchkin's conclusion, *Postroenie sotsializma*, 517–520. A truncated discussion of the terror by one of the volume's authors blamed Stalin, who had allegedly wrested control over the NKVD from the party and subordinated it directly to himself (195–197).

32. A. P. Kuchkin, "Bol'shevistskaia organizatsiia v Viatke v nachale 1917 goda," in *Za vlast' sovetov: Sbornik vospominanii starykh bol'shevikov-uchastnikov Velikoi Oktiabr'skoi sotsialisticheskoi revoliutsii i Grazhdanskoi voiny v Viatskoi gubernii* (Kirov: Kirovskoe knizhnoe otdelenie, 1957), 5–29.

33. Kuchkin, "Bol'shevistskaia organizatsiia v Viatke," 17–18.

34. Kuchkin, "Bol'shevistskaia organizatsiia v Viatke," 27–28, quote on 27. Kuchkin's correspondence in 1961 with a fellow Viatka Bolshevik from 1917, Mikhail Popov, indicates that in all probability Kuchkin and Viatka's regional party committee made certain that the volume, *For the Power of Soviets*, presented no contrary opinion on Kuchkin's role and on the relationship between Bolsheviks and Mensheviks in early 1917. See Kuchkin's letters to Popov of March 15 and May 1, 1961, in GASPI KO, f. P-6807, op. 1, d. 24, ll. 23–24 ob. Popov had prepared in April 1957 a typescript covering Bolshevik activity throughout 1917 and beyond: GASPI KO, f. P-6807, op. 1, d. 7, ll. 33–49. However, only Popov's coverage of events from late May was submitted to the publisher at the end of July. The volume did not include his account on the months of March, April and May in which he largely ignored Kuchkin and emphasized that Viatka's Bolsheviks, himself included, had joined with Mensheviks in a united organization (ll. 39–49).

35. See Kuchkin's portrayal of his activity as represented by the character, Pavlov, in A. P. Kuchkin, *V te dni (1917 god): Iz vospominanii starogo bol'shevika* (Kirov: Kirovskoe knizhnoe izdatel'stvo, 1958), esp. 43–47. An instructor at Kirov's Pedagogical Institute, Evdokiia Stepanova Sadyrina, repeated Kuchkin's tendentious account in her E. S. Sadyrina, *Oktiabr' v Viatskoi gubernii* (Kirov: Kirovskoe knizhnoe izdatel'stvo, 1957), 38–39, 43, 46–48. She did so in part by relying on Kuchkin's article, "Bol'shevistskaia organizatsiia v Viatke," discussed above, that appeared in *PR*, no. 5 (64) (May 1927).

36. Kuchkin, *V boiakh i podkhodakh ot Volgi do Eniseia*, 44. For a more charitable assessment of Kuchkin's career, one that incudes his criticism of Khrushchev and Brezhnev, see the article by his daughter, a historian, O. A. Kuchkina, "O moem ottse," in *Istoriia i istoriki: Istoriograficheskii vestnik. 2005* (Moscow: "Nauka," 2006), 252–268, and the article by his colleague and friend, V. S. Zaitsev, "K 100-letiiu so dnia rozhdeniia A. P. Kuchkina," *Voprosy istorii*, no. 12 (December 1988), 158–161. Kuchkina discusses especially well her father's agony over Khrushchev's denunciation of Stalin at the Twentieth Party Congress in February 1956 (265–266).

Conclusion

AT ITS INCEPTION, ISTPART BELIEVED it possible to combine partisanship and scholarship. Such thinking was a heady brew. Its consumption prompted inspiring statements from Istpart's founders. And it encouraged tendentious but serious study of events in 1917 that embraced the role of spontaneity, emphasized the Bolshevik party's weakness, and proudly acknowledged Viatka's own version of events.

Istpart immediately found it difficult, if not impossible, to realize its dream on a national scale. Regional party committees refused to support Istpart branches. The number of locals, admittedly inflated, rapidly declined in the late 1920s. When Viatka's Istpart finally came to life, party organs and rank and file members showed little inclination to preserve the documentary record of the party's past. Those individuals who managed to write something produced little of value, as their leaders in Viatka contemptuously pointed out. Its Istpart printed work of uneven worth. In particular, its publications on the 1905 revolution were so uninspiring that they understandably remained unsold at sharply reduced prices. Soon both Moscow and Viatka grasped that the plans to celebrate revolutionary holidays in print fell short of the willingness of the party's faithful, let alone that of the broader public, to purchase and read the result. And yet Viatka's major publication on the 1917 revolution and civil war in the province had some value then and even now.

Regardless of the nobility of Istpart's intentions, its infectious faith in a symbiosis of scholarship and politics, and the value of many of its publications, Istpart's historians at the center and in Viatka were attempting to square the circle. Their party relied on an ideology that denied any epistemology that suggested nonideological and nonpolitical sources of truth. Except for the fleeting moment when Pokrovsky held an official position of leadership at Istpart, all of its chief administrators came from the Bolshevik world of propaganda. Ol'minsky had served as a journalist and editor of several of the party's newspapers. Kanatchikov, Savel'ev, and Gusev came to Istpart from either the Central Committee's Agitprop or its Press Department. In the early 1920s, Essen headed the Georgian Communist Party's agitprop. Viatka's Novoselov had led a district party committee's agitprop.[1]

Istpart's best representatives succumbed too readily to conduct that compromised their agency's admittedly improbable mission. Nevsky pressed his scholarly agenda in an imperious and counterproductive way. Ol'minsky hung on at Istpart literally for dear life and, in the process, prejudiced his own initial emphasis on the value of memoirs. Even as Pokrovsky and Piontkovsky promoted the scholarly canon, they grasped all too well that the borders separating ruthless politics and objective research were porous. In 1925, they wrote shrill pieces denouncing Trotsky's behavior in the past and present. Ol'minsky, Nevsky, Pokrovsky, Iaroslavsky, Novoselov, Kuchkin, and Kapustin engaged in pedantic and insulting behavior when evaluating each other's work and that of their fellow party historians. Many were all too quick to use atrocious language in denouncing their "bourgeois" colleagues.

Unlike Pokrovsky and Piontkovsky, Viatka's Novoselov may never have fully understood the predicament posed by Istpart's original mission. He had no historical training and perhaps never fully embraced in principle the traditional tenets of scholarship. More strikingly than Pokrovsky and Piontkovsky, Novoselov adopted inconsistent positions from one moment to the next that simultaneously displayed Istpart's dual agenda and the difficulty of its realization. In late 1926 and early 1927, as an amateur historian, he wrote in *Viatskaia pravda* of the numerical and organizational weakness of the Bolshevik party in Viatka and, by comparison, of the strength and popularity of Mensheviks and SRs. At the same time, in the same newspaper but now writing as Istpart's administrator, he stridently called on his agency to overcome "harmful academic deviation."

In 1927, Novoselov sharply condemned Kuchkin for inflation of Kuchkin's own role and that of the Bolshevik party in 1917. Once a party official who played a critical role in the party's limited history in 1917, Kuchkin had turned his back on the province with the warm embrace of an increasingly grand narrative that left little room for a distinctive local or regional history. In Moscow he was directly involved (as were other party historians) in writing a grand narrative (and, in Kuchkin's case, his alleged place in it). Novoselov objected. To be sure, he did so out of personal animosity toward Kuchkin, but he also acted out of acquaintance with documentary evidence. All three of his fellow members of Viatka Istpart's collegium, each a native son of the region, supported Novoselov in this war of words with the apostate in Moscow. They promoted Viatka's own distinct version of 1917 not because they wished to counter any other narrative for Petrograd or Moscow or for the country as a whole. Rather, as good Bolsheviks and as good citizens of Viatka, they believed it necessary and proper to provide a reasonably accurate account in their published work and at the regional Museum of the Revolution of developments in Viatka in 1917—a "little history," as I have put. It is worth noting, that Novoselov's work has recently been cited, among other sources, by Viatka's historian Iurii Nikolaevich Timkin to demonstrate the party's frailty in Viatka in 1917.[2] And yet as Novoselov repeatedly excoriated Kuchkin for embellishment of the party's role in 1917, he simultaneously complained of histories of the Viatka region, without mentioning his own, that underestimated the party's significance.

No doubt, Novoselov believed sincerely that Istpart should be, in his own words, an organ for the struggle against enemies and distortions of the party line. That sincerity metamorphosed into naivete when he failed to grasp that, for that very reason, his Istpart needed to rearrange events in the province in a way that he had not in his own work. In the unlikely event that Novoselov knew full well the deep contradictions in his own behavior, he would have been pleased to leave Viatka and its Istpart behind in 1927 for the Northern Caucasus.

In 1927, even as historians in Viatka and in Moscow (Genkina, Piontkovsky, and Pankratova, among them) published important work on 1917, Istpart jettisoned its mission to promote scholarship. Before the agency's demise at the center in 1928 and Stalin's letter to *Proletarskaia revoliutsiia* three years later, Istpart and its commanding party could no longer tolerate an interpretation that failed to demonstrate that the party had purportedly imposed its will in Petrograd, Moscow, and elsewhere. A history of 1917 increasingly became a story not of historical events but of party policy for the year, real and imagined. Such a prejudiced presentation of 1917 embodied the new meaning, repeatedly bandied about, of "objectivity" and "scholarship." When uncomfortable elements of Istpart's earlier versions of 1917 reappeared in 1929 in the fourth volume of the work edited by Iaroslavsky, a delayed but vicious attack from on high followed.

In the late 1920s, Istpart lost its initial mission to publish scholarly work, whether at the center or in the provinces. It also forfeited its goal of making a wide range of documents available. The agency and its successors might still collect material and deposit it in archives, but access became largely a thing of the past. Traditional research on the party's history had ceased to be essential even before Stalin declared it so in 1931.

In the 1930s, only some of the bourgeois historians who survived could make a public display, within prescribed limits, of scholarly standards. In so doing, they had to choose their subject matter carefully and, even then, risked denunciation and worse. Tarle was one such person. Released in 1932 from exile in Alma-Ata and the threat of imprisonment, he returned to Leningrad to continue his professional career. In 1935, Tarle began work on a biography of Napoleon, subsequently published in 1936.[3] It created an immediate sensation. But on June 10, 1937, *Pravda* (and *Izvestiia*) condemned it as "an example of a hostile sortie" written by "enemies of the people." The article ominously reminded its readers of Tarle's earlier arrest for alleged involvement in a plot to make him minister of foreign affairs in a new government.[4] Fearing arrest and worse, Tarle appealed to Stalin. Perhaps having orchestrated the whole affair, Stalin came to the historian's defense. On the very next day, *Pravda* printed a retraction of sorts. "Of non-Marxist works devoted to Napoleon," it concluded, "Tarle's book is the very best and closest to the truth."[5] During World War II, Tarle traveled by train in his own carriage to cities throughout the USSR to lecture on Napoleon's defeat in 1812 and, by analogy, Fascist Germany's own impending demise.[6] On November 1, 1942, in Viatka (now renamed Kirov), Tarle addressed an overflow crowd in the main library's large reading room.[7]

In conclusion, the party's leadership and its rank and file never embraced anything but a political mission for Istpart. In a one-party state, no ideological, institutional, or constitutional obstacles stood in the way of a thorough politicization of Istpart's work. I share the gloomy judgments reached by the Russian scholars Klopikhina and Mosolov and discussed in this book's introduction. "Istpart's functional principles," Klopikhina concluded, "gradually converted it into an ideological institute of state power."[8] Of the Institute of Marx and Engels, which began its life with a dual mission similar to Istpart's, Mosolov thought its failure "could only be such as it was."[9]

At its outset, Istpart was much more than a political exercise. At its end, it had become nothing but that. Initially, Istpart had thought of history in a traditional way: as choices to be made in the past by people, Bolsheviks included, when confronted with alternative paths of development and then by historians in interpreting those choices. But by the late 1920s, for historians of a party that could never err and, therefore, a party and historians without choice in the past or present, history ceased to exist.

NOTES

1. Another branch of the Central Committee's apparat, Zhenotdel, which had endeavored to delineate its own objectives and establish a measure of organizational independence, suffered much the same fate as Istpart. See Carol Eubanks Hayden, "The Zhenotdel and the Bolshevik Party," *Russian History* 3, no. 2 (1976): 150–173; Richard Stites, *The Women's Liberation Movement in Russia: Feminism, Nihilism, and Bolshevism, 1860–1930* (Princeton, NJ: Princeton University Press, 1978), 339–345.

2. Iu. N. Timkin, "Bol'shevistskie organizatsii Viatskoi gubernii vesnoi-osen'iu 1917 goda: Novoe prochtenie istochnikov," *Vestnik Permskogo Universiteta* 2 (37) (2017), 28.

3. E. V. Tarle, *Napoleon* (Moscow: Zhurn.-gaz. ob"edinenie, 1936).

4. A. Konstantinov, "Istoriia i sovremennost' (Po povodu E. Tarle 'Napoleon')," *Pravda*, June 10, 1937, 3.

5. *Pravda*, June 11, 1937, 4. *Pravda* noted that the publisher should have helped Tarle overcome his errors. For a discussion of the affair, see the preface by Sergei Goianov in E. V. Tarle, *Napoleon* (Rostov-on-Don: Izdatel'stvo "Feniks," 1996), 3–18; E. I. Chapkevich, *Poka iz ruk ne vypalo pero: Zhizn' i deiatel'snost' E. V. Tarle* (Orel: "Orel," 1994), 101–104; and B. S. Kaganovich, *Evgenii Viktorovich Tarle: Istorik i vremia* (Sankt-Peterburg: Izdatel'stvo Evropeiskogo universiteta, 2014), 186–188.

6. Chapkevich, *Poka iz ruk*, 146 and E. I. Chapkevich, *Evgenii Viktorovich Tarle* (Moscow: Izdatel'stvo "Nauka," 1977), 100.

7. GASPI KO, f. P-6818, op. 2, d. 24, l. 30.

8. Vasilina Sergeevna Klopikhina, "Deiatel'nost' istpartov na Severnom Kavkaze (1920–1939 gody)" (diss., Stavropol State University, Stavropol, 2011), 234.

9. V. G. Mosolov, *IMEL—Tsitadel' partiinoi ortodoksii. Iz istorii Instituta Marksizma-Leninizma pri TsK KPSS, 1921–1955* (Moscow: Novyi khronograf, 2010), 581.

GLOSSARY OF PROMINENT INDIVIDUALS

See chapter 9 for additional information on the fate of many of these individuals.

Dubrovsky, S. M. (1900–1970). Party historian, author of important works on the peasantry in 1917.

Elizarova, A. I. (1864–1935). Old Bolshevik, Lenin's sister, official at Istpart from 1921.

Essen, M. M. (1872–1956). Party journalist and propagandist, official at Istpart from 1927.

Falaleev, P. G. (1875–?). Bolshevik in the city of Viatka in 1917, minor party official in Viatka province during the 1920s.

Favorov, M. A. (1885–?). Historian in Viatka, author of an article on the city of Viatka in late 1917. Rector of Viatka's Pedagogical Institute, 1926–1930.

Genkina, E. B. (1901–1978). Party historian, author of an important study on the February 1917 revolution. Research associate of the History Institute of the USSR's Academy of Sciences and author of works on Lenin, the Russian Civil War, and collectivization.

Gorin, P. O. (1900–1938). Party historian and administrator at the Society of Marxist Historians.

Gusev, S. I. (1874–1933). Old Bolshevik, journalist, Istpart's head since August 1926.

Iaroslavsky, E. M. (1878–1943). Old Bolshevik, party historian, head of Society of Old Bolsheviks and Society of Former Political Prisoners and Penal Exiles.

Kamenev, L. B. (1883–1936). Old Bolshevik, head of Lenin Institute, 1923 to 1927. Executed in 1936.

Kanatchikov, S. I. (1979–1937, 1940?). Old Bolshevik, head of Istpart, 1925–1926.

Kapustin, P. P. (1889–1938). Bolshevik in the city of Viatka in 1917, antagonist of Viatka's Istpart.

Kin, D. Ia. (1899–1937). Party historian, author of several significant articles on 1917.

Kuchkin, A. P. (1888–1973). Bolshevik in the city of Viatka in 1917, party historian, antagonist of Viatka's Istpart.

Lenin, V. I. (1870–1924). Head of the Soviet state and Bolshevik party, originator of the idea for the creation of Istpart.

Lepeshinsky, P. N. (1868–1944). Old Bolshevik, official at Istpart.

Liubovikov, M. K. (1887–1974). Old Bolshevik, head of Viatka's Istpart, 1927–1928 and of Viatka's Museum of the Revolution.

Nevsky, V. I. (1876–1937). Old Bolshevik, party historian, head of Petrograd's Istpart to 1924.

Novoselov, A. A. (1902–?). Head of Viatka's Istpart,1924–1927, author of articles on Viatka in 1917. Purged from the party in 1935.

Ol'minsky, M. S. (1863–1933). Old Bolshevik, journalist, head of Istpart, 1920–1924, administrator at the Lenin Institute, 1928–1930.

Pankratova, A. P. (1889–1957). Party historian, author of important books on labor unions and factory committees in 1917. Editor of the journal *Voprosy istorii*, 1953–1957.

Picheta, V. I. Soviet historian, arrested in 1930, exiled to Viatka, freed in 1934.

Piontkovsky, S. A. (1891–1938). Party historian, author of significant books and articles on 1917.

Pokrovsky, M. N (1868–1932). Old Bolshevik, party historian, one of the founders of Istpart.

Riazanov, D. B. (1870–1938). Director of the Institute of Marx and Engels, 1921–1931.

Savel'ev, M. A. (1884–1939). Old Bolshevik, journalist, deputy head of Istpart from 1921.

Shestakov, A. V. (1877–1941). Party historian, author of important work on the Russian countryside in 1917.

Shliapnikov, A. G. (1885–1937). Old Bolshevik, memoirist and historian, author of four volumes and multiple articles on 1917, leader of the Workers Opposition.

Stalin, I. V. The party's general secretary intimately involved from 1931 to 1938 in the articulation of historical methodology and in the writing of the party's history.

Tarle, E. V. Soviet historian, arrested in 1930, freed in 1932, author of *Napoleon* (1936).

Tokarev, S. V. (1902–1958). Party historian in Viatka, educator, author of a controversial article on Viatka in 1917.

Trotsky, L. D. (1879–1940). Author of the controversial *Lessons of October*, antagonist of Istpart.

Tsaregorodtsev, S. V. (1902–1994). Party historian in Viatka, educator, author of a controversial article on Viatka in 1917.

Volkovicher, I. V. (1890–1952). Party historian, author and editor of work on the party's history.

SELECTED BIBLIOGRAPHY

The following abbreviations are used when citing Russian archival material: f. for collection (*fond*), op. for inventory (*opis'*), d. for file or folder (*delo*), l. (*list*) for page and ll. (*listy*) for pages, and ob. (*oborot*) for reverse side of a page.

ARCHIVES

f. 70. Commission for the Study of the October Revolution and the Russian Communist Party (Bolsheviks) (Istpart). Rossiiskii gosudarstvennyi arkhiv sotsial'no-politicheskoi istorii (RGASPI. Russian State Archive of Social and Political History), Moscow.

f. 72. Editorial Board of Istpart's journal, *Proletarskaia revoliutsiia*. RGASPI.

f. 89 (opis' 7). Emel'ian Mikhailovich Iaroslavsky. RGASPI.

f. 91 (opis' 1). Mikhail Stepanovich Ol'minsky. RGASPI.

f. 147 (opis'1 and 2). Mikhail Nikolaevich Pokrovsky. RGASPI.

f. P-1. Viatka's Provincial Committee of the Communist Party. Gosudarstvennyi arkhiv sotsial'no-politicheskoi istorii Kirovskoi oblasti (GASPI KO. State Archive of the Social and Political History of the Kirov Region), Kirov, Russian Federation.

f. P-45. Istpart. GASPI KO.

f. P-6864. Truzhenik. GASPI KO.

f. R-2221. Viatka's Museum of the Revolution. Gosudarstvennyi arkhiv Kirovskoi oblasti (GAKO. State Archive of the Kirov Region), Kirov, Russian Federation.

Kirovskii oblastnoi kraevedcheskii muzei, Otdel fondov (Kirov's Regional Museum of Local History, Collections Department), Kirov Russian Federation.

Rossiiskii gosudarstvennyi arkhiv kinofotodokumentov (Russian State Documentary Film and Photo Archive), Krasnogorsk, Russian Federation.

JOURNALS AND NEWSPAPERS

Biulleten' Istparta (BI)
Bol'shevik

Istorik-Marksist (IM)
Krasnaia letopis'
Pechat' i revoliutsiia
Pod znamenem marksizma
Pravda
Proletarskaia revoliutsiia (PR)
Sputnik bol'shevika
Viatskaia pravda
Viatsko-Vetluzhskii krai

REMINISCENCES, DIARIES, COLLECTIONS OF DOCUMENTS, AND STATISTICS

Dnevnik istorika S. A. Piontkovskogo (1927–1934). Kazan: Kazanskii gosudarstvennyi universitet, 2009.

Elizarova, A. "Retrospektivnyi vzgliad na Istpart i na zhurnal 'Proletarskaia revoliutsiia.'" *Proletarskaia revoliutsiia*, no. 5 (100) (May 1930), 156–162.

Kirovskaia oblast' k 50-letiiu Oktiabria: Statisticheskii sbornik. Gor'kii: Izdatel'stvo "Statistika," 1967.

Kirovskaia oblastnaia organizatsiia KPSS v tsifrakh, 1917–1985. Kirov: Volgo-Viatskoe knizhnoe izdatel'stvo, Kirovskoe otdelenie, 1986.

Kuchkin, A. "Bol'shevistskaia organizatsiia v Viatke v nachale 1917 g." *Proletarskaia revoliutsiia*, no. 5 (64) (May 1927), 174–194.

———. *V te dni (1917 god): Iz vospominanii starogo bol'shevika.* Kirov: Kirovskoe knizhnoe izdatel'stvo, 1958.

Ol'minsky, M. "Vozniknovenie Istparta i zhurnala 'Proletarskaia Revoliutsiia'." *Proletarskaia revoliutsiia*, no. 5 (100) (May 1930), 154–155.

Pokrovsky, M. N. "O vozniknovenii Istparta." *Proletarskaia revoliutsiia*, no. 7–8 (102–103) (July–August 1930), 138–139.

Trotsky's Challenge: The "Literary Discussion" of 1924 and the Fight for the Bolshevik Revolution. Translated by Frederick C. Corney. Boston: Brill, 2016.

Vo glave mass: Iz istorii Kirovskoi gorodskoi organizatsii KPSS. Kirov: Volgo-Viatskoe knizhnoe izdatel'stvo, Kirovskoe otdelenie, 1980.

Zelenov, M. V., ed. *I. V. Stalin: Istoricheskaia ideologiia v SSSR v 1920–1930-e gody: Perepiska s istorikami, stat'i i zametki po istorii, stenogrammy vystuplenii. Sbornik dokumentov i materialov.* Part 1. *1920–1930-e gody.* Sankt-Peterburg: "Nauka-Piter," 2006.

Zelenov, M. V., and D. Brandenberger, eds. *Kratkii kurs istorii VKP(b). Tekst i ego istorii.* Part 1. *Istoriia teksta "Kratkogo kursa istorii VKP(b)," 1931–1956.* Moscow: ROSSPEN, 2014.

ISTPART'S NATIONAL CONFERENCES

Second Istpart Conference, April 22–24, 1923. *Biulleten' Istparta*, no. 2 (1923), 3–43.

Third Istpart Conference, May 26–27, 1923. "Protokol 3-go soveshchaniia Istpartotdelov S.S.S.R. (sostavlennyi po stenogramme ot 26–27/V-1924 g.)." *Proletarskaia revoliutsiia*, no. 8–9 (31–32) (August–September 1924), 408–450.

Fourth Istpart Conference, January 4–8, 1927. "Stenogrammy zasedanii IV-go Soveshchaniia," RGASPI, f. 70, op. 1, dd. 33–36; "Kopiia protokola zasedaniia Kollegii Istparta po voprosu Vserossiiskogo Soveshchaniia zaveduiushchikh Istpartotdelov 1927 g.," f. 70, op. 4, d. 320; "Zapisi prezidiuma i voprosy, podannye v Prezidium IV Vserossiiskogo Soveshchaniia 1927 g.," f. 70, op. 4, d. 324.

MAJOR WORKS ON 1917 PUBLISHED IN THE 1920S

Dubrovsky, S. M. *Krest'ianstvo v 1917 godu*. Moscow-Leningrad: Gosudarstvennoe izdatel'stvo, 1927.

———. *Ocherki russkoi revoliutsii*. 2nd ed. Moscow: Izdatel'stvo Narkomzema "Novaia derevnia," 1923.

Genkina, E. B. "Fevral'skii perevorot." In *Ocherki po istorii Oktiabr'skoi revoliutsii: Raboty istoricheskogo seminariia Instituta krasnoi professury*, 2:3–110. Moscow-Leningrad: Gosudarstvennoe izdatel'stvo, 1927.

Iaroslavsky, Em. "Bol'sheviki v fevral'sko-martovskie dni 1917 g." *Proletarskaia revoliutsiia*, no. 2–3 (61–62) (February–March 1927), 36–60.

———, ed. *Istoriia VKP(b)*. Vol. 4. Moscow-Leningrad: Gosudarstvennoe izdatel'stvo, 1929.

———. *Partiia bol'shevikov v 1917 godu*. Moscow-Leningrad: Gosudarstvennoe izdatel'stvo, 1927.

Iugov, M. "Sovety v pervyi period revoliutsii (mart–iiun')." In *Ocherki po istorii Oktiabr'skoi revoliutsii: Raboty istoricheskogo seminariia Instituta krasnoi professury*, 2:113–253. Moscow-Leningrad: Gosudarstvennoe izdatel'stvo, 1927.

Kin, D. "Bor'ba protiv 'ob"edinitel'nogo ugara' v 1917 godu." *Proletarskaia revoliutsiia*, no. 6 (65) (June 1927), 3–17.

Lidak, O. "Iiul'skie sobytiia 1917 goda." In *Ocherki po istorii Oktiabr'skoi revoliutsii: Raboty istoricheskogo seminariia Instituta krasnoi professury*, 2:257–346. Moscow-Leningrad: Gosudarstvennoe izdatel'stvo, 1927.

Oktiabr' i Grazhdanskaia voina v Viatskoi gubernii. Viatka: Istpart, 1927.

Pankratova, A. M. *Fabzavkomy Rossii v bor'be za sotsialisticheskuiu fabriku*. Moscow: Krasnaia nov', 1923.

———. *Politicheskaia bor'ba v rossiiskom profdvizhenii, 1917–1918 gg*. Leningrad: Izdatel'stvo Leningradskogo gubprofsoveta, 1927.

Piontkovsky. S. A. *Oktiabr'skaia revoliutsiia v Rossii, ee predposylki i khod. Populiarno-istoricheskii ocherk*. Moscow-Petrograd: Gosudarstvennoe izdatel'stvo, 1923.

Pokrovsky, M. N. "Dva Oktiabria." In *Oktiabr'skaia revoliutsiia: Sbornik statei, 1917–1927*, 95–96. Moscow: Izdatel'stvo Kommunisticheskoi akademii, 1929.

———, ed. *Ocherki po istorii Oktiabr'skoi revoliutsii: Raboty istoricheskogo seminariia Instituta krasnoi professury.* Vol. 2. Moscow-Leningrad: Gosudarstvennoe izdatel'stvo, 1927.

———. "Prolog Oktiabr'skoi revoliutsiia." In *Oktiabr'skaia revoliutsiia: Sbornik statei, 1917–1927,* 73–85. Moscow: Izdatel'stvo Kommunisticheskoi akademii, 1929.

Shestakov, A. V. *Bol'sheviki i krest'ianstvo v revoliutsii 1917 goda.* Moscow-Leningrad: Gosudarstvennoe izdatel'stvo, 1927.

———. "Oktiabr' v derevne." *Proletarskaia revoliutsiia,* no. 10 (69) (October 1927), 91–109.

Shliapnikov, A. *Kanun semnadtsatogo goda.* Vol. 1. Moscow: Gosudarstvennoe izdatel'stvo, 1920.

———. *Kanun semnadtsatogo goda.* Vol. 2. Moscow: Gosudarstvennoe izdatel'stvo, 1922.

———. *Semnadtsatyi god.* Vol. 1. Moscow-Petrograd: Gosudarstvennoe izdatel'stvo, 1923.

———. *Semnadtsatyi god.* Vol. 2. Moscow-Leningrad: Gosudarstvennoe izdatel'stvo, 1925.

———. *Semnadtsatyi god.* Vol. 3. Moscow-Leningrad: Gosudarstvennoe izdatel'stvo, 1927.

Volkovicher, I. V. *25 let R.K.P. (bol'shevikov), 1898–1923: Illiustrirovannyi iubileinyi sbornik.* Moscow: Gosudarstvennoe izdatel'stvo, 1923.

SECONDARY WORKS

Allen, Barbara C. *Alexander Shlyapnikov, 1885–1937: Life of an Old Bolshevik.* Chicago: Haymarket Books, 2016.

Artizov, A. N. "M. N. Pokrovskii: final kar'ery—uspekh ili porazhenie?" *Otechestvennaia istoriia,* no. 1 (January–February 1998): 77–96.

———. "M. N. Pokrovskii: final kar'ery—uspekh ili porazhenie?" *Otechestvennaia istoriia,* no. 2 (March–April 1998): 124–143.

Bakulin, V. I. *Drama v dvukh aktakh: Viatskaia guberniia v 1917–1918 gg.* Kirov: ViatGGU, 2008.

Barber, John. *Soviet Historians in Crisis, 1928–1932.* New York: Holmes & Meier, 1981.

Brandenberger David. *Propaganda State in Crisis: Soviet Ideology, Indoctrination, and Terror under Stalin, 1927–1941.* New Haven, CT: Yale University Press, 2011.

———. "Stalin's Rewriting of 1917." *Russian Review* 76, no. 4 (October 2017): 667–689.

Burgess, William Francis. "The Istpart Commission: The Historical Department of the Russian Communist Party Central Committee, 1920–1928." PhD diss., Yale University, 1981.

Byrnes, Robert F. "Creating the Soviet Historical Profession, 1917–1934." *Slavic Review* 50, no. 2 (Summer 1991): 297–308.
Chernobaev, A. A. *"Professor s pikoi," ili Tri zhizni istorika M. N. Pokrovskogo*. Moscow: Izdatel'stvo "Lit," 1992.
Corney, Frederick C. *Telling October: Memory and the Making of the Bolshevik Revolution*. Ithaca, NY: Cornell University Press, 2004.
Dahlke, Sandra. *Individuum und Herrschaft im Stalinismus: Emel'jan Jaroslavskij (1878–1943)*. Munich: R. Oldenbourg Verlag, 2010.
David-Fox, Michael. *Revolution of the Mind: Higher Learning among the Bolsheviks, 1918–1929*. Ithaca, NY: Cornell University Press, 1997.
Drabkina, Elizaveta. *A. I. Ul'ianova-Elizarova*. 2nd ed. Moscow: Izdatel'stvo politicheskoi literatury, 1979.
Enteen, George M. *The Soviet Scholar-Bureaucrat: M. N. Pokrovskii and the Society of Marxist Historians*. University Park: Pennsylvania State University Press, 1978.
———. "Writing Party History in the USSR: The Case of E. M. Iaroslavskii." *Journal of Contemporary History* 21, no. 2 (April 1986): 321–339.
Evtuhov, Catherine. *Portrait of a Russian Province: Economy, Society, and Civilization in Nineteenth-Century Nizhnii Novgorod*. Pittsburgh, PA: University of Pittsburgh Press, 2011.
Gorodetsky, E. N. *Sovetskaia istoriografiia Velikogo Oktiabria*. Moscow: Izdatel'stvo "Nauka," 1981.
Hickey, Michael C. "Paper, Memory and a Good Story: How Smolensk Got Its 'October.'" *Revolutionary Russia* 13, no. 2 (December 2000): 1–19.
Holmes, Larry E. "Soviet Rewriting of 1917: The Case of A. G. Shliapnikov." *Slavic Review* 38, no. 2 (June 1979): 224–242.
Holmes, Larry E., and William Burgess. "Scholarly Voice or Political Echo? Soviet Party Historians in the 1920s." *Russian History* 9, pts. 2–3 (1982): 378–398.
Kaganovich, B. S. *Evgenii Viktorovich Tarle: Istorik i vremia*. Sankt-Peterburg: Izdatel'stvo Evropeiskogo universiteta, 2014.
Klopikhina, Vasilina Sergeevna. "Deiatel'nost' istpartov na Severnom Kavkaze (1920–1939 gody)." Diss., Stavropol State University, 2011.
Korovainikov, V. Iu. "Gruppy sodeistviia Istpartu TsK VKP(b)." *Voprosy istorii KPSS*, no. 1 (January 1991): 112–123.
Kuchkina, O. A. "O moem ottse." *Istoriia i istoriki: Istoriograficheskii vestnik*, 2005, 252–268. Moscow: "Nauka," 2006.
Lezhava O. and N. Nelidov. *M. S. Ol'minskii: Zhizn' i deiatel'nost'*. 2nd ed. Moscow: Izdatel'stvo politicheskoi literatury, 1973.
Litvin, Aleksei. *Bez prava na mysl': Istoriki v epokhu Bol'shego Terrora. Ocherki sudeb*. Kazan: Tatarskoe knizhnoe izdatel'stvo, 1994.
———. "Vvedenie." In *Dnevnik istorika S. A. Piontkovskogo (1927–1934)*, 3–63. Kazan: Kazanskii gosudarstvennyi universitet, 2009.

1905 god v Viatskoi gubernii. Viatka: Truzhenik, 1925.

Mosolov, Vladimir Gavrilovich. *IMEL—Tsitadel' partiinoi ortodoksii. Iz istorii Instituta Marksizma-Leninizma pri TsK KPSS, 1921–1955*. Moscow: Novyi khronograf, 2010.

Nevsky, V. *Ocherki po istorii Rossiiskoi kommunisticheskoi partii*. Vol. 1. Petrograd: Priboi, 1923.

Oktiabr' i Grazhdanskaia voina v Viatskoi gubernii. Viatka: Istpart, 1927.

O sud'bakh i mgnoven'iakh proletevshikh . . . Ocherki istorii Gosudarstvennoi arkhivnoi sluzhby Kirovskoi oblasti. Kirov: "O-Kratkoe," 2008.

Retish, Aaron B. *Russia's Peasants in Revolution and Civil War: Citizenship, Identity, and the Creation of the Soviet State, 1914–1922*. New York: Cambridge University Press, 2008.

Russia's Home Front in War and Revolution, 1914–1922. Bk. 1, *Russia's Revolution in Regional Perspective*, edited by Aaron Retish, Sarah Badcock, and Liudimila Novikova. Bloomington, IN: Slavica, 2015.

Sadyrina, E. S. *Andrei Kuchkin, 1888–1973*. Kirov: Volgo-Viatskoe knizhnoe izdatel'stvo, Kirovskoe otdelenie, 1982.

———. *Oktiabr' v Viatskoi gubernii*. Kirov: Kirovskoe knizhnoe izdatel'stvo, 1957.

Shteppa, Konstantin. *Russian Historians and the Soviet State*. New Brunswick, NJ: Rutgers University Press, 1962.

Szporluk, Roman. "Introduction." In *M. N. Pokrovsky, Russia in World History: Selected Essays*, 1–46. Edited by Roman Szporluk. Translated by Roman and Mary Ann Szporluk. Ann Arbor: University of Michigan Press, 1970.

Timkin, Iu. N. "Bol'shevistskie organizatsii Viatskoi gubernii vesnoi-osen'iu 1917 goda: Novoe prochtenie istochnikov." *Vestnik Permskogo Universiteta* 2, no. 37 (2017): 27–33.

———. *Smutnoe vremia na Viatke: Obshchestvenno-politicheskoe razvitie Viatskoi gubernii vesnoi 1917-osen'iu 1918 gg*. Kirov: Izdatel'stvo VGPU, 1998.

Za Leninizm: Sbornik statei. Moscow-Leningrad: Gosudarstvennoe izdatel'stvo, 1925.

Zelenov, M. V. *Apparat TsK RKP(b)-VKP(b), tsenzura i istoricheskaia nauka v 1920-e gody*. Nizhnii Novgorod: Volgo-Viatskaia akademiia gosudarstvennoi sluzhby, 2000.

———. "Kontseptsiia, rozhdennaia v bor'be (Istoriko-partiinoe tvorchestvo V. I. Nevskogo)." *Voprosy istorii KPSS*, no. 8 (August 1991): 121–135.

Zelnik, Reginald E. *The Fate of a Russian Bebel: Semen Ivanovich Kanatchikov, 1905–1940*. Pittsburgh, PA: Center for Russian and East European Studies, University of Pittsburgh, 1995.

———. *Perils of Pankratova: Some Stories from the Annals of Soviet Historiography*. Seattle: Herbert J. Ellison Center for Russian, East European, and Central Asian Studies, University of Washington, 2005.

INDEX

Note: Photographs are identified by italicized page numbers followed by *f*.

1905 in the Viatka Province, 90, 100n15, 100n18
1917 (Semnadtsatyi god), 57, 113

academicism, 106, 116, 133, 172
agitprop: celebrations by, 43; historians' roots in, 40, 69, 94, 172; Istpart branches and, 36, 38, 39
Andreev, Andrei, 18, 38
anti-Communist army, 72–73
Antselovich, Naum Markovich, 71, 76, 86n33, 119, *120f*
archives: collection and use of records, 21, 37–38, 77; discarding of records, 42; politicization of, 111; purging of, 116
Artizov, A. N., 138n23

Bakhrushin, Sergei Vladimirovich, 136
Bakulin, V. I., 84n21
Barber, John, 6, 104, 139n34
Baturin, Nikolai Nikolaevich, 33n54
Bernstein, Frances Lee, 12n17
Billington, James, 64n43
Biulleten' (Viatka), 90
Bol'shevik: Iaroslavsky's confessions in, 146, 147; Iaroslavsky's *History*, 147; Iaroslavsky's role on, 53–54; Stalin's view of October revolution in, 115

Bolshevik party: demands to focus on, 9, 43–44, 45, 49n53, 52; depictions of, 64n45; and documentation of the past, 171; focus in October revolution's decennial celebration, 112; gaining control in Viatka, 71–73, 76, 128n98; and Istpart's mission, 174; Kin's comments regarding Lenin and, 143; Kuchkin's promotion of, 80; military records in Viatka, 116; and overthrow of tsarist government, 54; and policy as history, 173; purging of membership, 167nn5–6; in regional publications, 121; reliance on military support, 84n21; and revisions of revolutionary history, 114–15; role in Viatka's revolutionary history, 67, 69, 70–71; and Soviet history, 5, 6–7; and Stalin, 13n19; support for Istpart, 42; view of October revolution, 56; weakness of, 55, 57, 60, 83n10, 84n21, 144, 172; "Workers Opposition" in, 56–57; workers' support of, 57–58. *See also* grand narrative of revolutionary history; united Bolshevik-Menshevik organization
Brandenberger, David, 150, 151n1, 156n50
Bubnov, Andrei, 92, 101n29
Bukharin, Nikolai, 18, 49n61, 92
Bundists, 113

Burgess, William, 6, 49n61
Byloe, 17
Byrnes, Robert, 5–6

Central Committee of the Communist Party: appointment of Gusev to Istpart, 45; campaign to place Istpart under control of, 28; and changes to Istpart's structure, 43; condemnation of Trotsky, 19; directives on archives, 111; hopes for Istpart, 15; Iaroslavsky's joining, 157; Istpart's absorption into the Lenin Institute, 131–32; and Istpart's leadership, 34n68; limitation on publishing imposed by, 92, 95; and local branches of Istpart, 30n2, 130, 137n16; support for Istpart, 37
The Civil War in the Urals, 1917–1919 (Podshivalov), 75
Commissariat of Enlightenment (Narkompros), 15, 16, 27, 34n64, 34n67, 105, 132
Commission for Celebrating the October Revolution (Moscow), 92
Commission for Celebrating the October Revolution (Viatka branch), 66–67, 82n1, 85n30, 96, 97–98, 131, 137n8
Communist Academy, 133, 157
Corney, Frederick C., 49n53, 62n21, 116; *Telling October*, 4
Council of Peoples Commissars, 1

Dahlke, Sandra, 134, 139n34, 154n38
Decembrists, 44
Dela i dni, 17
Demidov, M. A., 129n99; *The Year 1917* (painting), 119
Deniken, A., 31n9
Department for Agitation and Propaganda (Agitprop), 15, 54, 55. *See also* agitprop
Derishev, Ivan Ipatovich, 40, 71, 77
Drabkina, Feodosiia Il'inichna, 43–44, 50n61, 112
Dubrovsky, Sergei Mitrofanovich, 54, 56, 62n18, 157; *The Peasantry in 1917*, 55
Dzerzhinsky, Feliks, 42, 73, 92, 118

Eisenstein, Sergei, *October* (film), 111
Elizarova, Anna Il'inichna: and Istpart, 28, 34n68, 35n84; on Narkompros, 34n67; on Ol'minsky's working climate, 27; support of Lenin Institute, 29; support of research articles, 23–24, 32n42
Engels, Friedrich, 17
Enteen, George, 104, 139n34, 153n15; *The Soviet Scholar-Bureaucrat*, 4–5
Essays on the History of the October Revolution (ed. Pokrovsky), 58–59, 64n43
Essen, Mariia Moiseevna, 94, 114, 132, 137nn17–18, 172
Evtuhov, Catherine, 2, 3

Falaleev, Petr Grigor'evich, 41f, 77
Favorov, Mikhail Aleksandrovich, 98, 103n63, 127n84; "October in Viatka," 67, 117
February revolution (1917): celebrations of, 43; criticism of Kin's account of, 145; Kin's scholarship on, 143; relationship with October revolution, 56
Finkel'shtein, Ida, 94, 106, 122n14
Finland and grand narrative, 121
First All-Russian Congress of Peasant Deputies, 80
Fishkin, 113
Flerovsky, Ivan Petrovich, 112
For Leninism: A Collection of Articles, 18–19
Fourth Istpart Conference: attendance at, 137n16; comments on *Katorga i ssylka*, 134; and Istpart's dual mission, 137n16; politicization of Istpart demanded at, 105–8; postponement of, 92–93; publication disaster shared at, 93–94; reduction of branches called for, 136n1; resolutions on museum exhibits, 109; restrictions on October jubilee literature, 94–95; statements on historical methodology at, 108–9
From the Revolutionary Past of Viatka Province's Youth (Viatka's Istpart), 75

Genkina, Esfir' Borisovna, 58, 96
Golos minuvshego, 17

Gorin, Pavel Osipovich, 108–9, 123n26, 133
Gorodetsky, E. N., 62n18
Gorodilova, N., 103n63
Gosizdat (State Publishing House): and commission to study the past, 14; on *Proletarskaia revoliutsiia*, 96; reliability of, 28, 91; and sales of publications, 90–91, 94, 96; and Shliapnikov's volumes, 113, 153n22; Trotsky's *1917*, 18
grand narrative of revolutionary history: criticism of provincial literature and, 108; inapplicability of, 60, 104, 108, 109, 112; Istpart's demands for, 8, 9, 44, 111, 112, 115–16, 118; museums and, 109; *Proletarskaia revoliutsiia* and, 121; Stalin and, 141, 150–51. *See also History of the Communist Party* (ed. Iaroslavsky); Kuchkin, Andrei Pavlovich
Great October Socialist Revolution. *See* October Revolution
The Great Soviet Encyclopedia, 67, 145
Groups of Assistance, 113, 114
Gusev, Sergei Ivanovich: agitprop roots of, 172; biographical information about, 50n61; on celebration commissions, 92, 101n29; death of, 157; on financial problems and publication, 93–94; as head of Istpart, 45; on local Istpart branches, 39; "On Jubilee Literature," 95; photograph of, *93f*; politicization of Istpart demanded by, 106, 122n12; on publication limits, 112; on publication plans for 1917 commemoration, 94

Hickey, Michael C., 116
historical scholarship and historians. *See* regional histories; Soviet historians; Soviet historical scholarship
History Institute, 133
History of the Communist Party (ed. Iaroslavsky): as challenge to grand narrative of 1917, 141; Iaroslavsky's mea culpa, 147–48, 155n40; Iaroslavsky's responses to criticism, 143–44, 145, 146–47, 148–50, 154n27; Istpart and editing of, 142–43; Kin's account of February revolt in and responses to Stalin, 143, 144, 145–46, 153n19; reviews of, 147, 148, 153n15, 155n41; Stalin's objections to, 142, 143, 144–45, 147, 173
History of the Communist Party: A Short Course (Stalin and historians), 141, 150–51, 156n50

Iakovlev, V., memoir by, 107–8
Iaroslavsky, Emel'ian Mikhailovich: archival sources for, 7; attacks on Stalin's rivals, 112; on Bolshevik party, 54–55, 57, 62n21; criticism of fellow historians by, 172; death of, 157; defense of *Katorga i ssylka*, 134, 154n38; despondency and bitterness of, 146, 155n47; dispute with Pokrovsky, 132, 138n19; and "hallelujah chorus" on a note from Institute of Red Professors, 150, *150f*, 155n47; and historical scholarship, 139n34; on October revolution, 56; *The Party of Bolsheviks in 1917*, 144; photographs of, *146f*, *158f*; placing blame on others, 143–44, 145, 148, 153n23; and rewrite of party history, 150; on Shliapnikov's work, 144; "Stalin as a Historian of the Party's History," 157; survival of, 9. *See also History of the Communist Party* (ed. Iaroslavsky)
Institute of Marx and Engels, 6, 174
Institute of Red Professors on Iaroslavsky's *History*, 147
International Organization for Aid to Revolutionary Fighters (MOPR), 118, 128n93
Istpart (Commission for the Collection, Study, and Publication of Materials on the October Revolution and History of the Communist Party): animosity among leaders of, 8; archival sources for research about, 7; and control of historical narrative, 11n12; decline of, 173–74; documents of interest to, 42–43, 48n47; dual mission of partisanship and scholarship, 3, 6–7, 9, 15–18, 22, 130, 171–72; formation and existence of, 1–2, 14–15; historical assessment of, 4–6; and

Istpart (*Cont.*)
  Iaroslavsky's work on *History*, 142–43;
  on museum exhibits, 109–10; personality
  conflicts in, 20–27; politicization of
  history, 173; publication issues of, 27–28,
  91–95, 97; questionnaires regarding
  October revolution, 113, 124n53; and
  regional histories, 126n74; reports
  demanded from, 36–37, 46n4; source
  material collected by, 3–4; support for
  researched articles, 23; threats to mission
  and existence of, 104; working conditions,
  support, and staffing for, 27–30, 46n2.
  See also grand narrative of revolutionary
  history; Gusev, Sergei Ivanovich;
  Kanatchikov, Semen Ivanovich;
  local Istpart branches; Ol'minsky,
  Mikhail Stepanovich; Pokrovsky,
  Mikhail Nikolaevich; Soviet historical
  scholarship; Viatka's Istpart
Istpart Conferences, 37, 38, 111. *See also*
  Fourth Istpart Conference
Iugov, Mikhail Simonovich, 58–59,
  64–65nn45–46, 96
Izvestiia's publication of Trotsky letter, 19

Kadets (of the Constitutional Democratic
  Party), 70
Kaganovich, Lazar, 27, 144–45, 147
Kalinin, Mikhail, 92
Kamenev, Lev: and Bolshevism, 58;
  on celebration commission, 92;
  denouncement of, 112; Kin's blaming
  of, 146, 147; on Lenin Institute, 29;
  opposition to Lenin's directives, 59;
  relationship with Ol'minsky, 35n85;
  treachery of, 156n50; as Trotsky opponent,
  18–19
Kanatchikov, Semen Ivanovich: agitprop
  roots of, 172; on celebration commission,
  92; as director of Istpart, 43; letter on
  Istpart locals and agitprop, 38; likely
  execution of, 161; memorandum to
  local Istpart branches, 43–44, 49n53,
  52; and October revolution's decennial
  celebration by locals, 112, 124n45; and
  removal from Istpart, 44–45, 49n61;
  response to complaint from Viatka's
  Istpart, 39; as Trotsky opponent, 20
Kapustin, Petr Pavlovich: about, 73–75;
  article reviews by, 73, 76–77, 79–80;
  criticism of fellow historians by, 172;
  execution of, 161; memoirs of 1917, 79;
  photographs of, 74f, 119, 120f, 162f; request
  for Central Committee assistance, 71;
  review of Popov article, 80; review of
  Solonitsyn article, 79–80
Katorga i ssylka: defense and disposition of,
  154–55n38; denunciations of, 147; memoirs
  in, 134
Kautsky, Karl, 141–42
Kerensky, A., 31n9
Khabas, R., 52, 61n14
Khlevniuk, Oleg, 2
Khorobrykh, Fedor Aleksandrovich,
  126–27n81
Kiev, histories of, 121
Kin, David Iakovlevich: blaming Istpart
  for his errors, 145–46; execution of, 161;
  "Party History as a Science," 133; response
  to Stalin, 147; "The Struggle against the
  Intoxication of Unification," 55; work in
  Iaroslavsky's *History*, 143, 144, 153n19
Kirov. *See* Viatka
Kliuchevsky, Vasilii Osipovich, 16, 17, 26
Klopikhina, Vasilina Sergeevna, 6, 174
Kolchak, Aleksandr, 72–73
Kotkin, Stephen, 13n19
Kotsonis, Yanni, 116
Krasin, L. B., 119, 120f
Krasnaia letopis': limitation on content in, 23;
  Nevsky and, 21, 33n45; praise for inclusion
  of memoirs and documents, 17
Krupskaya, Nadezhda (Lenin's wife), 18,
  92, 134
Kuchkin, Andrei Pavlovich: about, 73;
  article reviews by, 73, 75, 76; concessions
  by, 168–69n17; continued self-promotion
  by, 77, 79, 80–81, 87n47; and cooperation
  with Mensheviks, 75–76, 77, 78, 81–82;

criticism of, 164–65; criticism of fellow historians by, 172; criticism of Khrushchev and Brezhnev by, 170n36; death of, 166; dispute with Novoselov, 130, 165, 172–73; final historical work of, 163–66; *The Formation of Socialism in the USSR, 1933–1941*, 165; *The Great October Socialist Revolution*, 164; "July Days in Beloretsk," 80; on Kazakh resistance, 169n26; photographs of, 74f, 119, 120f, 129n99; relationship with Mensheviks, 88n63, 164–65; response to Novoselov's criticism, 77, 81; reviews by, 88n55, 163; signature on Menshevik proclamation, 75–76, 77, 78, 81–82, 165–66; "The Sovietization of the Kazakh Countryside," 164, 165

Latvia and grand narrative, 121
Lelevich, G. (Laborii Gilelevich Kalmanson), 59
Lenin, Vladimir: appointment of Shliapnikov, 56; "April Theses," 55; biography of, 26; criticism of Stalin by, 113; desire for official history, 14; and October revolution, 115, 164; opposition to directives of, 59; on petty bourgeois democrats, 65n50; seizure of power by, 18; Slutsky article downplaying, 141–42
Lenin Institute (later Marx-Engels-Lenin Institute): creation and mission of, 29–30, 35n83; directives on museums, 133; Istpart's incorporation into, 9, 130, 131–32, 137n14; Kuchkin at, 164; Savel'ev's role at, 157
Leninism: objectivity and Bolshevik politics, 17–18; Petrov on October revolution and, 145; Trotsky on, 19, 20
Lenin on Trotsky and Trotskyism, 19
Lentsner, Naum Mikhailovich, 59, 64–65n50
Lepeshinsky, Panteleiman Nikolaevich, 22–23, 24, 142–43
"Lessons of October" (Trotsky), 17, 18–20, 130
Lidak, Otto Avgustovich, 58, 59, 96
Litvin, Aleksei, 5, 104

Liubovikov, Mikhail Konstantinovich, 41f, 77, 78f, 118, 131, 157
local Istpart branches: and agitprop, 38, 39; demise of, 130, 137n16; final conference of, 132, 137n17; funding and central control of, 37, 39; and Istpart's grand narrative, 44, 49n55; Kanatchikov and Drabkina memorandum to, 43–44, 49n53, 52; Moscow's relationship with, 3; numbers and staffing of, 36, 45–46nn1–2; and October revolution's decennial celebration, 112; publication limits for, 94–95, 101n38; publishing with own resources, 95, 101n44; and regional history, 119; regional party committees' support of, 171; resources for, 38, 39, 47n16, 47n22; and revisionist history of October revolution, 116; scolded for poor work, 114; tasks of, 36–37
Lukomsky, A., 31n9
Luxemburg, Rosa, 141–42, 155n40

Main Archival Administration, 27, 34n64
Maksakov, Vladimir Vasil'evich, 48n47
Marx, Karl, 17
Marx-Engels-Lenin Institute. *See* Lenin Institute
Marxism and Marxist methods: and criticism of Kapustin, 76; and historical scholarship, 30n5, 105; in the History Institute, 133; objectivity and Bolshevik politics, 17–18; scientific method for history, 108
Marxist Historians, Conference of, 133, 138n23
Mekhlis, Lev Zakharovich, 148
memoirs in historical scholarship: campaign against, 133–34; denouncement of, 113–14; and Istpart's grand narrative, 60; Nevsky's views of, 21–22; of non-Bolsheviks, 17, 59; Novoselov's support for, 102nn51–52; Ol'minsky on, 139n31; Piontkovsky on, 17; *For the Power of Soviets*, 165, 170n34; from Society of Old Bolsheviks, 60; support by Istpart for, 60; Viatka Istpart's publication of, 96

Mensheviks: and betrayals of socialism, 114; condemnations of, 70; control and dominance of, 60; influence of, 121; and Istpart's focus on Bolsheviks, 44, 54; memoirs of, 113; in regional publications, 121; support for, 85n25; and unity with Bolsheviks in Viatka, 76; in Viatka, 67, 69, 70, 71, 85n25, 172; Viatka's acknowledgment of, 52, 57. *See also* Favorov, Mikhail Aleksandrovich; Kuchkin, Andrei Pavlovich; Sukhanov, Nikolai Nikolaevich; united Bolshevik-Menshevik organization
Mints, I. I, 152n10
Mishin, Ivan Vasil'evich, 94
Mitskevich, Sergei Ivanovich, 109, 134
Molotov, Viacheslav, 18, 92, 101n29, 111
MOPR. *See* International Organization for Aid to Revolutionary Fighters (MOPR)
Mosolov, Vladimir Gavrilovich, 6, 174
Mstislavsky, S., 31n9
museum exhibits: Istpart's directives on, 109–11; photograph of, *110f*
Museum of the Revolution (Moscow), *107f*, 109
Museum of the Revolution (Viatka branch): displays and visitors' response to, 118–19; later disposition of, 128n98; revised displays in, 119; size of, 128n91; "The Revolution in Viatka" (exhibit), 119, *120f*; and Viatka's version of 1917, 173

Narkompros. *See* Commissariat of Enlightenment
Nelidov, N., 83n10
Nevsky, Vladimir Ivanovich: arguments for nonpartisan scholarship, 20–23; on the Bolshevik party, 33–34n63; criticism of fellow historians by, 172; critics of, 22–23, 33n54; *Essays on the History of the Russian Communist Party*, 23–26, 27, 33n49; execution of, 161; and focus on serious research by Istpart, 36; and *Krasnaia letopis'*, 32n26, 33n45; other publications by, 26, 33n62; relationship with Ol'minsky, 130; scholarly mission of, 172. *See also* Ol'minsky, Mikhail Stepanovich
New Economic Policy (NEP), 56–57
Nizhnii Novgorod (Nizhnegorod): documents in, 38; enlargement of, 131; provincial attachment in, 2
Notes on the Revolution (Sukhanov), 59
Novoselov, Aleksandr Abramovich: on *1905*, 100n15; and academic deviations in Viatka's work, 116; after leaving Viatka, 9; agitprop roots of, 172; appeals to Moscow for help, 39, 40–41, 98; applications for party card, 159–61, *160f*, *161f*; on commission to celebrate October revolution, 66–67; contradictions in work of, 172, 173; criticism of fellow historians by, 172; departure from Viatka, 81, 82, 88n59, 131, 159, 173; dispute with Kuchkin, 75–76, 77–79, 81, 130, 172–73; and document collection, 43; on errors in celebration materials, 52; on February 1917 in Viatka, 67, 98; at Fourth Istpart Conference, 93; as head of Viatka's Istpart, 40, 47n31, 167n7; and Istpart's dual agenda, 172; objections to rejection of draft article, 75, 76; "October in Viatka," 67; photograph of, *41f*; publication agenda for October jubilee, 96–97; purging of, 159–61, 167n6; rebukes by, 42, 48nn45–46; response to Moscow's instructions about *The Year 1905*, 52–53; and Viatka's experience of October revolution, 119; and weakness of Bolshevik party, 117. *See also October and the Civil War in the Viatka Province* (ed. Novoselov)

October and the Civil War in the Viatka Province (ed. Novoselov): on Bolsheviks and cooperation with Mensheviks, 78–79, 83n12; cost and reprinting of, 102–3n62; cover of, *68f*; criticism of, 83n10; cuts made to, 98, 126n81, 127n83; funding of, 96, 97; initial plans for, 102n59; Moscow's response to, 116–17; overview and Novoselov's contribution to, 67

October at Military Headquarters (Lelevich), 108

October revolution (1917): assumed inevitability of, 53; celebrations of, 43; criticism of local publications about, 114; criticism of Piontkovsky's account of, 145; features of, 55–56, 63n35; historical revision as proletarian revolution, 114–15; impact on global politics, 1; Istpart's commemoration plans, 92, 111; party historians' view of, 56; Piontkovsky on study of, 17; publications on Viatka's history during, 66–67, 73–75; restrictions on celebration of, 94–95. *See also October and the Civil War in the Viatka Province* (ed. Novoselov); "The Prerequisites of October in the Viatka Province" (Tokarev and Tsaregorodtsev)

Office for Regional Branches (Istpart), 37

Okhranka (tsarist police), 24, 26, 38, 43

Ol'minsky, Mikhail Stepanovich: agitprop roots of, 172; appointed head of historical commission, 14; archival sources for, 7; and changes to Istpart's structure, 43, 49n50; complaints about support for Istpart, 28, 29; compromises made by, 172; conflict with Nevsky, 20–23, 24–26, 32n32, 130; criticism of fellow historians by, 45, 50n62, 81, 172; criticism of *Katorga i ssylka* by, 134; death of, 157; denunciation of police records by, 26; and Gosizdat, 91; on Iaroslavsky's work on *History*, 142; and Lenin Institute, 131–32; on Lepeshinsky, 24, 33n53; management of Istpart office, 27, 34n66, 34n76; on memoirs, 59, 139n31; and obligations of local branches, 46n11; personality and leadership characteristics of, 20, 31–32n25; photograph of, 25f; publication of branches' materials, 91; publication of Trotsky's letters, 19;

relationship with Kamenev, 35n85; role in Istpart, 15, 43, 50n64

"On Guardists," 59

Pankratova, Anna Mikhailovna: *History of the Kazakh Republic from the Earliest Times to the Present*, 163, 164; *The Political Struggle in the Russian Labor Movement, 1917–1918*, 57–58, 63n40, 96; and socieconomic conditions, 54; and Tarle, 168n14; Zelnik on, 168n15

paper shortages, 92, 111

The Party of Bolsheviks in 1917, 55, 56

peasants and grain confiscation, 72, 79–80, 87n51

peasant's revolutionary movement: Dubrovsky's historical view of, 53; and October revolution, 55–56; political desires for history of, 53; as unorganized, 62n20

Pedagogical Institute (Kirov), 2

Petrov, Fedor Nikolaevich, 145

Petrov, G., 145

Petrov, Zakhar Semenovich, 94, 106

Picheta, Vladimir Ivanovich, 135–36

Piontkovsky, Sergei Andreevich: account of Stalin-Iaroslavsky dispute, 144; booklet on February Revolution, 60; condemnations of historians, 136; contribution to politicization of scholarship, 104, 105; criticism of, 167n8; duality of conduct of, 5; execution of, 161; on Iaroslavsky's despondency, 146, 154n27; on Kin, 153n23; "Mistakes in Trotsky's 'Lessons of October,'" 20; on October revolution, 56, 153n26; *October Revolution in Russia, Its Prerequisites and Progress*, 54; on Pokrovsky, 161; and politics in scholarship, 172; review of memoirs, 17, 30–31n9; revision of work, 114; on Stalin and the armed revolt, 112; use of memoirs by, 59

Platonov, Sergei Fedorovich, 136, 140n38

Pokrovsky, Mikhail Nikolaevich: on 1905 revolt, 51; address to Conference of Archivists, 111; apology for encouraging Shliapnikov's work, 113; archival sources for, 7; on Bolshevik party, 64n45; career and impact of, 4–5; on celebration commissions, 92, 101n29; conflict with Iaroslavsky, 132; contribution to politicization of scholarship, 104–5; criticism of fellow historians by, 138n20, 172; death of, 135, 161; denunciation of, 163; on history and historians, 1, 10n1, 16–17, 30n5; and imprisoned historians, 135–36, 140n38, 140n40; and Lenin Institute, 131–32; and locals' decennial celebrations, 112; and Marxism in Soviet history, 133; on October revolution, 56, 58; photograph of, *16f*; and politics in scholarship, 16, 172; and restrictions on publication, 95, 96; and revisionist history of 1917, 115, 126n73; role in Istpart, 15; scholarly and political credentials of, 16; and Soviet scholarship, 138n23; and truth, 172; on use of police records, 26; vision of historical work, 14–15
Popov, Ivan Vasil'evich, 79–80, 83n12
Popov, Mikhail Mikhailovich, 67, 119, *120f*, 170n34
Popov, N., 155n41, 155n43
Populist movement, 34n63, 44, 155n40
Poroshin, Stefan Nikolaevich, 40, 41, *41f*, 47n31, 52, 66
power, decentralization of, 2
Pravda: editor of, 50n61; Iaroslavsky's mea culpa in, 147–48; publication of Trotsky letter, 19; review of Iaroslavsky's *History*, 145; on Tarle, 174, 175n5
"The Prerequisites of October in the Viatka Province" (Tokarev and Tsaregorodtsev): content of, 73, 75, 86n32; intended publication of, 85n30; Istpart requests vetting of, 73; Kuchkin-Novoselov continuing dispute, 77–78; Kuchkin's and Kapustin's opposition to publication of, 73–75; Novoselov's commentary on reviews of, 75–76; omission of in *October*, 116–17; vetting of, 86n33

proletarian revolution: Bolshevik views of, 56; and bourgeois-democratic movement, 142, 145; in historical revisions, 114–16; Pokrovsky on, 126n73
Proletarskaia revoliutsiia: archival collection for, 7; articles denouncing Stalin's political rivals, 112; changes to, 106; condemnation of Trotsky by, 19–20; criticism of *Katorga i ssylka* by, 134; criticism of locals for regionalism in publications, 119, 121; downsizing of, 96; editor of, 45; first issue, 28; intended publication agenda, 15; under Kanatchikov's tenure, 50n64; Kapustin's and Kuchkin's self-promotions in, 77, 80–81; memoirs in, 21–22, 60, 134; and Novoselov-Kuchkin dispute, 75, 77–78, 79, 81; praise for Piontkovsky, 60; promotion of October revolution's decennial celebration, 111–12; publication delays, 79, 81, 88n57; review of Iaroslavsky's *History*, 143; sales of, 91; Slutsky's article in, 141–42, 152n10; Stalin's letter to, 3, 6, 142, 146, 147, 150, 152nn9–10, 157; survey of events after revolt in Petrograd, 60; tolerance for departures from grand narrative, 121; unsold copies, 100n20
provinces: histories of non-Russian provinces, 164–65; party's history in, 2; political agenda setting in, 2; relationship to central power, 2–3. *See also* local Istpart branches; Viatka's Istpart
Pugachev, Emel'ian, 44
Put' prosveshcheniia, 89, 90

RANION. *See* Russian Association of Research Institutes of the Social Sciences (RANION)
regional histories: Kuchkin's dismissal of, 172; local Istparts' pursuit of, 2, 3; in museum exhibits, 109, 119. *See also 1905 in the Viatka Province; From the Revolutionary Past of Viatka Province's Youth;* grand narrative of revolutionary history; Novoselov, Aleksandr Abramovich; *October and the Civil War in the Viatka Province;* "The Prerequisites of

October in the Viatka Province"; Viatka's Istpart; *The Year 1905 in the Viatka Region*
Revolutionary Russia's special centennial issue, 1
"The Revolution in Viatka" (exhibit), 119, 120f, 129n99
Riazanov, David Borisovich, 6
Rodzianko, M., 31n9
Romanovskaia, Nadezhda Vasil'evna, 109
Rubach, Mikhail Abramovich, 106
Russian Association of Research Institutes of the Social Sciences (RANION), 132–33
Russian revolution of 1905: criticism of histories of, 52–53, 108; directives on celebration of, 44, 51; glut of publications on, 94; local funding for celebration materials, 41; publications to commemorate, 90, 92
Russian revolution of 1917: conflict over Viatka's decennial celebration of, 66; guidelines for work on, 45; Istpart and historians' writing about, 53; local funding for celebration materials, 41; Novoselov's history of, 67; revised narrative for histories of, 114; value of Viatka's publication on, 171. *See also* February revolution; October revolution
Russian State Archive of Social and Political History (Moscow), 7
Russkaia letopis', 22
Rykov, Aleksei, 18, 92

Saar, Gustav Petrovich, 38
Sakwa, Richard, 63n35
Saltykov-Shchedrin, Mikhail, 159
Saratov, histories of, 121
Savel'ev, Maksimilian Aleksandrovich: about, 25, 50n61; activity in his last years, 157; agitprop roots of, 172; and archives, 111; criticism of locals by, 114; as Gusev's deputy and editor of *Proletarskaia revoliutsiia*, 45; on Iaroslavsky's work on *History*, 142; and Lenin Institute, 132, 137n17; on locals' publishing with local resources, 101n44; photograph of, *107f*; on politicization of publications, 106;

and publication of branch materials, 91; rejection of memoirs, 114; and restrictions on publication, 94, 112; support for locals, 37
Shestakov, Andrei Vasil'evich, 53, 56, 60, 157
Shevchenko, Taras, 44
Shliapnikov, Aleksandr Gavrilovich: criticism of account of, 113; *The Eve of 1917*, 57, 91, 125nn58, 144; execution of, 161; further publishing of, 153n22; histories based on, 143, 144; influence of, 58; work of, 56–57
Shlikhter, Aleksandr Grigor'evich, 79–80, 87n52
Shteinman, E. E., 37, 112, 121
Shteppa, Konstantin, 13n21
Sitnikova, S., 119, 128n98
Slutsky, Anatolii Grigor'evich, 141–42, 151n4, 152n10
Social Democratic Party, 23, 34n63
Socialist Revolutionaries (SRs), 70; at All-Russian Congress of Peasant Deputies, 80–81, 172; and betrayals of socialism, 114; condemnations of, 70; control and dominance by, 59, 60; memoirs of, 113; in museum exhibits, 52; in regional publications, 44, 121; in Viatka, 71, 72, 117
Society of Marxist Historians, 105, 108, 121n9
Society of Old Bolsheviks, 60
Society of Political Prisoners and Exiles, 134
socioeconomic reforms, desires for, 52, 54, 57, 58, 70
Solonitsyn, Nikolai Karpovich, 79, 99n14, 117
Soviet historians: disputes among, 132, 134, 172; imprisonment of, 135–36; rebuked by Stalin, 142, 152–53n11. *See also* Iaroslavsky, Emel'ian Mikhailovich; Kapustin, Petr Pavlovich; Kin, David Iakovlevich; Kuchkin, Andrei Pavlovich; Nevsky, Vladimir Ivanovich; Novoselov, Aleksandr Abramovich; Ol'minsky, Mikhail Stepanovich; Pankratova, Anna Mikhailovna; Pokrovsky, Mikhail Nikolaevich; Shliapnikov, Aleksandr Gavrilovich; Tokarev, Sergei Vasil'evich; Tsaregorodtsev, Ivan Vasil'evich

Soviet historical scholarship: class identity and political revolution in, 53–54; and compatibility with political ends, 3, 18; contested discussion regarding, 2; criticism of idealism in, 105, 108; critiques of, 4–6; Iaroslavsky's view on, 143; and Istpart's mission, 22, 38; Marxism in, 133; objectivity and political expediency, 152n10; Pankratova's role in control over, 163; Pokrovsky on history, 1; politicization of, 5–7, 9, 13n24, 104, 173. *See also* Istpart; regional histories

Soviet of Workers and Soldiers Deputies (Viatka), 71

spontaneity: and Bolshevik influence, 58, 107; importance of, 2, 8, 112, 125n58, 171; in the October revolution, 45, 54, 55, 56; and politicization of history, 6, 104; and revisions to histories, 114, 151; of workers and peasants, 58, 64n46, 150

Sputnik bol'shevika, 67, 98

SRs. *See* Socialist Revolutionaries (SRs)

Stalin, Iosif (Joseph): alternative policies to, 13n19; on celebration commission, 92; comments on 1917, 151n1; criticism of Iaroslavsky by, 142–43; defense of Tarle, 174; denouncement of Trotsky's essay, 18; empowerment of, 3; and Istpart's demise, 5; Kuchkin's lauding of, 164, 165; letter to *Proletarskaia revoliutsiia*, 3, 6, 142, 146, 147, 150, 152nn9–10, 157; and party history, 141, 150–51, 155n48 (*see also History of the Communist Party: A Short Course*); photograph of, *146f*; and power struggle in Viatka, 73; rebuke of Iaroslavsky, 144–45, 147, 150, 155n46; rebuke of Slutsky article, 142; relationship with Lenin, 59, 112; and revision of revolution's narrative, 114, 115; and the terror, 169n31; Trotsky on, 113

Stalin Prize, 163

State Archive of the Social and Political History of the Kirov Region (Kirov), 7

State Publishing House. *See* Gosizdat

Stepanov, A. A., 87n51

Sukhanov, Nikolai Nikolaevich, 31n9, 58, 65n50; *Notes on the Revolution*, 58–59

Supreme Soviet of Viatka province, 71, *72f*, 119

Sverdlov, Ia. M., 119, *120f*

Tarle, Evgenii Viktorovich, 135, 140n40, 168n14, 174

Teachers of Leninism, Party History, and the History of the Comintern, Conference of, 133

the terror, 10n5, 160, 169n31

Tillett, Lowell, 164–65

Timkin, Iurii Nikolaevich, 72, 84n21, 173

Tokarev, Sergei Vasil'evich, 73, 97, 117–18, 127n87, 157, 159

Tompkins, Stuart R., 140n40

Tomsky, Mikhail, 92

Trotsky, Leon: on Bolshevik seizure of power, 18; and Bolshevism, 58; on celebration commission, 92; condemnation of, 18–20, 112, 172; and Kanatchikov, 43; on Lenin, 19, 59; "Lessons of October," 17, 18–20, 130; on October Revolution, 113; and power struggle in Viatka, 73, 87n55; quoted by Solonitsyn, 117

Trotskyism, accusations of, 159. *See also History of the Communist Party* (ed. Iaroslavsky)

Truzhenik (publisher): closing of, 89–90; and Istpart, 7; sale of *1905*, 90–91

Tsaregorodtsev, Ivan Vasil'evich, 73, 117, 157, 159

tsarist police records, 24, 26, 38, 43

Twelfth Party Congress, 37

Ukraine's Istpart, 44

united Bolshevik-Menshevik organization: appeal for membership by, 86n41, 117; denials of, 73, 75–76, 77, 78, 143; due to Bolshevik weakness, 54–55, 57, 60, 67, 143; extent of, 164; Popov and, 170n34

urban communes and communards, 12n17

Verevkin, B. P., 31–32n25
Viatka (later, Kirov): condemnation of Bolshevik takeover in Petrograd, 71; Congress of Archivists, 41, 41f; description of population and economy of, 70; Municipal Party Committee, 74f; power struggle in, 71–72, 85n26, 88n55; proletariat and peasant desires for change in, 52–53; relationship with Moscow, 2; secret archive in, 111
Viatka Historical Society, 126n74
Viatka regional party committee (later Kirov regional party committee): 1928 agenda, 131; archival sources for, 7; book of memoirs sponsored by, 165; commission for decennial celebration of the October revolution, 66–67, 82n1; and financial retrenchment, 89, 99nn5–6, 103n63; and sale of literature, 90–91; statute establishing local Istpart branch, 39–40, 47n28
Viatka's Istpart: commemoration of the 1905 revolution, 51–52; continuing hostility with critics, 81; demise of, 2, 131, 136n2; disagreement with Istpart (Moscow), 3; emphasis on local history, 3, 70, 118; and halt of publishing for, 89–90; historical work of, 3, 171; Moscow's criticism of, 7, 52; on Novoselov-Kuchkin dispute, 77; Novoselov's role at, 39–40; objections to rejection of draft article, 75; party members' interest in, 42; plans for decennial celebration of the October Revolution, 66–67; and politicization of its work, 116; printing of publications by, 7; resources and mission of, 39–40; support of Novoselov, 173; work of, 41–42, 43. *See also* Novoselov, Aleksandr Abramovich

Viatskaia pravda: complaints about, 99n6; and criticism of Istpart, 42; Novoselov's work in, 67, 116, 172; retrenchment for, 89–90

Viatsko-Vetluzhskii krai, 79, 98, 117–18

Volkovicher, Isidor Vladimirovich: changing attitudes of, 108; on correct use of resources, 106–7, 108; criticism of Novoselov by, 52, 108; and local Istpart branches, 61n9; and October celebrations, 112; and Polish socialism, 122n21

Volodarsky, V., 119, 120f

Volosevich, Vladislav Ottonovich, 152–53n11

Voprosy istorii, 163

Vorovsky, Vatslav Vatslavovich, 42–43, 118, 119, 120f

Vylegzhanina, Matrona Ivanovna, 81, 88n59

workers: political amorphousness among, 58; wages and working conditions, 52, 54, 57, 58, 70

Workers Opposition and Democratic Centralists, 15

The Year 1905 in the Viatka Region: controversy over contents of, 52–53

Young Communist League, 97

Zapol'skikh, Nikolai Nikiforovich, 42, 48n45–46

Zelenov, Mikhail, 11n12, 111, 136n1

Zelnik, Reginald E., 168n15

Zemstvo Assembly, 71

Zhenotdel, 175n1

Zinoviev, Grigorii, 18, 59, 92, 112

LARRY E. HOLMES is Professor Emeritus of History at the University of South Alabama. He is author of *Kremlin and the Schoolhouse: Reforming Education in Soviet Russia, 1917–1931* (1991); *Stalin's School: Moscow's Model School No. 25, 1931–1937* (1999); and *Stalin's World War II Evacuations: Triumph and Troubles in Kirov* (2017).

www.ingramcontent.com/pod-product-compliance
Lightning Source LLC
Chambersburg PA
CBHW031816220426
43662CB00007B/672